CHINUA ACHEBE'S

Things Fall Apart

◆ ◆ ◆

A CASEBOOK

Edited by
Isidore Okpewho

OXFORD
UNIVERSITY PRESS

2003

OXFORD
UNIVERSITY PRESS

Oxford   New York

Auckland   Bangkok   Buenos Aires   Cape Town   Chennai
Dar es Salaam   Delhi   Hong Kong   Istanbul   Karachi   Kolkata
Kuala Lumpur   Madrid   Melbourne   Mexico City   Mumbai   Nairobi
São Paulo   Shanghai   Taipei   Tokyo   Toronto

Copyright © 2003 by Oxford University Press, Inc.

Published by Oxford University Press, Inc.
198 Madison Avenue, New York, New York 10016

www.oup.com

Oxford is a registered trademark of Oxford University Press

Library of Congress Cataloging-in-Publication Data
Chinua Achebe's Things fall apart : a casebook / edited by
Isidore Okpewho.
p. cm. — (Casebooks in criticism)
Includes bibliographical references (p.).
ISBN 0-19-514763-4; 0-19-514764-2 (pbk.)
1. Achebe, Chinua. Things fall apart.   2. Igbo (African people) in
literature.   3. Nigeria—In literature.   I. Okpewho, Isidore.
II. Series.
PR9387.9.A3 T52397 2003
823'.914—dc21   2002013555

1 3 5 7 9 8 6 4 2

Printed in the United States of America
on acid-free paper

Credits

Contents

Chinua Achebe's
Things Fall Apart

A CASEBOOK

Introduction

ISIDORE OKPEWHO

❖ ❖ ❖

THERE ARE FEW WORKS outside of the Western canon
that have received anything close to the attention given to
Things Fall Apart, and for good reasons. In its home continent of
Africa, it is arguably the most widely read book, next to the Bible
and the Quran. Outside Africa, it has become part of a global
literary canon; it exists in close to sixty languages (including English), with total sales of nearly nine million copies since its publication in 1958, and it is included in some of the most prestigious
literary series across the world. It would be hard to find many
institutions of higher learning in the English-speaking world that
have not listed the novel in courses across the humanities and
social sciences, at both undergraduate and graduate levels; at the
secondary school level, it is also a highly favored text. It occupies
an important place in critical as well as cultural discourse because
it inaugurated a long and continuing tradition of inquiry into
the problematic relations between the West and the nations of
the Third World that were once European colonies. In many

crucial senses, therefore, *Things Fall Apart* is a classic that deserves to be read and discussed again and again.

In his delightfully pious portrait, *Chinua Achebe: A Biography*, the Nigerian scholar Ezenwa-Ohaeto has produced a document that will be of signal service to those investigating the development of the writer, not least in assessing the place of Achebe's art in the context of his many commitments, both national and international. We follow Achebe's growth from his native Igbo homeland, through his education in Nigeria, his early career in the country's broadcasting corporation, his links with the first generation of the local intelligentsia, right to his current status as a highly respected voice in world cultural circles. Those of us who grew up in Nigeria's small towns and villages are especially touched with a certain nostalgia for the curious postcolonial climate that framed our lives: masquerade outings and missionary obligations vying for our undecided loyalties; colonial pomp and authority claiming our awed regard quite as much as the hallowed traditions of our people; the masterpieces of colonial education stirring questions in our minds about the folk images so deeply ingrained in us. I should stress both the curiosity of the moment and the nostalgia we feel about it now, for the wonder is that we survived the intense trauma to which we may have been exposed and can today identify, with mingled awe and gratitude, the contending forces of the time.

We have learned in recent times to read literature with a certain postmodernist cynicism toward anything that claims to represent reality. This is as it should be, given the tricks that have often been played on us by those pretending to conduct our affairs with honest intentions. But when Achebe tells us in "The Novelist as Teacher" that, as a writer, he takes his obligation to educate his readers about the real lives and problems of Africans with the same commitment as physical and social scientists addressing the same issues, we are obviously entitled to take the images he conjures in his works with the seriousness of one who has lived through the harsh realities the images project. Ezenwa-Ohaeto frequently succeeds in teasing out the histories of those images. In his equally well targeted ethnographic study, *Achebe's*

World, Robert Wren has succeeded in drawing attention to the enabling social and cultural contexts that shed valuable light on our reading of Achebe's fiction.

An honest assessment of Achebe's work should therefore begin by exploring the interplay between his personal background and the succession of forces controlling his development as a writer. As his biographers have amply attested, he was born in a village (Ogidi) in Igbo country where traditional African customs were still vibrant but at a moment when the colonial presence was increasingly making itself felt in the fabric of the people's lives. There was something about the brand of imperialism practiced by the British in Nigeria that disposed the young Achebe to cultivate an even-tempered approach to the cultural ferment into which he had been born. Unlike the French system of *assimilation* which was designed to force upon indigenous African youth an adoption of French cultural identity, the British policy of indirect rule allowed indigenous African leaders to stand as brokers between the imperial will and the ways of their people. The result was that, although the youth in a country like Nigeria were almost as likely to be tempted away from traditional mores as the youth in a country like Senegal, the former were inclined to a more dispassionate approach to matters of culture than their counterparts in Francophone Africa.[1] Hence Chinua, though born (1930) to first-generation Christian parents, Isaiah Okafor and Janet Achebe, continued to address, admittedly with guarded reverence, the hallowed traditions of the folk despite his formal education in Nigeria's elite secondary and tertiary institutions.

After a brilliant record at Government College, Umuahia (1944–1948), one of a handful of privileged secondary schools established by the colonial government and staffed predominantly with expatriate graduates, Achebe proceeded to the newly constituted University College, Ibadan. He was initially admitted to study medicine, but interactions with cultural circles in the university awakened an underlying interest in the humanities. He ended up taking a bachelor's degree in the arts (1948–1953).

The reorientation was responsible, in a pivotal way, for Achebe's future career, thanks to the position of the university in the cultural politics of the time. By the 1940s and 1950s, Western scholars were slowly shifting their perception of "other" cultures from a superior conception of them as "primitive" to a more or less liberal view, in which each culture was seen in terms more of how its values and usages satisfied its needs than of how it measured up to standards set by the more "advanced" cultures of Europe. This relativist view of culture aided the growing science of human societies—anthropology—in directing its attention toward studying the functions served by the various things done in each society and how those functions help to define and unify the society. Functionalist anthropology was countered, soon enough, by a view within its ranks that a society does not always stay united; there are often internal problems and frictions that prompt disunification—that cause things to "fall apart"—at some level.

These trends in social thought are relevant here because Ibadan, one of several university colleges set up by the colonial government in selected outposts of the British empire,[2] was staffed predominantly with graduates of major British universities, including Oxford, Cambridge, and London, where they had been influenced or taught by key theorists in the discipline: Malinowski, Radcliffe-Brown, Evans-Pritchard, Leach, Firth, and so on. Ibadan thus became a major laboratory for testing and perhaps refining the central strands of the new social thought. The structural-functionalist view of society, which more deeply probed its internal organization as well as the functions that defined it, may well be deemed to represent a more progressive approach to the study of human societies. Unfortunately, it remained largely an academic tool of analysis and did little to arrest prejudices too deeply enshrined in the relations between the expatriate community and the Africans they had come to rule or to investigate. The structure of education in the institutions that Achebe and his contemporaries attended was still solidly geared to privilege the dominant European culture. A rather interesting phenomenon emerged with the arrival at Ibadan of Geoffrey Parrinder, a scholar of religions who took—and awakened in students like Achebe—a deep "interest in our gods and religious systems"

(Wren 60). Otherwise, the books they read invariably portrayed Africans in unflattering terms. In his literature courses, Achebe "read some appalling novels about Africa (including Joyce Cary's much praised *Mister Johnson*) and decided that the story we had to tell could not be told for us by anyone else no matter how gifted or well intentioned" ("Named for Victoria" 25).[3]

Achebe had published a few short stories in student periodicals and was evidently biding his time. He graduated from Ibadan (1953) into the Nigerian work force, first as a high school teacher in eastern Nigeria and later (mid-1954), on the recommendation of some of his teachers, as a trainee broadcaster in the fledgling Nigerian Broadcasting Service, which was seeking young indigenous graduates to groom for future assumption of positions still predominantly filled by expatriate personnel. Here, Achebe gave a good account of himself, rising through the ranks and eventually becoming (1961) director of external broadcasting. But not long after joining the broadcasting service, he had begun writing the novel that would make such a difference to the lives of so many. He completed the first draft of *Things Fall Apart* early in 1956, but it was not until 1958, with the mixed fortunes of friendly help and a near loss of the original manuscript,[4] that the novel was published by Heinemann in London.

Achebe was not the first African or even Nigerian writer to publish a work of imaginative literature in English. In West Africa alone, there had been a generation of "pioneer poets," who put some of their creativity to the service of anticolonial contestation; some of them were indeed Nigerians, like Nnamdi Azikiwe and Dennis Osadebay, who would play key roles in the political life of the nation. Even as a work of prose fiction, *Things Fall Apart* had been preceded by Amos Tutuola's first three folk fantasies, *The Palm-Wine Drinkard and His Dead Palm-Wine Tapster in the Deads' Town* (1952), *My Life in the Bush of Ghosts* (1954), and *Simbi and the Satyr of the Dark Jungle* (1955), and by Cyprian Ekwensi's first three novellas, *When Love Whispers* (1948), *The Leopard's Claw* (1947), and *People of the City* (1954). But what marked Achebe's novel as a pioneering effort was the seriousness of purpose and the depth of vision contained in his reaction to the European novel of Africa. True, like his

Nigerian predecessors in this genre, he had before him the formal and stylistic achievement even of British authors with whom he took issue, like Joyce Cary and Joseph Conrad (see Achebe, "An Image of Africa"). But while his predecessors used their models simply as springboards for creative experiments, Achebe transcended form and style for a more revisionist representation of the peculiar conditions and outlook of an African society in ways that the British authors could never have conceived. While his predecessors treated issues of daily existence in more lighthearted picaresque or journalistic veins, Achebe tackled the historical and contemporary predicaments of his people with a more fitting tragic seriousness.[5]

Things Fall Apart is basically a story about the first encounters between a traditional African (Igbo) community and the encroaching British colonial presence, a presence that brings into tragic confrontation two highly valued ideals of Igbo society: on one hand, the republican ideal of success through earnest individual effort and, on the other hand, the democratic ideal of harmony through the acknowledgment and resolution of disparate interests. The first ideal is represented by the community's principal warrior, Okonkwo, who sets himself with such singleminded fierceness against the encroaching colonial power that he runs afoul even of the second ideal, which is championed, unfortunately, by the rest of his people. Although they are no less protective of their freedom, they are nevertheless inclined to treat the newcomers with some guarded curiosity. This conflict of approaches ultimately facilitates the victory of the invaders. Written on the eve of Nigeria's liberation from colonial rule, in the period of experimental "self-government" designed to prepare the country for managing its unwieldy sociopolitical organization, the novel reveals Achebe's deep concern for the destiny of the nation amid the distinct outlooks and expectations evident within its segments. Its title "alluded not only to the fast pace of political events but also to the endemic internal pressures that were emerging, with the Eastern and Western regions in Nigeria asking for independence and the Northern region reluctant to take it" (Ezenwa-Ohaeto 60–61). However we read the novel, it nonetheless proclaims a writer cautiously observing the turn of events in his country, aware of the historical complications and anxious to see it move into the future with well-considered steps. As a Nigerian living and working in a cosmopolitan setting, rather than an Igbo man in his limited clan enclave, Achebe was well aware of the altered climate of relationships in the new political union. Though set in the Igbo hinterland, *Things Fall Apart* may thus be seen, in this sense, as a microcosmic portrait of the problems of social and political engineering in a society struggling to reconcile its internal tensions under an arrangement dictated by an external force.

Achebe's second novel, *No Longer at Ease*, was published in 1960, the year of Nigeria's political independence from Britain. Although the nation was awash with the euphoria of liberation, the writer had a clearer perception of the trend of things. If anyone thought the title of the first novel rather pessimistic, the second may have been intended to drive home the writer's misgivings even more starkly. One thing, at least, was becoming increasingly clear with the publication of this second novel. Here was a writer with a committed sense of his country's historical fortunes, which he was proceeding to document with an imaginative representation of iconic figures. Here was not a mere storyteller trying his hand at a craft learned from his teachers.

Things Fall Apart portrays the systematic entrenchment in an African society of a colonial power, which progressively backs cultural arguments with military force; it is apparently set in the last two decades of the nineteenth century. In *No Longer at Ease*, the colony has been so firmly established that the youth of the land are being educated in Britain in readiness for assuming the government of their country on the impending termination of colonial status; the setting for the novel is evidently the 1950s. This apprenticeship is, sadly, rather ill-starred. Obi Okonkwo, the story's principal character, is unable to live up to either of the expectations imposed upon him. On the one hand, his clansmen have put their resources together for his education abroad in the hope that, when he returns home and assumes his position in the nation's power structure, he will reward the clan interests that helped achieve that position. But he fails his clan in several respects. First, he gives scant comfort to those who hoped he would secure their children privileges, like scholarships; more seriously, he defies his people's traditions by falling in love with, even pressing his plans to marry, a girl from a family on whom an ancient religious taboo had been imposed; on the whole, he turns his back on the people's communalistic ethos by cultivating the individualistic lifestyle of the new European-influenced elite. On the other hand, in giving him a responsible place in its administration, the colonial government had expected of him a level of probity befitting someone with so much education, but he is caught taking bribes to award scholarships. At the trial in which Obi is sentenced to jail, most people—both his colonial bosses and his compatriots—wonder why a young man who showed so much promise should come to such a pass.

This novel should have confirmed Achebe's growing skill and sensitivity to the state of the health of his society as it was emerging into independence from foreign rule. But it has frequently been seen as an inferior effort to *Things Fall Apart*, particularly with respect to the novelist's handling of the principal character. Obviously with Okonkwo of the earlier novel in mind, David Carroll laments the "absence of any graspable self" in Obi, an "absence of particularity which, according to the paradoxical logic of fiction, limits in a drastic way the general significance of the hero's career and the novel as a whole" (Carroll 86–87). This seems to me a rather harsh judgment. If we accept the single-mindedness of Okonkwo as a credible character scheme, it makes sense, at any rate, as a unified cultural trait, uncomplicated by outside influences and posing a challenge to an equally determined intruder. The world of Obi Okonkwo, however, has been thoroughly unsettled by the contending claims of two cultures. To the extent that character is determined as much by context as by anything else, there seems little room in *No Longer at Ease* for the sort of stability and certainty we find in the representation of Okonkwo in *Things Fall Apart*.

Given that Obi Okonkwo in *No Longer at Ease* is the grandson of Okonkwo in *Things Fall Apart*, it is clear that Achebe intended the former novel as a sequel to the latter in his portrait of the historical fortunes of his society. However, in conceiving his third novel, *Arrow of God* (1964), he must have felt a certain gap in his time scheme. Obi Okonkwo is the culmination of a process by which the colonial dispensation methodically took firm control of the land and schooled the youth of the land in the ways of the foreign culture. But the traditional leaders of the land, who watched this process unfold, had not been adequately represented. It is quite possible that Achebe, who at this point was coming into senior leadership positions in the establishment, had begun to see the problems of Nigeria as rooted in the failures of its leadership, as revealed by the outcome of the federal elections (1959) that ushered in the first post-independence government of the country. To be sure, even *Things Fall Apart* is in part an interrogation of the kind of leaders by whom a society allows itself to be governed. In *Arrow of God*, Achebe turns his lights fully on the psychology of power and the consequences of its exercise, factors crucial to the destiny of a society in the grip of inevitable change.

There are three key players in the system set up by Achebe in his anatomy of power in *Arrow of God*. First, there is the indigenous society of Umuaro, under the paramountcy of Ezeulu, a priest-king who, as servant of the community's guardian deity (Ulu), conducts the rituals (festivals of cleansing and renewal) defining the annual life cycle of his community; as the mouthpiece of the god, he is thus invested with a tremendous power to be exercised in the interest of his people. Second, there is the colonial administrator, Winterbottom, servant of the Brittanic majesty, who is charged, at this point in the empire's history, with the responsibility of establishing the system of indirect rule by which Britain hopes to divest itself of some of the burdens of empire by appointing indigenous African rulers as brokers between the imperial will and the welfare of their people. Finally, there is the Christian missionary enterprise in the colonized society, treading a discreet middle ground between the other two forces but ushering in an alternative cultural and spiritual system which, in the final analysis, subserves the empire's agenda of domination.

On the surface, the colonial authority and the indigenous African leadership seem to be diametrically opposed to one another. But in this brilliant anatomy of power, Achebe succeeds in demonstrating, through his careful dissection of the personalities of the two representative figures Ezeulu and Winterbottom, the basic truth about the willful exercise of power, no matter by whom or on whose behalf. Charged to implement the policy of indirect rule, whereby colonial rule is filtered through local African leaders, Winterbottom resents a system that will only diminish the more *direct* authority a man in his position had over those he considered less than human. He is no less imperious in his relations with the colonial officers under him, insisting on the hierarchical structure of their relations as well as on their superior attitudes toward the African natives they have come to govern. A figure very much in the racist mold of Joseph Conrad's Marlow, he is both arrogant and high-handed in his dealings with Ezeulu. When Ezeulu does not embrace the position Winterbottom offers him as warrant chief of his people, the district commissioner does not hesitate to throw him into prison. Winterbottom succeeds only in isolating himself by his stubborn pursuit of power, until illness incapacitates him, and he loses grip on that power.

A rather similar fate overtakes Ezeulu. As chief priest of the community's protective deity, Ulu, he arrogates to himself the absolute authority for setting the terms of the traditional rituals and indeed of determining the god's interests even against the less doctrinaire inclinations of his people. He is so self-righteous about his authority that he does not hesitate to oppose his village (Umuaro) in its dispute with another (Okperi) and finds himself in sympathy with the colonial judgment against his people in the dispute. He consistently resists any attempt by his people to interfere with the power and authority he is convinced the god has put in his charge, unaware that in pressing too hard on them he is testing their patience with the old ways and driving them to consider more viable alternatives.

For Christianity has begun to make serious claims upon the community's attention, to the extent that even Ezeulu, seeing the disturbing trend, sends one of his sons to infiltrate the new dispensation to see what may be gained, more by him than by anyone else. But the decline has become irreversible, not only in the powers of Ezeulu as mouthpiece of the god but indeed in the hold of the god over the people. A man who has long isolated himself from his people in his quest for absolute authority loses not only that authority but his sanity: Ezeulu lives out his days "in the haughty splendour of a demented high priest," a state of health not unlike what finally befalls his antagonist and kindred spirit, Winterbottom.

Arrow of God is, clearly, one of Achebe's most sensitive portraits of the ugliness of egomaniacal leadership and absolute power. Set, like his previous novels, in pre-independence Nigeria but published in the early years of the republic, it is the work of an intellectual "present at the creation," as it were, and concerned that the nation examine carefully the dispositions and backgrounds of leaders to whom it entrusts the control of its destiny.[6] Although *No Longer* succeeds *Arrow* in terms of historical setting, it is no less a comment on the emergent leadership, considering that Obi Okonkwo is among the first generation of the British-trained elite poised to assume the mantle of control from the soon-to-abdicate colonial administrators.

At the end of this trilogy, we may safely ask if Achebe has reasonably delivered on his commitment to rewrite the story of Africa from a truer perspective than that adopted by earlier, European writers like Cary and Conrad. Although from early in his career as a writer, Achebe has been showered with superlative praise across the world, it is significant that, even among his fellow Africans, some questions were raised about the validity of his writing. Perhaps the most resounding doubts were raised by a fellow Nigerian, the critic Obi Wali, who took exception to the new effort by Achebe and others in writing works with what he judged a non-African sensibility. In a paper titled "The Dead End of African Literature," presented at the first major conference on the new African writing at Makerere University in Uganda, Wali charged that no literature could legitimately claim to be *African* unless written in an African language. In another paper published not long after, "The Individual and the Novel in Africa," he went on to observe the limitations of characterization in works like *No*

Longer at Ease. In traditional African society, according to Wali, "the individual does not exist in his own right but is compelled to lose his identity for the sake of social cohesion...yet the African novelist in order to make his craft possible is forced to hammer out characters from this social block which is amorphous in many ways" (31).

These were hard words at the time, and they made a lasting impression on a young student at Makerere present in the audience, (James) Ngugi, who adopted that perspective later in his own career.[7] I shall have more to say about Achebe's use of language later in this introduction. The verdict of time has, however, favored Achebe's record as a revisionist novelist who has given a more credible picture of the African world than anything to be found in the antecedent European fiction of Africa. Where the latter was remarkable for its almost total erasure of the indigenous African presence, Achebe has succeeded in reestablishing that presence most convincingly: *people* live here, he has committed himself to stressing. Indeed, with regard to Wali's point about the collective sensibility in traditional African society, in every one of his works, Achebe has given forceful acknowledgment to the influence of the collective will in African social life. The dictum that resounds in *Arrow of God*—"no man however great was greater than his people"—is just as true for the protagonists of the two other novels, who try to go against the grain of their people's interests. What Achebe has done is to put credible faces to the contending forces that drive social life, often to painful ends. Even more, he has enabled us to appreciate the peculiar contexts—environmental, cosmological, cultural, political, economic, and otherwise—that enable human life and fate in Africa. Here is no longer, in Carroll's words, the "landscape without figures, an Africa without Africans" (2) that we find in the fictions of Cary and Conrad.

Not long after independence in 1960, the progress of social and political life in Nigeria confirmed the fears that Achebe and others had articulated. In a sense, the colonial presence was castigated by writers like him not simply because it destabilized societies working out their destinies along peculiar paths of existence, but especially because it created conditions that had consequences more favorable to the colonizers than to the colonized. The negative image of indirect rule in *Arrow of God* reflects the resentment of a people (the Igbo) to a policy that treated their more republican institutions as inferior to the feudalistic and monarchical traditions of what Winterbottom calls "the more advanced tribes" elsewhere in the country. By the end of the 1950s into the early 1960s, it became clear to not a few Nigerians that the organs of colonial policy were on the whole intended to leave a legacy of conflict between one sector of the country (the North) and the other (the South), driven especially by differences in religious and ideological orientations. This became clear in the electoral crisis (1959) between the North—whose feudal institutions appealed to the British—and the South, which nearly upset the plans for Britain's transfer of power in 1960. A compromise was reached only by making the leader of a southern political party (Dr. Nnamdi Azikiwe) the country's governor-general—a rather hollow title, with far less authority than was wielded by the last British administrator to have it—while bestowing the real executive powers on a northerner (Alhaji Abubakar Tafawa Balewa) as prime minister.

With the North firmly in control, the scene was inevitably set for a game of affiliations between parties in the South eyeing a share of the power held by the North and those determined to wrest that power in the next elections. In the circumstances, the nation was steadily losing, so early in its life, any chance of cultivating a political will that would bring some cohesion to the unwieldy structure left behind by the British. Nigerians, on the whole, now felt far less committed to a united nation than they had before the political union was handed to them. The accumulated wealth from the extensive geographical reaches of the land were seen not as a reserve to be invested for the common good but as bounty to be looted at will. Increasingly, the idea of "our share of the national cake" became the defining frame of reference as much in the general social discourse as in the politicians' management of the country's resources. Corruption was steadily establishing itself as an acceptable mode of conduct in various facets of life.

Achebe had long seen all of this developing. In *No Longer at Ease*, Obi Okonkwo's clanspeople marvel at his downfall not because they think he erred in accepting bribes but because he bungled what most people easily accomplished: he "tried to do what everyone does without finding out how it was done." That novel, thus, may be seen as Achebe's exegesis both of the growing dis-ease in the random union set in place by the colonial dispensation and of the despair—even dissociation of political sensibility—inevitably created in the discerning citizen. In his fourth novel, *A Man of the People*, these dispositions are underlined both by its general tone of disgust and by the self-withdrawal signified by the first-person narration.

A Man of the People is essentially designed to show that things had become so bad in the new nation as both to pervert the cherished values of the past and to frustrate the idealism of a still committed few. On one side is Odili Samalu, the narrator, a university graduate and high school teacher with an honest desire to promote the common good. On the other is Chief the Honorable M. N. Nanga, parliamentarian and cabinet minister, a most amoral politician dedicated to reaping the utmost personal gain from his position and scornful of the idealism of the educated class. But Nanga is a most charismatic fellow, so that he succeeds in disarming Odili, who condemns what he stands for, with a show of friendship that is really patronage. For a while, Odili basks in this relationship and even sees some appeal in the likes of Nanga. But when Nanga seduces Odili's lover, Odili plots revenge by joining a rival political party (of radical pretensions) and vowing to expose Nanga before the electorate. Nanga still hopes to persuade the young idealist to leave the more pragmatic turf of national politics to those, like himself, best suited to it; he even tempts him with the offer of a scholarship for advanced study abroad. When nothing he does can persuade the young man, Nanga lets loose his thugs, who beat Odili to within an inch of his life. Unfortunately for Nanga and the amoral machine he serves, the politicians can hardly control the monster they have let loose. Violence erupts between the thugs of the rival parties; in the ensuing anarchy, the prime minister unilaterally reappoints his old cabinet. When the turmoil still does not abate, the army stages a coup and throws the leaders in jail.

There is an interesting subplot, which signifies the decline of the old morality in the new nation. A village trader, Josiah, steals a blind beggar's walking stick with which he makes a charm to draw buyers to his wares. But the people discover this and boycott his store, driving Josiah to economic ruin and disgrace. However, at the height of Nanga's political power and appeal, Josiah is enlisted as one of the politician's trusted confidants; it is he, in fact, who sets Odili up for the drubbing that lands him in the hospital.

And yet *A Man of the People* is as remarkable for the image it presents of the "discerning" intelligentsia as of the insensitive political leadership. Killam has made the interesting observation that "Odili is the man Obi [*No Longer at Ease*] might have become" (87). I would go further and say that, given the historical trajectory Achebe set himself in chronicling the fortunes of his society, Odili *is* the man Obi finally became. In all four novels, the educated Africans who represent the new dispensation are every bit as responsible for the derailment of their society as the ones much closer to the traditional outlook. In *Things Fall Apart*, those Africans aiding the evangelization of Igboland show greater zeal in dismantling the indigenous religion than the white missionaries they serve. Moses Unachukwu in *Arrow of God* adopts a more restrained approach, but even he is no less committed to the erosion of the hold of the god Ulu over Umuaro society. In *No Longer at Ease*, Obi Okonkwo is clearly unwilling to abdicate his privileged membership in the colonial elite; his education has, in fact, disposed him to treat his fellow citizens with nearly the same contempt as do the colonialists. And in *A Man of the People*, it is clear from Odili Samalu's reflections that there is precious little separating him from Nanga; if there were no personal grudge involved in his relations with the chief, he might easily be drawn, for all his cute diagnosis, into Nanga's corrupt political machine.

So what is it that separates the Obis and Odilis from their

fellow citizens, whom they so readily despise? In his *Reading Chinua Achebe*, Gikandi makes an interesting analysis of the ironies and paradoxes undergirding *A Man of the People*, suggesting that Achebe adopts this scheme because of "his need to develop an alternative way of representing the postcolonial state" (113). Yet it would appear that the same strategy is at play even in the first three novels (Gikandi 114). The fact is, Achebe has been castigating the Western-educated elements in African society all along, in rather subtle moves. By the time we get to the last two books of the carefully modulated quartet, he has allowed this foreign factor among the citizens to build itself up to a point where it proclaims not only its misfit with the rest of the society but indeed its complicity in the final disorientation of the communal will. This mode of irony argues for a brutal honesty on Achebe's part, for it is a self-reflective irony that enables him to observe the risks attendant on educated men like him in African society, on whom seems to lie the burden to steer their society through the stormy waters of the new, postcolonial culture. Does our education, he seems to be asking, make us *that* different from the rest of our fellows? When we scratch the surface, as Achebe does with characters like Obi and Odili, we find it does not. The "Manichean aesthetics" on which, as JanMohamed has ably argued, Achebe has constructed his representation of the dilemmas inherent in postcolonial society is true essentially as a paradigm of exposition; in the final analysis, Achebe has demonstrated in the confrontations between Ezeulu and Winterbottom in *Arrow of God* and between Odili and Nanga in *A Man of the People* that there is a rather thin line between the two approaches to reality.

The closing section of *A Man of the People* presents a military coup in which soldiers shut down the country's civilian government and throw the leaders in jail. The book was published two days after Nigeria's first military coup in January 1966, prompting suspicions within both official quarters (Ezenwa-Ohaeto 115) and the general public that Achebe had *some* inside knowledge of plans for the coup; indeed, Achebe has had to confront open questions on the subject and to offer a rather testy defense of himself ("The Truth of Fiction" 104–5). Whatever Achebe's position on the matter, it was clear things had gone so far wrong with the management of the country's affairs that it was heading for some form of catastrophe. As one of Nigeria's educated elite, he was very much part of the national conversation on the problems of the country. Not only was he director of one of its major official communications organs, but he was part of a circle of creative artists who met periodically at the Mbari Club in Ibadan, western Nigeria—whose membership included visual artists like Demas Nwoko, poets and dramatists J. P. Clark, Wole Soyinka, and Christopher Okigbo, and others—to present their works and no doubt to share thoughts on the state of the nation. There was rampant violence, in social as well as political life, of the kind that had precipitated military take-overs elsewhere in the world, so a suggestion of it by a discerning writer was not such a farfetched thing, after all.[8]

The January 1966 military coup spawned another, in July of the same year, led by officers from northern Nigeria who feared the entrenchment of a southern, and specifically Igbo, bias in the emergent military leadership. In *No Longer at Ease*, the phenomenon of an ethnic association (the Umuofia Progressive Union), committed to guaranteeing the clan's interests through the agency of civil servants like Obi Okonkwo, portrayed the country more as a patchwork of ethnic factions than as a nation linked by unified goals. Evidently, not even the national army was immune to this fractious outlook. From 1966, the country teetered from one crisis to another, not the least of which was ethnic violence in several towns north and south, which culminated in the dissolution of all mutual trust among both the leadership and the general citizenry. Many Igbo living and working in several parts of Nigeria— including Achebe and his family in the capital city, Lagos—fled to their ancestral homes in the East to avoid threats to their lives; numerous others were killed. The Igbo, much the majority in the population of Nigeria's eastern states, were so incensed by the colossal body count of kinfolk returning to the heartland, dead and alive, that their leaders severed the region from the rest of the federation, declaring an independent nation of Biafra. The result of it all was an enormously costly civil war (1967–1970), which ended with the capitulation of Biafra to the federal army and the restoration, considerable if not complete, of the Igbo into the structure of things as they were before the war. The poet Okigbo, an old friend of Achebe's from their days in secondary school and university, died fighting on the frontlines early in the war.

In the thirty months that the war lasted, Achebe found himself mobilized, like many other prominent Igbo citizens in the embattled enclave, in keeping Biafra alive and especially in enlisting the sympathy of the outside world in its fight against the superior war machine of federal Nigeria. This was no time for an extended project like a novel. A minor fiction that Achebe wrote at the time (with John Iroaganachi) and later published as *How the Leopard Got Its Claws*, was a folk story, ostensibly for children but essentially an allegory on the tyranny of power, with a glance at power configurations in the Nigerian federation. Otherwise, Achebe occasionally wrote pieces of poetry, later collected in the volume *Beware Soul Brother*,[9] some of them dealing with the tragedy of the civil war and others exploring issues of a more or less philosophical character. The civil war ended in 1970. Rather than seek reabsorption into federal service, Achebe opted for appointment as a writer in residence and researcher at the University of Nigeria, Nsukka (in Igbo country), an institution struggling to recover from the devastation it suffered during the war.

Achebe spent the initial years of this period not in recovering his momentum as a novelist, but in attending to projects that would reestablish interest in the culture of his people, which had been severely threatened by the war,[10] as well as encouraging the emergence of new literary voices. In the latter connection, he founded the journal *Okike: A Nigerian* (later, *An African*) *Journal of New Writing* (1971) as a forum for new initiatives in creative (poems, short stories) and critical writing. But with his entry into the academic world, Achebe became more deeply involved with the discourse than the actual practice of creativity. True, he had published a few essays before the war on the responsibility of African writers like himself and other articles of a somewhat journalistic nature. Now, however, he began to take a more controversial stand in the terrain of postcoloniality defined by his earlier

essays. An extended American leave (1973–1975) offered him opportunities to give talks of a more combatively ideological character, some of them devoted to addressing the image of Africa as
presented in works by Africans and non-Africans alike. In one of
them, "Africa and Her Writers," he laments the smug universalism of some African writing, which shies away from confronting
the problems of the continent in a direct and committed way,
preferring rather to see them in the context of a larger "human
condition." In this context, Achebe condemns Ayi Kwei Armah's
modernist novel *The Beautyful Ones Are Not Yet Born*, which uses a
lot of scatological imagery in portraying the moral decay of
Ghana, as a book "sick, not with the sickness of Ghana, but with
the sickness of the *human condition*" (39). In another talk, "An Image
of Africa," Achebe denounces the racist outlook of Joseph Conrad's novel of Africa, *Heart of Darkness*. Needless to say, he drew
angry responses from the admirers of Conrad and, of course, from
Armah himself.

Returning to Nsukka in 1975 from his American leave, Achebe
continued to use the academic environment to familiarize himself
with the issues of the day, cultural and political. As references
especially in his second volume of essays (*Hopes and Impediments*)
suggest, he was reading widely on a great variety of subjects. In
addition to creative writing from inside and outside Africa, he was
exploring the economic thought of Arthur Lewis and J. Kenneth
Galbraith, psychoanalytic scholarship in the *Proceedings of the Modern
Language Association* of America, the structural anthropology of
Claude Lévi-Strauss and Edmund Leach, the colonialist discourse
of Fanon and Mannoni, African ethnography by both native and
foreign scholars, the criticism of African creative writing by both
African and non-African scholars, and so on. Consequently, his
essays in this period display an erudition that mark him more as
a scholar in the academic tradition than an essayist in the general
sense. He also continued to publish the journal *Okike* and other
derivative works,[11] thus keeping abreast of new trends and styles.
As if he were not busy enough, Achebe was so concerned with
troubling trends in Nigerian society that, in the prospect of a
return to civilian rule in 1983, he proceeded to join one of the

more progressive political parties in the country committed to somewhat egalitarian goals: the People's Redemption Party, of which Wole Soyinka was also a member. On the uneven playing fields of Nigerian politics, Achebe had of course little chance of influencing any real change. But his experience here enabled him at least to see the troubles of the country as rooted in the insensitivity and incompetence of its leadership, in the face of the mutual distrust and intolerance among the country's ethnic groups. This essentially is the burden of the slim volume Achebe put out in 1983, *The Trouble with Nigeria*.

By the time he published his fifth novel, *Anthills of the Savannah*, in 1987, Achebe had been exposed to several trends—in literature, culture, politics, and so on—that his imagination needed to process. Take literature, for instance. Although his earlier novels revealed a genuine attachment to the oral culture of his people, his acquaintance with the growing scholarly interest in African oral literature (an interest indebted, in turn, to his own creative example) seemed to have confirmed him in his commitment. There was also a growing vogue of Marxist-socialist praxis among writers and scholars on the continent that Achebe could hardly ignore. Then there was a growing interest in feminist issues, inspired of course by the rise of female African writing since the 1960s but aggressively driven by an awareness, especially among female scholars, of long-standing gender inequities in African life and thought. Achebe had himself been taken to task by various feminist critics (e.g., Carole Boyce Davies) for giving women short shrift in the male-dominated world of his novels.

There was a final issue, related to a central preoccupation in his fiction, that Achebe must have been pressed to address. I have already spoken of the failure of the educated class, in his first four novels, in its relations with both the colonial and the traditional orders of life in contemporary society. But surely the creative artist does not share this guilt to the same degree as others? If there is a larger, elemental truth to art, as Achebe suggests in one of his essays, that projects itself in images that life is ultimately driven to reflect, then there must be a place for art in any agenda of social restoration. Yet the artist has been

systematically sidelined, silenced, and even destroyed by the political authorities in postcolonial African society. In Nigeria alone,
Soyinka was jailed by two successive administrations, one civilian
and the other military. Within the Nigerian army, the one officer
who showed any real creative genius, the poet Mamman Vatsa,
was judged by his superiors to know too much: charged with
complicity in a plot to overthrow the leadership, he was executed,
against all counsel from distinguished citizens (including Achebe
and Soyinka), before any evidence could be adduced to his defense. But perhaps the experience closest to Achebe's feelings on
the matter was the death of his friend Christopher Okigbo early
in the civil war. Shortly before his death, and amid the turbulent
days of the dying first republic, Okigbo was gradually moving
from the arcane idiom of his earlier poetry (inspired largely by
his readings in literate European and other traditions) to a more
declamatory voice deeply influenced by Igbo oral tradition. So
conscious was he of the growing menace to the voice of the
popular will that, in one of his last poems, he could not help
proclaiming:

> If I don't learn to shut my mouth I'll soon go to hell,
> I, Okigbo, town-crier, together with my iron bell.
>   ("Hurrah for Thunder" 94)

What makes these lines so significant is that, quite soon after the
civil war began, Okigbo gave up all thoughts about writing and
joined the Biafran army, dying in an early encounter with the
federal forces and demonstrating, it would seem, that at that
crucial moment in the fortunes of his people the man of action
was more desperately needed than the man of words.[12] Achebe
may have asked himself: Is the artist really irrelevant to our lives?
Must art, under the pressure of the times, yield to tools of life
denial the pride of place accorded it in the traditions of our
people?

These questions enable us to appreciate why in *Anthills of the
Savannah*, a novel in which he endeavors to come to terms with
issues that defined the period since the publication of *A Man of*

the People, Achebe has chosen to foreground the voice of the storyteller. Framed by the troubled political history of a fictive African nation, Kangan (a thinly veiled Nigeria), *Anthills* sets out to explore the questions: How did we get to this sorry state? And what can be done to prevent it from becoming an endless cycle? Like *A Man of the People*, the novel is an anatomy of the ugliness of absolute power and its destructive effect on the communal will, not least in erasing the creative potential of alternative voices. Abandoning the tyranny of the monologic view in *A Man of the People*, Achebe allows the story of *Anthills* to be told by several voices. There are three principal ones (Chris, Ikem, and Beatrice), and they are all writers. Here, it seems, Achebe seeks to establish that Western education need not destroy the innate usefulness of the indigenous African to his society. But they are not the only voices heard here. There are also the proletarian elements in the society: in this book, pidgin enjoys a prominence it never received in Achebe's earlier fiction, so much so that it is the voice that concludes the novel. Finally, there is the voice of oral tradition, represented by a delegation of elders from the community of Abazon, whose proverbial wisdom proffers the foundation on which the future salvation of Kangan may be built.

These various characters narrate stories, which are presented somewhat in the form of testimonies in a putative trial investigating the roles and careers of various elements of society—leaders and subjects, males and females, and so on—in the troubled history of Kangan. Why does the novel privilege the act of narration? Stories, the novel stresses, are the repositories of our collective memory, containing the wisdom that will guide us in our present and future courses, so that we do not foolishly repeat the mistakes of the past. The title of the novel comes from a proverb about "anthills surviving to tell the new grass of the savannah about last year's brush fires," underlining the usefulness of the narrative tradition in bearing the seeds of future renewal. Neither the testimonies nor their bearers are, of course, flawless; from *A Man of the People*, we have been conditioned to read the narratives of individuals with some caution. But in *Anthills*, we see the characters lose their unhealthy dispositions and come to terms with their fellows. Chris graduates from his complicity with tyrannical authority to a commitment to the lot of his fellow citizens. Ikem descends from his elitist high horse to make his wisdom available to a wider spectrum of the population and even rethinks his gender attitudes. A notable element in this novel is the prominence of the female narrative, not only in the person of Beatrice (Chris's fiancée), who provides some of the key testimonies and ultimately initiates a rethinking of roles guaranteed to males in the traditional culture (e.g., child naming), but also in the voice of collective womanhood as an equal partner with males in the quest for change and a new social order. Equally striking in *Anthills* is Achebe's effort in moving beyond the limited Igbo paradigm of his earlier novels to project a larger national community, varied as much in ethnicity as in class.

In *Anthills*, therefore, Achebe gives us the fruits of his fellowship in the academy as well as his exposure to the much wider theater of experience in Nigerian, African, and global politics and culture. He remains committed to the goal of upholding the validity of our native traditions and especially the relevance of the artist to the restorative goals first of his native country but ultimately of the larger human society. By the time he came to write *Anthills*, his accumulated wisdom had deepened his critical outlook on the world so much as to render the book a work—to borrow a phrase from Lyn Innes's notable study of Achebe's writing—of "the critic as novelist" (150). It is not clear what kind of fiction Achebe will write next. A motor accident in 1990 has greatly limited his mobility, and for this and other reasons he has found it convenient to live in the United States (he is a professor of English at Bard College). But if his recently published series of lectures, *Home and Exile*, is any guide to his thinking on the matter, he is no less committed to "the reclamation of the African story" (73) than he was when he wrote his first novel.

THE MOST STRIKING QUALITY of *Things Fall Apart* is, in fact, its empathic account of the Igbo society of its setting. Achebe has not quite gone out of his way to romanticize traditional Igbo culture and may indeed have shown it incapable of withstanding the unforeseen dangers posed by the encroaching colonialism. But in many respects he presents the indigenous way of life as altogether well founded in its religious and ethical systems and traditions. For instance, there is a studied ontological balance between male and female principles, especially in respect of the major divinities of the land: the goddess of the Earth (Ani) has a male (Ezeani) as chief priest, while the male Oracle of the Hills and the Caves (Agbala) is served by the priestess Chielo. Aspects of the traditional belief system that may be dismissed as superstitious are presented as having an internal logic, which serves the needs of the people in metaphysical realms: thus, the recurrent cycle of death and rebirth (*ogbanje*), which torments Ekwefi's child Ezinma, is summarily arrested when a diviner digs up the item (a pebble) binding her to the cycle. In the debate between the British missionary (Brown) and a local savant (Akunna), it becomes clear to the former that the foreign culture has little to teach the indigenous African in terms of theological sophistication; the goals of domination will have to be achieved by other methods. Even the myths bolstering certain aspects of the traditional metaphysics are presented by Achebe almost as articles of faith: one of the *egwugwu* (spirit masques) is said to have "only one hand and with it carried a basket full of water" (85).

Igbo society is also shown to have worked out a well-regulated system for harmonizing relations between its citizens in interpersonal, domestic, and larger societal spheres. There is, for instance, engaging poetry in the sheer etiquette of hospitality: kola nuts and alligator pepper are shared and prayers offered to the ancestors before any serious discussion is initiated, whether the business is agreeable, like the marital negotiations between Obierika and his prospective in-laws, or less auspicious, like Okoye's luckless attempt to collect a debt from the shiftless Unoka. The seven-year exile of Okonkwo in his maternal home of Mbanta gives us a most touching portrait of a society in full, civilized awareness of its moral as well as affinal responsibilities. Although the somber lessons of the sojourn seem lost on Okonkwo upon his return to Umuofia, the interlude does reassert the humane outlook with which the average citizen in Okonkwo's Igbo society is traditionally raised. Whether or not we accept the mytho-logic of spirit masques dispensing justice in human society—even Achebe sometimes indicates that citizens of Umuofia are fairly certain who are under those masks—the decision of the *egwuwgu* in the case between the wife-beating Uzowulu and his in-laws seems well founded enough. On the whole, the society is shown to be fundamentally guided by democratic principles of reasoned debate and recognition of alternative points of view.

Achebe's empathy with his ancestral culture is even more evident in the harmonies that he reveals between the people and their environment. It is not without reason that such harmonies are predicated on the music of drums, which helps to convey a sense of the rhythms regulating the structures of feeling that have defined the culture of the people over time. Significantly, one such moment of drum music prefaces a scene of conjugal harmony in Okonkwo's polygamous household: "The drums were still beating, persistent and unchanging. Their sound was no longer a separate thing from the living village. It was like the pulsation of its heart. It throbbed in the air, in the sunshine, and even in the trees, and filled the village with excitement" (31).

In a somewhat different scene, a wrestling match in which two evenly matched wrestlers parry each other move for move, the attending crowd is shown to have become interwoven with the musical accompaniment: "The crowd had surrounded and swallowed up the drummers, whose frantic rhythm was no longer a mere disembodied sound but the very heart beat of the people" (37–38). Even when instrumental music is not specifically mentioned, we still feel the rhythm of vibrant life in the play of the elements:

At last the rain came. It was sudden and tremendous. For two or three moons the sun had been gathering strength till it seemed to breathe a breath of fire on the earth. All the grass had long been scorched brown, and the sand felt like live coals on the feet. Evergreen trees wore a dusty coat of brown. The birds were silenced in the forests, and the world lay panting under the live, vibrating heat. And then came the clap of thunder. It was an angry, metallic and thirsty clap, like the deep and liquid rumbling of the rainy season. A mighty wind arose and filled the air with dust. Palm trees swayed as the wind combed their leaves into flying crests like strange and fantastic coiffure. (91–92)

In this passage, Achebe uses the word "moons" where conventional English prose would say "months." In defining what he calls "the African imagination," Abiola Irele has argued, quite cogently, that "the problem of the African writer employing a European language is *how to write an oral culture*" (16). Indeed it seems to me that the most visible revolution effected by Achebe in *Things Fall Apart* is on the level of language: here, the English language has been forced to assume lexical and semantic burdens for which it was never designed. It is clear from what Achebe says in his essay reprinted here, "The African Writer and the English Language," that language was an integral part of his resolve to rewrite the story of Africa in new terms. "What I do see is a new voice coming out of Africa, speaking of African experience in a world-wide language," Achebe tells us, and he is speaking here as much of the medium as the message. He goes on to illustrate what he means by quoting a character's speech from *Arrow of God*, reconstructing it the way it would sound in standard English, then concluding with a statement that defends his preference: "The material is the same. But the form of the one is *in character* and the other is not." From this we can understand why Achebe has chosen to punctuate his prose every so often with indigenous Igbo words. For some of them, he gives an English translation in parentheses, prompted perhaps by his publishers to do so. For many others, he could have found quite usable English equivalents but has chosen to keep the original Igbo, no doubt under an antihegemonist urge to deconstruct the dominance of the empire in the linguistic landscape of his work.

Equally calculated is the use of nuggets of folk wit in spicing up statements or else clinching the messages they convey. There is hardly a novel by Achebe in which we do not find a healthy recourse to proverbs and proverbial expressions: from *Things Fall*

Apart to *Anthills of the Savannah*, they are used, especially by elderly characters or those well grounded in the culture, to lend pointedness to their speech. A key moment of proverb use in *Things Fall Apart* concerns Okoye's visit to Unoka to try to collect a debt the latter has owed him for more than two years. It is here that Achebe makes his classic statement about the place of proverbs in Igbo speech:

> Having spoken plainly so far, Okoye said the next half a dozen sentences in proverbs. Among the Ibo the art of conversation is regarded very highly, and proverbs are the palm-oil with which words are eaten. Okoye was a great talker and he spoke for a long time, skirting round the subject and then hitting it finally. In short, he was asking Unoka to return the two hundred cowries he had borrowed from him more than two years before. (5)[13]

Not to be outdone, Unoka laughs heartily and shows Okoye a long tally of debts on a wall of his hut, which leaves Okoye in no doubt how low he stands on the scale of Unoka's indebtedness; he then clinches the point by reminding Okoye, "Our elders say that the sun will shine on those who stand before it shines on those who kneel under them. I shall pay my big debts first." What else is there to say? "Okoye rolled his goatskin and departed" (5–6).[14]

In writing his fiction, Achebe was clearly determined to remind his readers that he comes from a culture with established narrative traditions. The celebration of storytelling, in *Anthills of the Savannah*, as a timeless and invaluable cultural resource really goes back to *Things Fall Apart*, where the fortunes of Okonkwo and his fellows are presented within a narrative format that recalls their familiar mythic conventions, until the world they knew and cherished becomes steadily overtaken by a system of cold, impersonal documentation typical of the invading culture. *Things Fall Apart* begins, in fact, with the tale of Okonkwo's triumph in a wrestling contest over the legendary Amalinze the Cat. Thereafter, at measured intervals, the novel is punctuated with stories and storytelling situations in which the elderly and wise draw lessons from past events or a family basks in the poetry of their folk traditions. In these traditions, songs are frequently used by the storyteller to renew the attentiveness of the audience by drawing their participation into the lyric performance. In writing his story Achebe is, of course, operating within the conventions of print culture. Still, in interjecting nuggets of song here and there in the story, he evidently has in mind their old ventilatory role in oral narrative performances.

What I have said in the last few paragraphs bears some witness to an ethnographic design that has enabled Achebe to indulge a certain nostalgia for a way of life and an environment that helped to shape his outlook on the world. Once we move beyond this level, however, and venture into the artistic techniques that he has used in conveying the fortunes of that world, we find he is forced by the imperatives of art—or what elsewhere he has called the "truth of fiction"—to adopt a certain objective stance in interrogating the choices made by personalities guiding the affairs of that world. Here, no doubt, we are inclined to take seriously the point made by Ato Quayson in his contribution to this volume that *Things Fall Apart* can hardly be treated as a realistic portrait of the Igbo universe if it makes any claims at all to us as a work of art. Take the issue of proverb use as a central factor in Igbo speech. It is not without reason that in the third and final part of the book, when Okonkwo returns from exile to find that the foreigners have taken control of his village, there is a precipitous decline in the use of proverbs. Of course, the vibrancy that marked the life of the place is no more, and the people are somewhat shell-shocked. But I think that Achebe has deliberately drained the narrative, at this point, of the vigor of the traditional discourse to signal its powerlessness within the emergent structures of control. For all his loyalty to the traditions of his people, that old style of speech would ring hollow in the context of the dominant discourse.

I have called Achebe's attitude here an objective *stance*. But if we look carefully at some of the earlier episodes in the story, the word *distance* is a more fitting description of his approach to aspects of his culture. Take the scene in which the spirit masques (*egwugwu*) of Umuofia sit in judgment over the wife-beater Uzowulu. Achebe tells us of the crowd viewing the scene from a distance:

> Okonkwo's wives, and perhaps other women as well, might have noticed that the second *egwugwu* had the springy walk of Okonkwo. And they might also have noticed that Okonkwo was not among the titled men and elders who sat behind the row of *egwugwu*. But if they thought these things they kept them within themselves. The *egwugwu* with the springy walk was one of the dead fathers of the clan. (63–64)

Only a non-African, perhaps, would be fooled by the attempt in that last sentence to cover up a secret the writer has virtually given away: the *egwugwu* are really human beings masquerading as ancestors. Few native sons would be so bold as to reveal one of the fundamental secrets they had sworn in the cult enclave to keep. Perhaps Achebe, growing up in the strictly Christian household of his catechist father, was never initiated into any of these cults.[15] Fair enough. But the problem with revealing such a secret is that the *egwugwu*'s integrity is somewhat compromised. Given the intricate play of interests even in the collective life of rural societies, why should we as readers trust that the *egwugwu* would be impartial in a dispute?[16] After all, they are humans themselves. If we seek further evidence of this objective distance in Achebe, we will find it in the passages where he gives us a direct ethnographic insight into Umuofia life, as in the following:

> Fortunately, among *these* people a man was judged according to his worth and not according to the worth of his father. (6)
>
> Darkness held a vague terror for *these* people, even the bravest among *them*. (7; emphases mine)

It seems obvious that, in these instances of objective distance, Achebe has chosen to step back a little for some critical interrogation of the outlook he has undertaken to defend. Irele has characterized *Things Fall Apart* as "nothing less than an uncom-promising reappraisal of the tribal world" in light of the emergent postcolonial reality:

> Rather than a unilateral revaluation of the past, the central preoccupation of this novel, as indeed of Achebe's entire pro-duction, revolves around the deeply problematic relationship of past to present in Africa. What is at issue here, in the most fundamental way, is the bearing of that past upon the present, fraught as it is with implications for the future prospects of the continent. (Irele 144–45)

Given what I said earlier of the historical trajectory of Achebe's writing, I could hardly disagree with Irele's position. But if we consider the environment in which Achebe wrote the novel, we can understand why he may have adopted such an attitude in the cited passages. Earlier in this essay, I indicated some of the forces at play in the circumstances of Achebe's growth. For one thing, colonial culture had the insidious power to plant in the native African youth seeds of skepticism if not apostasy from their indigenous traditions. But Achebe must have faced an even greater challenge as he advanced further in the colony's intellec-tual culture. As an undergraduate at University College, Ibadan, he studied under (mostly British) scholars trained in the relativist discourse on the "primitive" Other. When he came to write his first novel shortly after graduation, it was too soon for him to realize that, in referring to his own people as *them*, he was un-wittingly identifying with an *us* who did not look too kindly across the divide.

With these considerations in mind, we may understand why we can hardly pretend to be on firm ground as we discuss the characters and events within the artistic economy of the novel. Take the character of the protagonist, Okonkwo. In more than ten years of teaching *Things Fall Apart* in the United States, I have encountered an array of responses to his representation in the novel. By far, the majority of these have been from young Amer-

icans vigorously defending his "heroic" violence against the agent
of the colonial administration that cost him his life. Yet the bias
of scholarly opinion appears to lean toward denouncing him as
a loose cannon, a character so driven by his self-importance that
all of his energies are devoted to defending no other interests but
his own. Or take his friend, Obierika. He has often been construed
as a foil to the personality of Okonkwo, a man who, while not
lacking in the manly virtues upheld by his society, nonetheless
represents a quality of pragmatic reason that has helped his culture to entertain and absorb successive changes in its outlook on
the world. Yet the question has just as often been asked, as hinted
in Harold Scheub's contribution to this volume: How well have
Obierika's touted qualities served his community as it capitulates
to a forced change it could scarcely have foreseen? After beheading the white man's messenger, Okonkwo, seeing that no one
will join him in fighting the white man, "wiped his matchet on
the sand and went away" (145). In the threnodic denouement of
the story, when the district commissioner visits the scene of
Okonkwo's suicide, Obierika finally announces the community's
plans for his friend's last rites: "When he has been buried we will
then do our duty by him. We shall make sacrifices to cleanse the
desecrated land" (147). At this point, one cannot help wondering,
with David Cook, "Which is the real desecration—Okonkwo's
stoic death, or the meek acceptance of humiliation at the hands
of the white man?" (80).

Easily the most controversial scene in *Things Fall Apart* is the
killing of the hostage boy, Ikemefuna. Again, Okonkwo's agency
in this has been denounced by an all-too-strident chorus of
(mostly Western) moral indignation. I have included, in this casebook, a contribution by an Igbo scholar, Damian Opata, who
stoutly defends the propriety of Okonkwo's act. It may be well
also to recall the statement on this issue by the distinguished Igbo
critic Emmanuel Obiechina:

> Ikemefuna's murder at the instigation of the Oracle of the Hills
> and the Caves (who is also the Oracle of the Earth Goddess)
> revolts the conscience of the reader who has followed his "in-

nocent" and vivacious young life throughout the three years in which he has integrated himself into Okonkwo's household. "Innocent" is put advisedly in quotation marks because he is innocent only in the sense that he has done nothing wrong. Our feeling for him should not obscure the fact that as soon as his people hand him over to Umuofia as a recompense for their murdered kinswoman, Ikemefuna loses his innocence. He becomes the bearer of the guilt of his whole people and must be sacrificed to expiate their crime of homicide. When he falls, he does so by the operation of the lex talonis, for many traditional Africans like the Jews of old believed in an eye for an eye and a life for a life, especially in their dealings with those outside their own corporate groups. No one is better suited to take the dreadful decision than the oracle of the goddess whose duty it is to see to the security of the community and its members and to demand expiation when one of her children has been murdered. The earth requires that justice should be done, and it is done. (*Culture, Tradition and Society* 213)

Yet none of this sanctimony resolves the dilemma created by the delicate artistry of the scene. The journey to kill Ikemefuna on the outskirts of Umuofia is a tightly drawn episode, with a great deal of grim suspense built into it, as befits a truly tragic undertaking. But somehow we are scarcely led to suspect that Okonkwo will be the one to kill the boy, especially since he has been warned by the respected Ezeudu to have no hand in killing a child who calls him "father." We may well be justified in assuming that Okonkwo follows the executioners just to make sure they carry out their hard but sacred duty. Still, he goes ahead and kills Ikemefuna, and the reason the writer gives us for Okonkwo's act is that "he was afraid of being thought weak" (43)! I, for one, would have defended Okonkwo on the ground that, seeing the executioners have done such a poor job with a blow that leaves Ikemefuna reeling in a miserable half-life, Okonkwo has done well to save the boy from further suffering. But, to be "afraid of being thought weak"! Would it make sense to surmise that Okonkwo is unable to control himself in the frenzy of Ikemefuna's dash toward him; that, surprised by the menacing stampede of the sacrificial animal, Okonkwo decides to terminate its life before it gets out of control; or that, having abdicated the protective instincts of a father (as Ikemefuna calls him), he is left with nothing but the killing urge of a gore-blinded warrior? These are scary thoughts, whichever one we choose.

The callousness and precipitancy of the act clearly becomes a man who has taken a gunshot at his own wife and later beheads an unarmed messenger.[17] But if we look beyond the explanation given by Achebe, we cannot help recalling vignettes of domestic relations between Okonkwo and Ikemefuna from earlier in the novel and asking a few questions. For instance, when Ezeudu visits Okonkwo and warns him that, though the clan has decided to kill Ikemefuna, he should have no hand in the boy's death, what *really* does Okonkwo begin to tell the old man before he is interrupted (40): that the boy should be spared the fate everyone has long known to have been appointed for him? Is there something in the relations between Ikemefuna and Okonkwo's son, Nwoye—with whom Ikemefuna has been particularly close— that may be a factor at the point when the boy is being sacrificed? We are told Okonkwo likes Ikemefuna very much as his own son, and particularly appreciates Ikemefuna's role in encouraging manly instincts in an otherwise tender-hearted Nwoye, lover of "women's" tales. When Ezeudu comes to announce Umuofia's decision about Ikemefuna, does Okonkwo try to interrupt him because he fears the boy is being taken away before he has quite fulfilled the role he has been playing in Okonkwo's family? It is quite curious that, as Ikemefuna is being led through the bush toward his death, Okonkwo does not say a word nor does Achebe give us the faintest clue what thoughts are on his mind. So, when Okonkwo deals Ikemefuna that decisive deathblow, is he perhaps taking his frustration out on the poor boy over his unfinished role in Okonkwo's household?

Given Okonkwo's masculinist paranoia about Nwoye's future as heir to his household (37, 107–9), these are hardly idle questions to ask. They certainly bear some witness to the way Achebe has problematized the character of Okonkwo in this story. And if we still wonder at Ato Quayson's plea that we not treat *Things Fall Apart* as a realistic portrait of Igbo society, perhaps we should ask ourselves one final question: In view of the ethnographic picture Achebe presents of Umuofia as a society tolerant of diverse voices and open to reasonable changes in its outlook, are there other than artistic grounds for justifying the role of such a deviant within it?[18] When we ask such a question, we will begin to appreciate the novel more as an allegorical response to the peculiar (postcolonial) environment in which Achebe conceived the work, than as what Obi Wali thought it was: a failed attempt to create an individualist in an entirely collectivist society.

There are other problems in *Things Fall Apart* that various contributions in this casebook will address. One of these is the image of the female in the novel's gendered economy. Evidently, Umuofia recognizes some balance between male and female entities in its ontology—or does it? The beauty of the harmonious partnership between Ogbuefi Ndulue and his senior wife, Ozoemena (47–48), appears to be qualified by its uniqueness. Certainly, the logic of Okonkwo's role in the story problematizes the prospects of gender harmony within it. In their contributions here, Rhonda Cobham and Biodun Jeyifo raise some ground-breaking questions, from uncommon ideological and pedagogical angles, about the female factor in the novel.

I would like to conclude by interrogating the title Achebe has chosen for this novel. Do things *really* fall apart and, if so, in what sense? Of course, the old mythology and religion lose some of their hold: there may now be some misfit between one's wishes and those of one's personal god (*chi*); the *egwugwu* have been exposed to public gaze by overzealous converts; and though Okoli dies not long after he kills a sacred python, the new mission thrives, within the dreaded Evil Forest, with a growing number of converts. Of course, the colonial presence aggravates the latent divisions within Umuofia by quietly encouraging the self-serving instincts of some of its citizens: with the establishment of schools that breed a new indigenous leadership and trading stores that create a new economic elite, a new power structure emerges that relegates the old titled class to the background. Most of all, the white man has come with weapons of mass destruction for which the indigenous African arms are no match. But do these things *really* destroy the nerve center of the Igbo world?

In their contributions here, Clayton MacKenzie and Neil ten Kortenaar take two somewhat divergent positions on the issue, and I think they make compelling arguments about the fate of the Igbo society of *Things Fall Apart*. However, in light of Achebe's programmatic interest in history, I would like to step a little outside the ambit of fiction and address the concept of "falling apart" in the larger postcolony. If, following Achebe's lead, we review the history of the Nigerian nation from pre-independence to the present day, we will agree that though the nation continues to hang together in some desperate half-life, the constitutional and other ties fashioned by well-meaning nationalists to hold the loose federation securely together have hopelessly slackened; the organs within the debilitated body have pretty much fallen apart. But somehow, those organs have managed to reinvigorate themselves and take on lives of their own in the absence of a leadership committed to their corporate existence. In other words, the political entities in present-day Nigeria are behaving as though they no longer owe their existence to the political union of which they were supposed to be a part. The constituent states of the country are vitalized more by pristine ethnic loyalties than by nationalist ideologies of more recent history.

While, therefore, things may have fallen apart in the federation, they have hardly done so in its respective ethnic cocoons. The tribe—to recall a word that was banished from currency in the heady days of nationalist zeal—is alive and well with a vengeance in Nigerian political life. It is relevant to bring these issues to an interrogation of the concept of "falling apart" in Achebe's novel, if we seriously mean to understand what becomes the real fate of Umuofia in light of the dissolution of its old structures of existence. Does a people "fall apart" just because it has been overrun by a new power and culture? So the old religion loses its hold; a new economic structure comes into place; the old leadership is superseded by a class of competent young men trained in the ways of the foreign culture. But do the new elite suddenly lose a sense of who they *really* are? After all, as we learn from the reflections of Obierika and Ezeudu in the novel, things in their day are not what they were like in the past; new systems and usages enter the lore of the clan, which absorbs them and carries on life with a duly adjusted outlook. More important, the language of the clan, which is the final distillate of its composite outlook, does not disappear but simply finds a place for the new cultural elements. Today, language continues to be the basis of cohesion of the respective political units in Nigeria, and this with a vengeance. The last few years have seen the rise of ethnic organizations in Nigeria, not unlike the Umuofia Progressive Union of *No Longer at Ease*, each one adopting a name that announces a separatist identity: in the Hausa North, *Arewa*; in the Yoruba West, *Afenifere*; in the Igbo East, *Ohaneze*; and other, less-prominent, "minority" associations. Worse still, these bodies have affiliated organs, in various ethnic constituencies of the new African diaspora in North America and Europe, which are busy utilizing the new electronic media as much for fanning the flames of interethnic conflict back home as for keeping alive a sense of their cultural identity.

To understand in what sense "things fall apart" in Achebe's novel, therefore, it is not out of place to step a little outside the ambit of fiction and take a long look at social and political developments in the country where the novel has been set. It is a view that the nationalist writer in Achebe would happily endorse.[19]

MY CHOICE OF CONTRIBUTIONS to this casebook is aimed at exploring the diversity of issues that have been raised over time in the study of *Things Fall Apart*. I have given the first statement to Achebe himself, so as to foreground the nationalist project he set himself in writing the novel. We then move through essays that provide a variety of insights: ethnography, literary and critical analysis, ideology, pedagogy, and theory. We end with an interview in which Achebe addresses a variety of questions that students and general readers, especially in the West, have asked of this engaging novel.

Things Fall Apart is an unusual novel not only for the "strange" world it portrays but equally for the unfamiliar touch Achebe brings to the English medium of his writing. Indeed, with this novel, Achebe intiated a vogue in postcolonial African literature whereby writers, while representing their societies in a European language, endeavored to create a space for their indigenous sensibilities in both sound (African words inserted here and there) and sense (peculiar ways of meaning). In "The African Writer and the English Language," Achebe explains and defends the logic of the choices he had to make in his peculiar use of English. This early (1964) essay, which establishes Achebe's mission as champion of an integral African cultural sensibility, has influenced a good deal of assessment of the content and style of *Things Fall Apart* and other Achebe fiction.

In "Igbo Cosmology and the Parameters of Individual Accomplishment," Clement Okafor offers a neat ethnographic introduction to Achebe's fiction, especially *Things Fall Apart*, putting many of its concepts in their proper contexts. He presents Igbo society as historically egalitarian and democratic, with no tradition of rulers having anything like autocratic powers. Instead, it is marked by an ideology of duality or pairing, which ensures a sense of balance in all human undertakings and relationships. Okonkwo's failure to recognize this ideology becomes "a major handicap" in his personality. Destiny is seen as a prenatal choice that determines the course of an individual's life but need not preclude the exercise of individual initiative. This ethnographic survey hardly pretends to be exhaustive, nor does it try to account for adjustments to these concepts in diverse segments of Igboland. Still, whatever discursive strategy any critic may adopt in looking at the novel, this essay, by an Igbo scholar, should provide "an appropriate epistemological framework" for the exercise.

It is generally agreed that Okonkwo is destroyed by his high-handedness and *hubris*. Damian Opata's contribution, "Eternal Sacred Order versus Conventional Wisdom," nevertheless addresses Okonkwo's behavior in what is perhaps the most controversial episode in the story: his killing of the hostage boy, Ikemefuna.

While not denying the basic character flaws in the hero, Opata argues that there are controlling forces at play in Okonkwo's conduct, which leave him no choice but to do what he has done. Not only is Okonkwo, as one of the community's elders, obligated to carry out the order of the Oracle of the Hills and the Caves, but at the moment that he kills Ikemefuna he is under the control not of his own will but of the "capricious fates." As for the misfortunes that descend on Okonkwo subsequent to the act— for example, his accidental killing of Ezeudu's son at the old man's funeral—Opata suggests it is instructive not only that Ezeudu, the first man to caution Okonkwo against having a hand in Ikemefuna's death, loses his own life not long after the event, but indeed that it is his own son who is killed at his funeral. Clearly, there are forces at play here that transcend "human rationalization."

Harold Scheub's "When a Man Fails Alone" shows how Okonkwo so systematically isolates himself from the mores of his society that his tragedy is inevitable. Although he is the principal character in the novel and may be seen to epitomize the interests of his society, he is remarkably out of touch with the society's outlook and aspirations. Scheub methodically shows how Okonkwo, driven by fears of failure and dreams of success, continually upsets the balance sought by his people between material success and humane sensibility. "We do not, in this novel, witness the death throes of a society," he argues. What falls apart is not Umuofia society and culture—which have always survived by adjusting to ever-changing conditions—but Okonkwo, with his selfish goals of greatness.

Scheub's conclusions are complemented, in a fundamental sense, by Neil ten Kortenaar's "How the Center Is Made to Hold in *Things Fall Apart*." This essay interrogates Achebe's title for the novel by arguing that, contrary to the conventional view that the "homoeostatic" Igbo world disintegrates with the coming of Europeans, who proceed to incorporate it into a history predicated on literacy, there are certain internal dynamics in the traditional life of the Igbo that already identify them as active agents in the construction of their own history. By portraying the Igbo as a self-contained culture that nonetheless shares in a common humanity, Achebe succeeds immensely, argues ten Kortenaar, in demonstrating that the European intervention is by no means an unrelieved catastrophe for Igbo history and society. The Igbo are not just static subjects of the changes happening around them but participate actively by internalizing and reformulating their conceptual universe. "There is continuity and development, not just repetition and rupture. The Igbos chose Christianity, as Nwoye did, or rejected it, as Okonkwo did, because they were aware of themselves making their own world in time."

Contrarily, in "The Metamorphosis of Piety in *Things Fall Apart*," Clayton MacKenzie argues that in Umuofia "things have irrevocably fallen apart." The Christian mission aids the colonizing process by pursuing a process of "aggressive . . . proselytizing," which succeeds in two respects: first, weakening the hold of the traditional religion on the people, and second, offering the people surer routes of individual economic success. According to MacKenzie, Christianity does not at all coexist with traditional beliefs in a spirit of accommodation; rather, it aids the colonial enterprise by demanding "ideological substitution" and "metamorphosing piety against a backdrop of seemingly irresistible social and economic imperatives." There are at least two ways in which the new orientation wins against the old. First, "the real power of missionary proselytization lay in the breaking down of community norms. The Evil Forest became no longer evil; the outcasts became no longer outcasts; the objects and rituals of traditional sacrament were destroyed." Second, and perhaps more decisively, "the metamorphosis of piety is not a change from belief in one religious system to belief in another religious system but rather a switch from faith in a world where life is given, to commitment to one where security and achievement are measured and earned very differently."[20]

The next two articles in this collection deal with the gender outlook of *Things Fall Apart*. But far from roundly condemning Achebe for his marginalization of women in Igbo society, they view his novel against the background of the imperatives of his time and explore what lessons may be gleaned from it for a larger nationalist agenda.

Rhonda Cobham's "Problems of Gender and History" sees Achebe's work as a child of the dominant Euro-Christian cultural climate, to which it tries a little too hard to respond. For instance, in the episode of the killing of Ikemefuna, Cobham sees Achebe as trying to balance two outlooks: on the one hand, Achebe does his best to keep the ritual as close to the Igbo way of doing things while, on the other hand, he introduces into it the biblical motif of Abraham's sacrifice of his son, Isaac. The difference here is that there is no animal substitute. Cobham thinks that Achebe's selective use of cultural elements in the novel "speaks ably to his need to establish a view of a world, both modern and traditional, of which he can be a part." This becomes a problem, she suggests, only if we see the story as a "definitive, 'objective' account of the Igbo, not to say African, traditional past." Cobham does lament that, in his representation of the female factor in the novel, Achebe has not thought fit to consult traditions of female authority that are fairly well documented by anthropologists and made evident by the Aba Women's War of 1929.[21] Even here, she is not too hard on Achebe for selecting details that would help him tell the sort of tale of culture conflict he thinks suits a vision of the world he wants to project. "This [story] serves to remind us that literature, like anthropology or history, is a form of selective representation, replete with its inherent assumptions about authenticity and objectivity. Those of us who teach *Things Fall Apart* as literature in the hope of reaffirming traditional values may do well to bear in mind that the values we discover in the text will be most likely our own."

Biodun Jeyifo's "Okonkwo and His Mother" is a stimulating analysis of gender politics in *Things Fall Apart*—in his own words, a "radical feminist critique" intended as "an effective intervention in postcolonial African critical discourse." In this essay, Jeyifo concentrates his gaze on a single and often neglected reference to Okonkwo's mother in *Things Fall Apart*—regarding the story about Mosquito and Ear she told him in his youth—which for Jeyifo represents the hero's overall "phallogocentric" suppression of motherlore and the female personality, against the grain of traditional Igbo culture. Jeyifo acknowledges that Okonkwo's suppression of motherlore and femininity is, as especially female critics like Florence Stratton have pointed out,[22] a function of "fundamental male anxiety and insecurity about femaleness and its putative *primal* connection to creativity." Such "uterocentric" readings should not, however, ignore the more urgent challenge facing Achebe and his generation of writers at the critical point of history where they stood:

> The *nationalist* "master texts" of African postcolonial literature needed, as the basis of their self-constitution as *representative*, canonical works, to subsume gender difference under the putatively more primary racial and cultural difference of a resisting Africa from a colonizing Europe. By this occlusion of gender difference, Okonkwo's mother, his wives, and daughters recede into the *ground* which enables the *figure* of Okonkwo and his father and son to achieve their representational prominence.

Jeyifo identifies two basic failures in Achebe's characters. First, Okonkwo is so obsessed with his masculinist suppression of womanhood that he fails to see that his fight against the invading colonial presence is rendered futile thereby. At the same time, in disavowing "the national-masculine ethic that is embodied in his father's personality" and crossing over to the colonizers, his son, Nwoye, merely "embraces the colonialist ideology of the 'civilizing mission.' It is not overstating the case to observe that his feminization does not lead him to an adequate, critical comprehension of the invading colonial project." Both characters, argues Jeyifo, fail to recognize the insidious class and gender divisions inherent in the agenda of colonial capitalism. The point of this article is to seize the middle ground between the two positions represented by Okonkwo and his son and "rewrite national liberation as a historic phenomenon with a greater complexity in issues of gender and gender politics than a benighted, categorical phallocentrism." This is not, of course, a recommendation to rewrite *Things Fall Apart*, but a warning to "African male-centered writers and critics" against creating "a 'national' literature which, if not a mere appendage, a mere extension of metropolitan European traditions, is nevertheless imbricated in deeply gendered alienations and reifications whose genealogical roots go back to colonialism." This is a sound gender insight, though it is not pressed quite so firmly in respect of "uterocentric" feminist writers and critics.

Bu-Buakei Jabbi's "Fire and Transition" is one of the earliest discussions of *Things Fall Apart* to view it as serious literary art, motivated by the belief that criticism of African literature, rather than treating it as a "sociological handmaid" should "give riddance to a mere defensive pose" and "become truly literary and exploratory." In other words, Jabbi argues for a critical approach that balances the conventional interest in life and culture with an inquiry into the aesthetic design of the work. In examining the figurative economy of *Things Fall Apart* for symbols and images that encapsulate the central crisis of the story, Jabbi focuses on two of its most recurrent figures. One of these is fire: "By means of it, the novel manages to suggest how, unchecked or indulged, the manliness complex may blaze into a veritable *edax rerum*, working out a sinister scheme of suicide and disintegration from within." The other is the figure of water, especially of "rain water falling with relief on the sun-baked earth." It is significant that this figure of water is frequently juxtaposed with that of heat or fire, suggesting the prospect of a synthesis or fusion of the two contending forces in the world of the story (the traditional and the Euro-Christian) without going so far as to indicate a resolution. For example, in the portrait of a rain storm announcing the planting season in Mbanta (*Things Fall Apart* 115–16), we see "an effective imaginative projection of that ultimate adjustment and accommodation" that facilitates Nwoye's conversion to Christianity. Conversion does not, however, guarantee the resolution of the contending forces nor the society's adjustment to the new dispensation: the fusion of water with fire only symbolizes a transitional moment in the unfolding history, whereby Achebe "holds out a cautious optimism about the evolution of values" in the society. A critical voice like Jabbi's is seldom heard these days amid the buzz of postmodernist chatter. But its validity can hardly be questioned.

Ato Quayson's "Realism, Criticism, and the Disguises of Both" takes the artistic claims of *Things Fall Apart* quite as seriously and reinforces the caution sounded by Rhonda Cobham against treating the novel as a definitive picture of a particular society. Evidently because Achebe declared his mission to give a more accurate account of his society, earlier scholars tended to adopt one or another "representationalist" approach to discussing his fiction: by treating it as an anthropological portrait of the writer's immediate society; by seeing it as a more dependable account of an "African" reality than anything the colonial novelists ever wrote; or by hailing it for evincing authentic African aesthetics. Such fixations on Achebe as representing the *reality* of African life have, however, failed to address writings that adopt a more mythic than historical mode of representation, such as Amos Tutuola's romances or the more nuanced mythopoeic fiction of Soyinka, Armah, Okri, and others. Yet Quayson is no more sympathetic toward the kind of criticism that recognizes a supernal *text* from which the cultural matrix of a literary work can hardly be recovered.

Quayson identifies two levels at which a piece of fiction may be seen to be structured: one is the *metonymic* level, whereby the writer tries to mirror the cultural or anthropological reality (the "ethno-text") of its setting, and the other is the *symbolic/metaphoric* level, whereby the writer may manipulate a set of ironies[23] that subverts the ethno-text. In *Things Fall Apart*, Quayson argues although the ethno-text seems to privilege the female in the cosmogony of Umuofian society, the narrative consciously patriarchalizes its power structure; further, it sets up a pattern of antinomies that continually problematizes the relations between "male" and "female" values within Umuofian society and the relations between the society and the colonial presence. The important thing in this approach to criticism, argues Quayson, is to recognize that art is essentially based on a manipulation of reality.

The challenge is to examine the artistic statement closely enough to reveal those slippages whereby the artist achieves modes of signification that move the work beyond a facile representation of the world as we know it. "*Things Fall Apart*, like African novels in general," he suggests, "possesses a richly ambivalent attitude to its culture that can only be discovered by paying attention both to the reality processed and to the larger discursive strategies employed."

Charles Rowell's "Interview with Chinua Achebe" balances the overview of Achebe already given here. Like most interviews with African writers, this one touches on many subjects relating to the writer's creative career and the situation of African literature in an international context. The foci of the interview include issues like the role and sensibility of the African artist; African literature and its social responsibility; African literature and the Western canon, or "great tradition"; and especially certain positions Achebe has taken in various lectures, for example, in relation to European writers like Joseph Conrad, who have painted negative pictures of Africa in their works. There are a few questions directly related to *Things Fall Apart*, including Achebe's use of proverbs and patterns of irony in the story. The appeal of this interview is that Rowell does not make undue assumptions of readers' specialized familiarity with Achebe's work, as is often the case in interviews conducted by African intellectuals. In this way, Rowell succeeds in providing both a general insight into Achebe's art and thought and a specific focus on issues that will help especially the Western reader put *Things Fall Apart* in its proper perspective.

Most of the contributions to this casebook date from the 1990s, attesting to the continued appeal of *Things Fall Apart* as a classic literary statement and its significance as a paradigmatic comment on the postcolonial condition. As a pioneering work of contemporary African fiction, it remains the point of reference for anyone concerned with Africa's continued attempts to fashion a scale of values for itself in an increasingly complex global society. Beyond its African world, the novel is equally notable for the humane challenge it poses to our capacity to see ourselves in the predicaments of others. I have never ceased to marvel, as I teach the book year after year in the United States, at how forcefully young Americans debate the choices open to the people of Umuofia—and especially to its champion, Okonkwo—as they find themselves steadily losing their land, their dignity, and their way of life to foreign elements. In this sense, *Things Fall Apart* is not simply a contribution to a multicultural education. It is a challenge to all of us to reflect that we may someday find ourselves having to defend the freedoms we so easily take for granted.

Notes

1. We should not, of course, underestimate the active encouragement given by the British colonial leadership to the quest by some of the emergent Nigerian elite for acceptance into the privileged circles of the dominant culture, through efforts like the adoption of English surnames and European manners. Echeruo's *Victorian Lagos* gives ample documentation of such propensities. However, the earlier response by the Nigerian writer Wole Soyinka to the aggressive francophone ideology of Negritude—that the tiger need not proclaim its "tigritude"—is an eloquent measure of the anglophone African's attitude toward such matters at the time.

2. Some others were in Accra, the Gold Coast (later Ghana); Makerere, Uganda; and Kingston, Jamaica, all founded in 1948 as "external" campuses of London University.

3. For interesting, and somewhat varied, insights into Joyce Cary's fiction on Africa, see Mahood, *Joyce Cary's Africa*; Echeruo (Mahood's student at Ibadan), *Joyce Cary and the Novel of Africa*; and JanMohamed, *Manichean Aesthetics*, 15–48.

4. See Ezenwa-Ohaeto, 60–65, for a detailed account of the journey of the novel from manuscript to publication.

5. Achebe invokes Conrad's *Heart of Darkness* in his second and third novels, in each case projecting Conrad's major imperial characters (Marlow and Kurtz) as grotesque representatives of the racist mentality. There has, incidentally, been some effort in more recent times to credit the works of Ekwensi and Tutuola with a deeper sense of purpose. Achebe has himself published a paper ("Work and Play") which sees *The Palm-Wine Drinkard* as a castigation of contemporary society's abdication

of a traditional work ethic; see also Emenyonu's *Cyprian Ekwensi* for a fairly sympathetic discussion of the writer's stories. It is also worth noting that there was some prose fiction in indigenous Nigerian languages before Achebe. D. O. Fagunwa, acknowledged to be the model for Tutuola's picaresque fantasies, published three of his four novels in Yoruba between 1938 and 1954, the first of them translated by Soyinka as *The Forest of a Thousand Daemons*; the novels are the subject of an interesting study by Ayo Bamgbose. There was also Pita Nwana's Igbo novella, *Omenuko* (1933), and the Hausa *Shaihu Umar* (1955) by Abubakar Tafawa Balewa, who became Nigeria's first prime minister at independence (1960). Both works utilize the adventure format in highlighting the virtues of earnest perseverance.

6. A similar purpose is served by Wole Soyinka's first play, *A Dance of the Forests* (1963), which, offered as part of a state-sponsored program of events celebrating Nigeria's independence, spares no pains in warning the author's compatriots that, if history is any guide, there is little cause for optimism.

7. In *Decolonizing the Mind*, Ngugi (wa Thiong'o) took a firm nationalist stand to cease writing fiction in English and thenceforth adopt his native Gikuyu as his medium. *Petals of Blood* was the last novel he wrote in English.

8. In *A Man of the People*, "all the policemen turn round and walk quietly away" as Odili is being beaten unconscious by thugs at Nanga's political rally. In the real Nigeria of December 2001, it was reported that, when the assassins of the country's attorney general, Chief Bola Ige, arrived at his house to kill him, *all* the policemen on duty at the time left the place to have their dinner. It appears that life has a record of imitating art here; the artist is only being astute in reading trends in social and political behavior.

9. The American edition was given the title *Christmas in Biafra and Other Poems*.

10. I believe that Achebe wrote the seminal essay "*Chi* in Igbo Cosmology"—on a central concept in *Things Fall Apart*—during his early years (1970–1973) as a research fellow at the Institute of African Studies at Nsukka.

11. By "derivative" I imply works like the journal's educational supplement (under the editorship of Emmanuel Obiechina of the English department), poetry collections in English (*Don't Let Him Die*, dedicated to the late Okigbo) and Igbo (*Aka Weta*, an anthology of oral and written verses), and even the short story collection *Girls at War and Other Stories*, plus some material that was published in *Okike*.

12. Faint echoes of Lord Byron in Greece, perhaps, for a poet with a degree in the classics. The first time Wole Soyinka was thrown into detention (1965), it was for allegedly seizing a radio station to forestall the announcement of electoral victory by an unpopular government, which had evidently rigged the elections. He, too, may have tired of simply decrying injustice in his writing.

13. "Ibo" in this passage was the form preferred by the colonial authorities for the real name of the people, Igbo.

14. For an insightful discussion of proverb use in Achebe, see Bernth Lindfors's "The Palm-Oil with Which Achebe's Words Are Eaten." For a substantial discussion of language use by African novelists, including Achebe, see Obiechina, *Language and Theme*, 53–67.

15. In a somewhat similar moment in John Munonye's *The Only Son*, when a group of boys are being pressured by their schoolteacher to reveal the names of certain items pertaining to their masquerade cult, the novelist interjects a parenthetical comment that resolves an awkward cultural problem for himself and his characters: "The Nigerian Society for Preservation of African Culture forbids that the names be revealed" (153).

16. On page 121, Achebe recalls Okonkwo's place in the company of the spirit masques, which he abdicated as a result of being exiled from his community. Given the character of Okonkwo in the novel, the integrity of the *egwugwu*'s judgment is that much less beyond cavil.

17. The Igbo have a saying, *Ozi adi egbu uko*, which means "the message should not kill the messenger." The crowd may have fled from Okonkwo partly because they expect the grim response of the white man who sent the messenger, but partly also because Okonkwo, defender of his people and their values, seems to have taken full leave of his senses by breaking one of their hallowed taboos.

18. Compare Gerald Moore: "A point missed by many commentators is that Okonkwo is not 'a typical Igbo man.' If he had been, his example would have been followed by others. It is Obierika who really represents the more typical role. Okonkwo is more like a super-Igbo; an exaggeration of certain qualities admired by his people, but at the expense of others which the more rounded man is expected to possess" (127).

19. On Achebe's recommendation of the "long view of society," see his interview in Duerden and Pieterse, 17. Since the nation seems to thrive better at the level of ethnic or regional formations, perhaps a confederated union, which has often been recommended, is the best guarantee of its survival, after all.

20. MacKenzie seems to agree, to some extent, with Obiechina's conclusions on the factors leading to the capitulation of Umuofia society to the new dispensation; see Obiechina, *Culture, Tradition, and Society*, 232–33.

21. Cobham cites Leith-Ross's *African Women* on this subject, though the same account occurs in Perham's *Native Administration in Nigeria*. We should also add Green's *Igbo Village Affairs*, which contains some interesting observations on aspects of female empowerment in the specific community (Umueke Agbaja) she investigated, under commission from the colonial government, in the wake of the Aba Women's War. Of more recent studies of women's empowerment among the Igbo, Amadiume's *Male Daughters, Female Husbands* is a particularly engaging work.

22. Jeyifo specifically identifies Stratton's essay "Periodic Embodiments" in this connection.

23. In a 1989 interview, Achebe discussed with Bill Moyers the Igbo proverb "wherever something stands, something else will stand beside it" (Moyers 333) as not only codifying the Igbo belief in dualisms and alternative perspectives in life, but also as a guiding principle in his own writing. No doubt, this principle accounts for the centrality of ironies in the texture of his novels, especially in *Things Fall Apart*.

Works Cited

Achebe, Chinua. "Africa and Her Writers." In Achebe, *Morning Yet on Creation Day*, 29–45. New York: Anchor/Doubleday, 1975.

———. *Anthills of the Savannah*. London: Heinemann, 1987.

———. *Arrow of God*. London: Heinemann, 1964.

———. *Beware Soul Brother and Other Poems*. Enugu: Nwankwo-Ifejika, 1971.

———. "Chi in Igbo Cosmology." In Achebe, *Morning Yet on Creation Day*, 159–75. New York: Anchor/Doubleday, 1975.

———. *Christmas in Biafra and Other Poems*. New York: Anchor/Doubleday, 1973.

———. *Girls at War and Other Stories*. London: Heinemann, 1972.

———. *Home and Exile*. New York: Oxford University Press, 2000.

———. *Hopes and Impediments: Selected Essays*. London: Heinemann, 1988.

———. "An Image of Africa." In Achebe, *Hopes and Impediments*, 1–13. London: Heinemann, 1988.

———. *A Man of the People*. London: Heinemann, 1966.

————. *Morning Yet on Creation Day*. New York: Anchor/Doubleday, 1975.

————. "Named for Victoria, Queen of England." In Achebe, *Morning Yet on Creation Day*, 115–24. New York: Anchor/Doubleday, 1975.

————. *No Longer at Ease*. London: Heinemann, 1960.

————. "The Novelist as Teacher." In Achebe, *Morning Yet on Creation Day*, 67–74. New York: Anchor/Doubleday, 1975.

————. *Things Fall Apart* [1958]. London: Heinemann, 1962.

————. *The Trouble with Nigeria*. Enugu: Fourth Dimension, 1983.

————. "The Truth of Fiction." In Achebe, *Hopes and Impediments*, 95–105. London: Heinemann, 1988.

————. "Work and Play in Tutuola's *The Palm-Wine Drinkard*." In Achebe, *Hopes and Impediments*, 68–76. London: Heinemann, 1988.

Achebe, Chinua, and John Iroaganachi. *How the Leopard Got Its Claws*. Enugu: Nwamife, 1972.

Achebe, Chinua, and Dubem Okafor, eds. *Don't Let Him Die: An Anthology of Memorial Poems for Christopher Okigbo*. Enugu: Fourth Dimension, 1978.

Achebe, Chinua, and Obiorah Udechukwu, eds. *Aka Weta: Egwu Aguluagu, Egwu-Edeluede*. Nsukka: Okike, 1982.

Amadiume, Ifi. *Male Daughters, Female Husbands: Gender and Sex in an African Society*. London: Zed, 1987.

Armah, Ayi Kwei. *The Beautyful Ones Are Not Yet Born*. London: Heinemann, 1969.

Balewa, Abubakar Tafawa. *Shaihu Umar*. 1955. Reprint. London: Longmans, Green, 1967.

Bamgbose, Ayo. *The Novels of D. O. Fagunwa*. Benin City, Ethiope, 1974.

Carroll, David. *Chinua Achebe*. New York: St. Martin's, 1980.

Cook, David. *African Literature: A Critical View*. London: Longmans, 1977.

Davies, Carole Boyce. "Motherhood in the Works of Male and Female Igbo Writers: Achebe, Emecheta, Nwapa, and Nzekwu." In *Ngambika: Studies of Women in African Literature*, edited by C. B. Davies and A. A. Graves, 241–56. Trenton, NJ: Africa World, 1986.

Duerden, Dennis, and Cosmo Pieterse, eds. *African Writers Talking: A Collection of Radio Interviews*. London: Heinemann, 1972.

Echeruo, Michael J. C. *Joyce Cary and the Novel of Africa*. New York: Africana, 1973.

————. *Victorian Lagos*. London: Macmillan, 1977.

Ekwensi, Cyprian. *The Leopard's Claw*. London: Longmans, Green, 1947.

————. *When Love Whispers*. Onitsha: Tabansi, 1948.

————. *People of the City*. London: Dakers, 1954.

Emenyonu, Ernest. *Cyprian Ekwensi*. London: Evans, 1974.

Ezenwa-Ohaeto. *Chinua Achebe: A Biography*. Oxford: Currey, 1997.

Gikandi, Simon. *Reading Chinua Achebe*. London: Currey, 1991.

Green, Margaret M. *Igbo Village Affairs: Chiefly with Reference to the Village of Umueke Agbaja*. 1947. Reprint. London: Cass, 1964.

Innes, C. L. *Chinua Achebe*. Cambridge: Cambridge University Press, 1990.

Irele, F. Abiola. *The African Imagination: Literature in Africa and the Black Diaspora*. New York: Oxford University Press, 2001.

JanMohamed, Abdul. *Manichean Aesthetics: The Politics of Literature in Colonial Africa*. Amherst: University of Massachusetts Press, 1988.

Killam, G. D. *The Writings of Chinua Achebe*. New York: Africana, 1969.

Leith-Ross, Sylvia. *African Women: A Study of the Ibo of Nigeria*. London: Routledge, 1939.

Lindfors, Bernth. "The Palm-Oil with Which Achebe's Words Are Eaten." *African Literature Today* 1 (1968): 3–18. Reprinted in *Critical Perspectives on Chinua Achebe*, edited by C. L. Innes and B. Lindfors. Washington, DC: Three Continents, 1978.

Mahood, Molly. *Joyce Cary's Africa*. 1964. Reprint. Boston: Houghton Mifflin, 1965.

Moore, Gerald. *Twelve African Writers*. Bloomington: Indiana University Press, 1980.

Moyers, Bill. "Interview with Chinua Achebe." In *A World of Ideas*, edited by B. Flowers. Garden City, NY: Doubleday, 1989.

Munonye, John. *The Only Son*. London: Heinemann, 1966.

Ngugi wa Thiong'o. *Decolonizing the Mind*. London: Currey, 1986.

———. *Petals of Blood*. London: Heinemann, 1977.

Nwana, Pita. *Omenuko*. London: Longmans, Green, 1933.

Obiechina, Emmanuel N. *Culture, Tradition, and Society in the West African Novel*. Cambridge: Cambridge University Press, 1975.

———. *Language and Theme: Essays on African Literature*. Washington, DC: Howard University Press, 1990.

Okigbo, Christopher. "Hurrah for Thunder." In *Christopher Okigbo: Collected Poems*, edited by A. Maja-Pearce, 94. London: Heinemann, 1986.

Perham, Margery. *Native Administration in Nigeria*. London: Oxford University Press, 1937.

Soyinka, Wole. *A Dance of the Forests* [1963]. In *Wole Soyinka, Five Plays*. London: Oxford University Press, 1964.

Soyinka, Wole, and D. O. Fagunwa. *The Forest of a Thousand Daemons*. London: Nelson, 1968.

Stratton, Florence. "Periodic Embodiments: A Ubiquitous Trope in African Men's Writing." *Research in African Literatures* 21 (1990): 111–26.

Tutuola, Amos. *The Palm-Wine Drinkard and His Dead Palm-Wine Tapster in the Deads' Town.* London: Faber, 1952.

———. *My Life in the Bush of Ghosts.* London: Faber, 1954.

———. *Simbi and the Satyr of the Dark Jungle.* London: Faber, 1955.

Wali, Obiajunwa. "The Dead End of African Literature." *Transition* 11 (1963): 13–15.

———. "The Individual and the Novel in Africa." *Transition* 13 (1965): 28–34.

Wren, Robert M. *Achebe's World: The Historical and Cultural Context of the Novels of Chinua Achebe.* Washington, DC: Three Continents, 1980.

The African Writer and the English Language

CHINUA ACHEBE

♦ ♦ ♦

IN JUNE 1962, there was a writers' gathering at Makerere, impressively styled: "A Conference of African Writers of English Expression." Despite this sonorous and rather solemn title, it turned out to be a very lively affair and a very exciting and useful experience for many of us. But there was something which we tried to do and failed—that was to define "African literature" satisfactorily.

Was it literature produced *in* Africa or *about* Africa? Could African literature be on any subject, or must it have an African theme? Should it embrace the whole continent or south of the Sahara, or just *black* Africa? And then the question of language. Should it be in indigenous African languages or should it include Arabic, English, French, Portuguese, Afrikaans, and so on?

In the end we gave up trying to find an answer, partly—I should admit—on my own instigation. Perhaps we should not have given up so easily. It seems to me from some of the things I have since heard and read that we may have given the impression of not knowing what we were doing, or worse, not daring to look too closely at it.

A Nigerian critic, Obi Wali, writing in *Transition* 10 said: "Perhaps the most important achievement of the conference . . . is that African literature as now defined and understood leads nowhere."

I am sure that Obi Wali must have felt triumphantly vindicated when he saw the report of a different kind of conference held later at Fourah Bay to discuss African literature and the university curriculum. This conference produced a tentative definition of African literature as follows: "Creative writing in which an African setting is authentically handled or to which experiences originating in Africa are integral." We are told specifically that Conrad's *Heart of Darkness* qualifies as African literature while Graham Greene's *Heart of the Matter* fails because it could have been set anywhere outside Africa.

A number of interesting speculations issue from this definition, which admittedly is only an interim formulation designed to produce an indisputably desirable end, namely, to introduce African students to literature set in their environment. But I could not help being amused by the curious circumstance in which Conrad, a Pole, writing in English could produce African literature while Peter Abrahams would be ineligible should he write a novel based on his experiences in the West Indies.

What all this suggests to me is that you cannot cram African literature into a small, neat definition. I do not see African literature as one unit but as a group of associated units—in fact the sum total of all the *national* and *ethnic* literatures of Africa.

A national literature is one that takes the whole nation for its province and has a realized or potential audience throughout its territory. In other words, a literature that is written in the *national* language. An ethnic literature is one which is available only to one ethnic group within the nation. If you take Nigeria as an example, the national literature, as I see it, is the literature written in English; and the ethnic literatures are in Hausa, Ibo, Yoruba, Efik, Edo, Ijaw, etc., etc.

Any attempt to define African literature in terms which overlook the complexities of the African scene at the material time is doomed to failure. After the elimination of white rule shall have been completed, the single most important fact in Africa in the second half of the twentieth century will appear to be the rise of individual nation-states. I believe that African literature will follow the same pattern.

What we tend to do today is to think of African literature as a newborn infant. But in fact what we have is a whole generation of newborn infants. Of course, if you only look cursorily, one infant is pretty much like another; but in reality each is already set on its own separate journey. Of course, you may group them together on the basis of anything you choose—the color of their hair, for instance. Or you may group them together on the basis of the language they will speak or the religion of their fathers. Those would all be valid distinctions, but they could not begin to account fully for each individual person carrying, as it were, his own little, unique lodestar of genes.

Those who in talking about African literature want to exclude North Africa because it belongs to a different tradition surely do not suggest that black Africa is anything like homogeneous. What does Shabaan Robert have in common with Christopher Okigbo or Awoonor-Williams? Or Mongo Beti of Cameroun and Paris with Nzekwu of Nigeria? What does the champagne-drinking upper-class Creole society described by Easmon of Sierra Leone have in common with the rural folk and fishermen of J. P. Clark's plays? Of course, some of these differences could be accounted for on individual rather than national grounds, but a good deal of it is also environmental.

I have indicated somewhat offhandedly that the national literature of Nigeria and of many other countries of Africa is, or will be, written in English. This may sound like a controversial statement, but it isn't. All I have done has been to look at the reality of present-day Africa. This "reality" may change as a result of deliberate, e.g., political, action. If it does, an entirely new situation will arise, and there will be plenty of time to examine it. At present it may be more profitable to look at the scene as it is.

What are the factors which have conspired to place English in the position of national language in many parts of Africa? Quite simply the reason is that these nations were created in the first place by the intervention of the British, which, I hasten to add, is not saying that the peoples comprising these nations were invented by the British.

The country which we know as Nigeria today began not so very long ago as the arbitrary creation of the British. It is true, as William Fagg says in his excellent new book, *Nigerian Images*, that this arbitrary action has proved as lucky in terms of African art history as any enterprise of the fortunate Princess of Serendip. And I believe that in political and economic terms too this arbitrary creation called Nigeria holds out great prospects. Yet the fact remains that Nigeria was created by the British—for their own ends. Let us give the devil his due: colonialism in Africa disrupted many things, but it did create big political units where there were small, scattered ones before. Nigeria had hundreds of autonomous communities ranging in size from the vast Fulani Empire founded by Usman dan Fodio in the north to tiny village entities in the east. Today it is one country.

Of course there are areas of Africa where colonialism divided up a single ethnic group among two or even three powers. But on the whole it did bring together many peoples that had hitherto gone their several ways. And it gave them a language with which to talk to one another. If it failed to give them a song, it at least gave them a tongue, for sighing. There are not many countries in Africa today where you could abolish the language of the erstwhile colonial powers and still retain the facility for mutual communication. Therefore those African writers who have chosen to write in English or French are not unpatriotic smart alecks with an eye on the main chance—outside their own countries. They are by-products of the same process that made the new nation-states of Africa.

You can take this argument a stage further to include other countries of Africa. The only reason why we can even talk about African unity is that when we get together, we have a manageable number of languages to talk in—English, French, Arabic.

The other day I had a visit from Joseph Kariuki of Kenya.

Although I had read some of his poems and he had read my novels, we had not met before. But it didn't seem to matter. In fact I had met him through his poems, especially through his love poem *Come Away My Love*, in which he captures in so few words the trials and tensions of an African in love with a white girl in Britain:

> Come away, my love, from streets
> Where unkind eyes divide
> And shop windows reflect our difference.

By contrast, when in 1960 I was traveling in East Africa and went to the home of the late Shabaan Robert, the Swahili poet of Tanganyika, things had been different. We spent some time talking about writing, but there was no real contact. I knew from all accounts that I was talking to an important writer, but of the nature of his work I had no idea. He gave me two books of his poems, which I treasure but cannot read—until I have learned Swahili.

And there are scores of languages I would want to learn if it were possible. Where am I to find the time to learn the half dozen or so Nigerian languages, each of which can sustain a literature? I am afraid it cannot be done. These languages will just have to develop as tributaries to feed the one central language enjoying nationwide currency. Today, for good or ill, that language is English. Tomorrow it may be something else, although I very much doubt it.

Those of us who have inherited the English language may not be in a position to appreciate the value of the inheritance. Or we may go on resenting it because it came as part of a package deal which included many other items of doubtful value and the positive atrocity of racial arrogance and prejudice, which may yet set the world on fire. But let us not in rejecting the evil throw out the good with it.

Some time last year I was traveling in Brazil meeting Brazilian writers and artists. A number of the writers I spoke to were concerned about the restrictions imposed on them by their use of the Portuguese language. I remember a woman poet saying she had given serious thought to writing in French! And yet their problem is not half as difficult as ours. Portuguese may not have the universal currency of English or French but at least it is the national language of Brazil with her eighty million or so people, to say nothing of the people of Portugal, Angola, Mozambique, etc.

Of Brazilian authors, I have only read, in translation, one novel by Jorge Amado, who is not only Brazil's leading novelist but one of the most important writers in the world. From that one novel, *Gabriella*, I was able to glimpse something of the exciting Afro-Latin culture which is the pride of Brazil and is quite unlike any other culture. Jorge Amado is only one of the many writers Brazil has produced. At their national writers' festival there were literally hundreds of them. But the work of the vast majority will be closed to the rest of the world forever, including no doubt the work of some excellent writers. There is certainly a great advantage to writing in a world language.

I think I have said enough to give an indication of my thinking on the importance of the world language which history has forced down our throats. Now let us look at some of the most serious handicaps. And let me say straightaway that one of the most serious handicaps is *not* the one people talk about most often, namely, that it is impossible for anyone ever to use a second language as effectively as his first. This assertion is compounded of half truth and half bogus mystique. Of course, it is true that the vast majority of people are happier with their first language than with any other. But then the majority of people are not writers. We do have enough examples of writers who have performed the feat of writing effectively in a second language. And I am not thinking of the obvious names like Conrad. It would be more germane to our subject to choose African examples.

The first name that comes to my mind is Olauda Equiano, better known as Gustavus Vassa, the African. Equiano was an Ibo, I believe from the village of Iseke in the Orlu division of Eastern Nigeria. He was sold as a slave at a very early age and transported to America. Later he bought his freedom and lived in England.

In 1789 he published his life story, a beautifully written document which, among other things, set down for the Europe of his time something of the life and habit of his people in Africa, in an attempt to counteract the lies and slander invented by some Europeans to justify the slave trade.

Coming nearer to our times, we may recall the attempts in the first quarter of this century by West African nationalists to come together and press for a greater say in the management of their own affairs. One of the most eloquent of that band was the Honorable Casely Hayford of the Gold Coast. His presidential address to the National Congress of British West Africa in 1925 was memorable not only for its sound common sense but as a fine example of elegant prose. The governor of Nigeria at the time was compelled to take notice, and he did so in characteristic style: he called Hayford's congress "a self-selected and self-appointed congregation of educated African gentlemen." We may derive some amusement from the fact that British colonial administrators learned very little in the following quarter of a century. But at least they *did* learn in the end—which is more than one can say for some others.

It is when we come to what is commonly called creative literature that most doubt seems to arise. Obi Wali, whose article "Dead End of African Literature" I referred to, has this to say:

> . . . until these writers and their Western midwives accept the fact that any true African literature must be written in African languages, they would be merely pursuing a dead end, which can only lead to sterility, uncreativity and frustration.

But far from leading to sterility, the work of many new African writers is full of the most exciting possibilities. Take this from Christopher Okigbo's *Limits*:

> Suddenly becoming talkative
>   like weaverbird
> Summoned at offside of
>   dream remembered

Between sleep and waking
I hand up my egg-shells
To you of palm grove,
Upon whose bamboo towers hang
Dripping with yesterupwine
A tiger mask and nude spear. . . .

Queen of the damp half light,
    I have had my cleansing.
Emigrant with air-borne nose,
    The he-goat-on-heat.

Or take the poem *Night Rain*, in which J. P. Clark captures so
well the fear and wonder felt by a child as rain clamors on the
thatch roof at night, and his mother, walking about in the dark,
moves her simple belongings

Out of the run of water
That like ants filing out of the wood
Will scatter and gain possession
Of the floor.

I think that the picture of water spreading on the floor "like
ants filing out of the wood" is beautiful. Of course, if you have
never made fire with faggots, you may miss it. But Clark's inspiration derives from the same source which gave birth to the
saying that a man who brings home ant-ridden faggots must be
ready for the visit of lizards.

I do not see any signs of sterility anywhere here. What I do
see is a new voice coming out of Africa, speaking of African
experience in a worldwide language. So my answer to the question *Can an African ever learn English well enough to be able to use it
effectively in creative writing?* is certainly yes. If on the other hand you
ask, *Can he ever learn to use it like a native speaker?* I should say, I hope
not. It is neither necessary nor desirable for him to be able to do
so. The price a world language must be prepared to pay is sub-

mission to many different kinds of use. The African writer should aim to use English in a way that brings out his message best without altering the language to the extent that its value as a medium of international exchange will be lost. He should aim at fashioning an English which is at once universal and able to carry his peculiar experience. I have in mind here the writer who has something new, something different to say. The nondescript writer has little to tell us, anyway, so he might as well tell it in conventional language and get it over with. If I may use an extravagant simile, he is like a man offering a small, nondescript routine sacrifice for which a chick, or less, will do. A serious writer must look for an animal whose blood can match the power of his offering.

In this respect Amos Tutola is a natural. A good instinct has turned his apparent limitation in language into a weapon of great strength—a half-strange dialect that serves him perfectly in the evocation of his bizarre world. His last book, and to my mind, his finest, is proof enough that one can make even an imperfectly learned second language do amazing things. In this book, *The Feather Woman of the Jungle*, Tutola's superb storytelling is at last cast in the episodic form which he handles best instead of being painfully stretched on the rack of the novel.

From a natural to a conscious artist: myself, in fact. Allow me to quote a small example from *Arrow of God*, which may give some idea of how I approach the use of English. The Chief Priest in the story is telling one of his sons why it is necessary to send him to church:

> I want one of my sons to join these people and be my eyes there. If there is nothing in it you will come back. But if there is something there you will bring home my share. The world is like a Mask, dancing. If you want to see it well you do not stand in one place. My spirit tells me that those who do not befriend the white man today will be saying *had we known* tomorrow.

Now supposing I had put it another way. Like this, for instance:

I am sending you as my representative among these people—just to be on the safe side in case the new religion de-
velops. One has to move with the times or else one is left
behind. I have a hunch that those who fail to come to terms
with the white man may well regret their lack of foresight.

The material is the same. But the form of the one is *in character*
and the other is not. It is largely a matter of instinct, but judgment comes into it too.

You read quite often nowadays of the problems of the African
writer having first to think in his mother tongue and then to
translate what he has thought into English. If it were such a
simple, mechanical process, I would agree that it was pointless—
the kind of eccentric pursuit you might expect to see in a modern
Academy of Lagado—and such a process could not possibly produce some of the exciting poetry and prose which is already ap-
pearing.

One final point remains for me to make. The real question is
not whether Africans *could* write in English but whether they *ought
to*. Is it right that a man should abandon his mother tongue for
someone else's? It looks like a dreadful betrayal and produces a
guilty feeling.

But, for me, there is no other choice. I have been given this
language and I intend to use it. I hope, though, that there always
will be men, like the late Chief Fagunwa, who will choose to
write in their native tongue and ensure that our ethnic literature
will flourish side by side with the national ones. For those of us
who opt for English, there is much work ahead and much excitement.

Writing in the London *Observer* recently, James Baldwin said:

My quarrel with the English language has been that the language reflected none of my experience. But now I began to
see the matter another way. . . . Perhaps the language was not
my own because I had never attempted to use it, had only
learned to imitate it. If this were so, then it might be made to

bear the burden of my experience if I could find the stamina to challenge it, and me, to such a test.

I recognize, of course, that Baldwin's problem is not exactly mine, but I feel that the English language will be able to carry the weight of my African experience. But it will have to be a new English, still in full communion with its ancestral home but altered to suit its new African surroundings.

Igbo Cosmology and the Parameters of Individual Accomplishment in *Things Fall Apart*

CLEMENT OKAFOR

◆　◆　◆

SINCE THE PUBLICATION OF *Things Fall Apart* in 1958, the novel has developed into a truly remarkable literary phenomenon; it is not only the most widely read book in Africa except for the Bible, but also is now part of the global literary canon. Furthermore, *Things Fall Apart* has sold more than eight million copies and has been translated into fifty-five languages of the world.

As the literary world celebrates the fortieth anniversary of the publication of this classic, it is more important now than ever before that we establish an appropriate epistemological framework that can profitably inform our critical discussions of *Things Fall Apart*.

Since literature is contextual, the interrogation of the setting of a literary opus creates opportunities for a deep and rewarding interpretation of the work under consideration. *Things Fall Apart* is set in Igboland in the second half of the nineteenth century, the time when Britain was in the process of colonizing, not only Igboland but also the other African territories allotted to it at the

Berlin Conference of 1884–1885. An exploration of traditional Igbo cosmology is, therefore, a valuable strategy for establishing the desired epistemological framework in which to place our further discourse on the novel.

Throughout this essay, the term *cosmology* is used to convey the sense of a society's perception of the world in which it lives. Such a concept usually explores the complex interlocking relationships between human beings and the pantheon of forces that function within their society's universe.[1]

First, a word about the Igbo. The Igbo inhabit the territory of southeastern Nigeria, and their homeland is located on both banks of *Orimili* (the great river), the River Niger, from which Nigeria derives her name. According to Basden, "the Ibo nation ranks as one of the largest in the whole of Africa" (xi). Igbo people now number about twenty-five million, a population larger than those of Norway, Sweden, and Denmark combined.

Igbo society is historically egalitarian and democratic in the sense that the people have never had rulers with anything approaching autocratic powers. According to Green, the Igbo "have no hierarchy of powers rising from a broad democratic basis through ascending levels to one central peak," rather, "Ibo democracy unlike English, works through a number of juxtaposed groups and a system of balances rather than on a unitary hierarchical principle" (145). This egalitarian principle is expressed in the famous statement: *Igbo enwe eze* (the Igbo do not have kings).

The town, which is the basic unit of Igbo traditional political organization, is made up of various villages that together comprise about twenty to thirty thousand people. Although these towns are "not united by central government authority, nor arranged in any political hierarchy they are nonetheless interlinked horizontally each with its neighbors by the social bonds of intermarriage," that is, based on the principle of exogamy; thus although the towns are politically independent, they are socially linked by a web of relationships centered around exogamous marriages, which means that everybody has links not only with his own hometown but also, as Green affirms, "with the birthplace of his mother, with that of his wife, and the various places into which his sisters have married"; 151), not to mention the towns into which his brothers have married. Every town has a market, which is held every four or eight days and is a socially unifying force; among the Igbo the market is also a place where people socialize.

As Simon Ottenberg has observed in his study,[2] the democratic nature of Igbo society—with its encouragement of healthy individual and group rivalry coupled with the premium it places on individual, personal accomplishment—has enabled its people to adapt rapidly to the modern, Western way of life.

Briefly, in Igbo cosmology, there is Chukwu, or *ama ama amasi amasi* (the one who can never be fully understood). Below him is a pantheon of deities whose domains may be limited to specific aspects of life on earth. Examples of these are Amadiora, the god of thunder, Ufiojioku, the god of the harvest, and Anyanwu, the sun god. Principal among these deities is Ani, the Earth goddess, who is the arbiter of ethical conduct. The major deities have special shrines and priests dedicated to their worship and it is the duty of human beings to strive at all times to live righteously by conducting their lives in accordance with the ethics of the community and by avoiding societal taboos. If for any reason human beings transgress these rules, they are expected to atone for their offenses by performing prescribed ritual acts of expiation.

When those who live well die, they become ancestors in *ani muo* (land of the dead) provided their living relatives have performed the appropriate funeral rites; it is these rites that initiate the dead into the company of the powerful ancestors. Such ancestors take an active interest in the welfare of the living members of their family, who pour libations to them and make offerings to their memories on certain occasions.

Igbo cosmology admits of the existence of evil spirits, *umunadi*, who are believed to live in the liminal, uninhabited spaces beyond the village settlements and also in the bad bush. It also admits of the existence of *ogbanje*, the spirits of children who reincarnate and are born to die, often in infancy, only to be born again by the same or another unfortunate mother.

Duality, or the phenomenology of pairing, is another very important aspect of Igbo cosmology. In Igbo thought, nothing can exist by itself, since wherever something exists, something else exists beside it. As the proverb says: *Ife kwulu, ife akwudebe ya* (when one thing stands, something else stands beside it). Thus, there can be no unpaired manifestation of any force or being.

Arising from the duality phenomenon is the Igbo concern for the maintenance of balance in one's life. Because Igbo cosmology envisages the simultaneous functioning of numerous and sometimes antagonistic forces, one is counseled to thread one's way cautiously so as not to offend any of the contending spirits. Extremism of any kind is thus perceived to be dangerous, as encapsulated in the following proverb: *ife belu n'oke ka dibia n'agwo* (the healer can cure only something within bounds).

Reincarnation is a cardinal principle in Igbo cosmology. Ancestors who are well cared for by their living offspring may take on new human bodies and be born as loving children to their former sons and daughters. However, reincarnation is not limited to the ancestors. As has been mentioned earlier, the spirits of some children are also believed to reincarnate only to die young.

Central to Igbo cosmology is one's choice of a destiny. This choice is made freely before the moment of incarnation and is witnessed and sealed by one's chi, or personal guiding spirit. The choice the individual makes usually compensates for the circumstances of his or her previous life. Thus, somebody who is killed by his jealous neighbors on account of his excessive wealth in one life may elect to be poor in his next incarnation. However, once the choice has been made and the child is born, his destiny is guarded throughout his life by his chi and cannot be changed. More important, once the child is born, he suffers total amnesia with respect to his chosen destiny.

As the child grows, he is socialized into the strong ethos of hard work for which the Igbo people are known, while the egalitarian organization of society encourages him to believe that there is no limit to what he can achieve in life. It is the same ethos of hard work and high self-esteem that Olaudah Equiano refers to in the following description of his Igbo people more than two centuries ago:

Agriculture is our chief employment; and every one, even the children and women are engaged in it. Thus we are all habituated to labour from our earliest years. Every one contributes something to the common stock; and as we are unacquainted with idleness we have no beggars. (145)

The amnesia at birth ensures that the pre-incarnation choice (as to whether the individual will be a success or a failure) does not deter the person from striving to achieve the best possible life, since only his chi knows what destiny he has chosen. Regardless of what one's conscious desires may be, the prior choice functions as the subconscious drive that predisposes the individual to acting in such a way as to fulfill the individual's destiny. This situation does not make the people fatalistic, however, because in the first place, no one remembers what manner of life he or she has chosen. In the second place, the Igbo also firmly believe that human agency is critical to the actualization of one's destiny and that hard work results in a better life. It is only after a person has been dogged by misfortune, despite his best effort, that he begins to suspect that he may not be destined for good things after all. Still, the final judgment is withheld until after the death of the individual. It is only after someone's death that the living can then assess his destiny fully. This practice is encapsulated in the proverb *Chi ejilu ada akalu ubosi* (one must not condemn the day until it is over).

The foregoing is a brief overview of the Igbo cosmology that was in place at the onset of British colonization of Igboland, the historical setting of *Things Fall Apart*. It remains for us to show how this paradigm is reflected in the novel itself.

Things Fall Apart is like an expansive epic narrative that uses its larger form to frame numerous smaller thematic strands. The main story of the novel is that of Okonkwo, the protagonist, who is introduced in the first word of the first paragraph of the text. At that point, Okonkwo is already famous on account of his personal accomplishments, especially for his earlier spectacular wrestling victory that is likened to that of the legendary founder of his hometown, who is reputed to have wrestled a spirit of the wilderness for seven days and seven nights. Okonkwo's victory over Amalinze the Cat, who has held the wrestling championship title for seven years, shows his affinity to his town's founding father. Thus, even at eighteen he has shown that he is a worthy son of Umuofia and appears to be marked for great achievements.

Sadly, Okonkwo's psyche is so traumatized by his father's penury and the poverty of his early childhood that his psyche remains mortally wounded throughout his life, although his hard work enables him to improve his material welfare; hence, he does not see the full range of dual possibilities inherent in every situation. Because he loathes his father, he instinctively hates everything that reminds him of Unoka. Because Unoka is weak, Okonkwo strives at all times to exhibit heroic courage, which pushes him to commit excesses, like killing Ikemefuna, that drive a wedge between him and his son, Nwoye. From the perspective of Igbo cosmology, Okonkwo's inability to recognize the duality and complexity of life situations is a major handicap, since it reveals a fundamental lack of balance in his life.

Okonkwo's problems also emanate from his inability to practice another Igbo ideal, balance in one's assessment of situations, since he usually takes extremist positions in life. For instance, he cannot understand how a strong man like Ogbuefi Ndulue can do nothing without consulting his wife first. Again, to Okonkwo, the new colonial dispensation is an unmitigated evil that should be expunged from his home and he does not realize that many of his people view it differently:

> There were many men and women in Umuofia who did not feel as strongly as Okonkwo about the new dispensation. The white man had indeed brought a lunatic religion, but he had also brought a trading store and for the first time palm oil and kernel became things of great price and much money flowed into Umuofia.
>
> And even in the matter of religion there was a growing feeling that there might be something in it after all, something vaguely akin to method in the overwhelming madness. (2583)

This difference in perception of the problem explains why Umuofia does not join Okonkwo in a battle to drive out the new colonial administration and the Christian missionaries. So in the end, Okonkwo's tragic demise arises from his lack of full understanding of his people and their culture.

However, *Things Fall Apart* is not only the story of the protagonist, Okonkwo; it is also the story of an African community, Umuofia. Contrary to the Hegelian ethnocentric theory of history, which posits that Africa has neither a history nor a future, the Igbo society that Achebe portrays in this novel is keenly aware of its history and the legendary feats of its founding fathers. It is a society in which someone at the beginning of his career can go to an elder and obtain without any collateral the resources with which to establish himself in life. Above all, it is a society that judges a man not by the size of his inheritance, but rather by his own personal accomplishments. Moreover, in Umuofia, the African community portrayed in the novel, there is marital amity and social problems are resolved on the basis of the consensus emanating from open public debate in a manner that protects not only the rights of the individuals concerned but also the corporate interests of the community.

What informs Achebe's portrait of Umuofia is not mawkish sentimentality, since he shows that the community has its share of internal contradictions, as is true of all human societies. These internal contradictions in all societies explain why new laws are being made to deal with new contradictions as well as to revisit old ones. What is remarkable in the African society portrayed in the novel is that it has achieved a great degree of stability by maintaining a balance between its centrifugal and centripetal forces. Indeed, what informs the novelist's portrait of the society is his conviction, which he has expressed on several occasions,[3] that the African needs to tell his own side of the colonial story himself:

> At the University I read some appalling novels about Africa (including Joyce Cary's much praised *Mr. Johnson*) and decided

that the story we had to tell could not be told for us by anyone else, no matter how gifted or well-intentioned. ("Named for Victoria," *Morning Yet on Creation Day*, 123)

Like the traditional epics that use the major narratives to frame the many minor ones, *Things Fall Apart* frames numerous minor stories within the major narratives about Okonkwo and his community. One of these minor narratives in the novel is the interrogation of the relationships between fathers and their sons. Igbo society is largely patriarchal and patrilineal; hence, families here depend on the male offspring for succession and the perpetuation of their names. This places a burden on the relationships between fathers and their sons, particularly their first sons. In the novel, Unoka is the founder of his lineage, but he is not successful in agriculture, the principal occupation of his people. His forte is music making and the happiest times of the year for him are those two or three moons after the harvest when the community relaxes from the rigors of farming and entertains itself with music and dance. Regrettably, he is so improvident that he owes his neighbors a lot of money. However, he has a tremendous sense of humor and drama, which he exhibits when one of his creditors, Okoye, asks him to pay him back the money he owes him:

As soon as Unoka understood what his friend was driving at, he burst out laughing. He laughed loud and long and his voice rang out clear as the ogene, and tears stood in his eyes. His visitor was amazed, and sat speechless. At the end, Unoka was able to give an answer between fresh outbursts of mirth.

"Look at that wall," he said pointing at the far wall of his hut, which was rubbed with red earth so it shone. "Look at those lines of chalk"; and Okoye saw groups of short perpendicular lines. There were five groups and the smallest group had ten lines. Unoka had a sense of the dramatic; and so he allowed a pause, in which he took a pinch of snuff and sneezed noisily and then continued: "Each group there represents a debt to someone and each stroke is one hundred cowries. You see, I owe that man a thousand cowries. But he has not come to wake me up in the morning for it. I shall pay you, but not today. Our elders say that the sun will shine on those who stand before it shines on those who kneel under them. I shall pay my big debts first." And he took another pinch of snuff, as if that was paying the big debts first. Okoye rolled his goat-skin and departed. (2506)

Furthermore, Unoka is undoubtedly a coward, and his people regard him as a failure. He is a burden on his son and the other members of his family; hence, Okonkwo is thoroughly ashamed of him.

Ironically, the dysfunctional relationship Okonkwo has with his father is duplicated in the one he has with his own son, Nwoye. Being an Igbo man, Okonkwo must have dreaded (even without admitting it to himself) the uncanny resemblance between Nwoye's temperament and that of Unoka. He must have feared that Nwoye may well be a reincarnation of his father. This may explain why Okonkwo tries to root out in his young son any personality trait he despised in his father. Hence, he encourages Nwoye to come to his dwelling place in order to imbibe the martial traditions of his people. However, the son prefers listening to the folktales, which the father despises as being fit for the ears of women only.

Because Nwoye has come to look up to Ikemefuna as if he were an elder brother, he is devastated by the ritual murder of this role model. This further aggravates the friction between father and son. In addition, there is something in Nwoye which cannot find fulfillment within the martial ethos of his society. It is indeed this search for something, which his community cannot satisfy, that leads Nwoye into an exploration of the new religion. Unfortunately, Okonkwo's handling of the news that his son has been seen in the company of the missionaries severs the already weak link between the two and emboldens the son to reject his father completely.

Another minor narrative in *Things Fall Apart* is the portrait of the relationships between fathers and their daughters. Igbo society is mainly patrilineal and succession is through the male offspring, who also perpetuate the family name. The society's concern for the survival of the lineage is expressed in such names as Amae-china (may the compound not perish/disappear) or Obiechina (may the household not perish). As is often the case with such patriarchal societies, they treasure their sons more highly than their daughters. Perhaps because these families expect more from boys than from girls, they exert greater pressure on the boys to succeed than on the girls.

The irony in *Things Fall Apart* is that the boy, Nwoye, runs away from his father, while his sister, Ezinma, dotes on Okonkwo. It is, thus, not surprising that there is a special bond between the father and his daughter and that Okonkwo wishes that Ezinma were a boy, as may be seen in the following dialogue:

> "You have not eaten for two days," said his daughter Ezinma when she brought the food to him. "So you must finish this." She sat down and stretched her legs in front of her. Okonkwo ate the food absent-mindedly. "She should have been a boy," he thought as he looked at his ten-year-old daughter. He passed her a piece of fish.
>
> "Go and bring me some cold water," he said. Ezinma rushed out of the hut, chewing the fish, and soon returned with a bowl of cool water from the earthen pot in her mother's hut. . . .
>
> "She should have been a boy," Okonkwo said to himself again. (2532)

Indeed, the bond between Okonkwo and Ezinma is so strong that later when they are in exile a mere word from Okonkwo, expressing his desire that she should hold off getting married until their return to Umuofia, makes Ezinma dismiss all good suitors from Mbanta, their place of exile. Thus, it is not unlikely that Okonkwo must have been frustrated that everything he has struggled to accomplish in life will be inherited by his sons, who may not be as deserving as this daughter.

The portrait of the relationships between husbands and their wives is yet another significant narrative framed in *Things Fall Apart*. In Umuofia, marriage is more than an affair between two individuals; it is a union of two family groups, which have a mutual interest in preserving that liaison. Marriages here are contracted after elaborate negotiations and public ceremonies, as is exemplified in the *uri* ceremony of Akueke, Obierika's daughter. On this occasion, Obierika's family entertains almost the entire village.

Like marriages all over the world, however, some of the marriages contracted in Umuofia later become dysfunctional, despite the best effort of the two families involved. Some are so bad that they are referred to the community elders for arbitration in the public square, as is the case with the dispute between Uzowulu and his wife. However, even Okonkwo, who abuses his wives, has a very endearing relationship with one of them, Ekwefi—his childhood sweetheart. She had been married before to someone else because Okonkwo was then too poor to finance the required ceremonies. That marriage notwithstanding, Ekwefi one day walked out on her husband and into Okonkwo's home. Thereafter, she became his wife. Not surprisingly, the special relationship that exists between Okonkwo and Ekwefi is transferred to their daughter, Ezinma.

Even truly romantic love affairs do exist among some married couples in this society, as is exemplified by the marital bliss of Ogbuefi Ndulue and his wife, Ozoemena. So strong is their love for one another that the husband never does anything without consulting his wife first. Indeed, so well known is their love for one another that their community has composed a song about them. The husband and wife are so inseparable, even in their old age, that when Ozoemena learns of the death of her husband, she immediately loses all interest in life. She walks to her house, lies down, and passes away that very day.

Another minor narrative that is framed in *Things Fall Apart* is the portrait of the relationships between leadership and followers. In the novel, the highest leadership positions are those of the nine *egwugwu*, who represent the nine villages of the town. Symbolizing the ancestors of the community, these elders arbitrate public disputes and their authority is never challenged, as may be seen in the following formulaic dialogue between Evil Forest, their spokesman, and Uzowulu:

> "Uzowulu's body, I salute you," he said. Spirits always address humans as "bodies." Uzowulu bent down and touched the earth with his right hand as a sign of submission.
> "Our father, my hand has touched the ground," he said.
> "Uzowulu's body, do you know me?" asked the spirit.
> "How can I know you, father? You are beyond our knowledge." (2545)

In such situations, the *egwugwu* first allow the contending parties to present their cases and thereafter pronounce a verdict that is not only fair to the parties, but helps to preserve the solidarity of the community.

In *Things Fall Apart*, matters of public concern are generally discussed at town meetings that are open to every male adult. Although the views of titled men carry infinitely more weight at such public gatherings, everyone who so desires can express his opinion. Eventually a consensus emerges through a reconciliation of the competing viewpoints, whereupon the consensus becomes the view of the entire community and is, thereafter, expected to be implemented without dissent. This is the case when Ogbuefi Udo's wife is killed in Mbaino. The consensus is that Umuofia should give Mbaino an ultimatum to choose either to pay the agreed-upon compensation or to go to war. On another occasion, when the peace of the community is threatened by the excesses of the fanatical Christians, a meeting is called and there is a consensus as to how the society should respond. Here again, the community acts as one and speaks with one unmistakable voice. One may rightly deduce then that this is the ideal Igbo political process. It follows, therefore, that good leaders among the Igbo must have consensus-building skills. Viewed from this perspective, Okonkwo's leadership skills fail when he is unable to build a consensus as to how Umuofia should respond to the district commissioner's imprisonment of the community's elders.

Thus far we have shown that in *Things Fall Apart*, there are many minor narratives that are framed by two major ones: the first portrays an individual's single-minded struggle to rise from the humble circumstances of his birth to a position of prominence in his community; the second is the narrative of a community that has evolved a civilization through the years as it struggles to adapt to colonial conquest and domination. These two narratives, however, merge into one, since that individual eventually becomes one of the six leaders imprisoned by the district commissioner.

It now remains for us to show that the universe of *Things Fall Apart* is a reflection of the Igbo cosmology described above. A close examination of the cosmos of *Things Fall Apart* shows that the world portrayed in the novel parallels very closely the universe of Igbo cosmology. For example, in both the Igbo paradigm and *Things Fall Apart*, the town is the unit of political organization. In *Things Fall Apart*, towns like Umuofia, Mbaino, Mbanta, Abame, etc., are also units of political organization since the people see themselves as citizens of these communities. Ordinarily, these autonomous communities live peacefully with one another, except when cordial relations are disturbed by the hostile actions of a neighboring town, as in the murder of an Umuofia woman by a citizen of Mbaino. Even in this case, the prompt payment of a ransom restores the good relations that had been consolidated over the generations through numerous exogamous intertown marriages. Furthermore, councils of elders rule these towns, as is the case in the real Igbo society.

In addition, the events in the lives of the characters in the novel resemble those of the people one encounters in the Igbo cosmos. For instance, the Igbo concept of reincarnation is reflected in Ezinma's life, since she is *ogbanje*—one of those children who are born to die in infancy and reenter their mothers' wombs to be born again and again. This explains the intervention of the medicine man who locates Ezinma's *iyi uwa* in his effort to enable her to break the cycle and live.

Furthermore, the marriages in *Things Fall Apart* are negotiated and celebrated in true Igbo manner. Again, the punishment for

Okonkwo's involuntary homicide in the novel is a replica of the Igbo response to such a crime. The corpse of someone who takes his or her own life is an abomination and a source of pollution not only to the earth but also to anyone who comes in contact with it. Indeed, the Igbo consider those who take their lives as being so despicable that they are not mourned and, as in Okonkwo's case, only strangers can handle their bodies. Above all, the pervasive role ascribed to Okonkwo's *chi* is a replica of the dominant role that is ascribed to that guardian spirit in Igbo cosmology. These examples demonstrate incontrovertibly that the universe portrayed in *Things Fall Apart* closely reflects the cosmos delineated above.

If, according to the Igbo paradigm, nobody can accomplish anything without the support of his *chi*, to what extent is Okonkwo then responsible for his tragic end? As Achebe himself explains, although no one can achieve anything without the assistance of his *chi*, the Igbo believe that human agency is essential to the realization of one's destiny. Again, in Igbo cosmology, amnesia at birth ensures that each person is unaware of the choice previously made and leads his life in accordance with the Igbo ethos encapsulated in the following proverb: *Onye kwe chi ya ekwe* (when somebody says yes, his *chi* says yes also).

A review of the career of the protagonist shows that he has a very high self-esteem. On account of his individual accomplishments, Okonkwo sees himself as the legendary lizard which jumped down from the high iroko tree and was able to escape from the seven agile men who were waiting to catch it. Indeed, Okonkwo seems to exemplify the Igbo ethos of hard work; by his hard work he has raised himself from the penury of his childhood to the highest leadership position in his society. He has said yes and it seems that his *chi* also supports his efforts, at least initially. Sadly, his traumatic childhood seems to have permanently wounded his psyche and endowed him with a one-dimensional perception of reality that makes him take the personal decisions that precipitate his calamitous end. The Igbo belief that a person cannot achieve anything without the consent of his *chi* must not mislead one to conclude that Okonkwo is merely a pawn in the hands of his guiding spirit. On the contrary, Okonkwo's personality flaws precipitate his catastrophic demise and nullify his individual accomplishments.

By situating *Things Fall Apart* in its cultural milieu, the exposition above has attempted to create for the ever-growing readership of the masterpiece an appropriate epistemological framework that should inform future discourse on its merits and meanings.

Notes

1. *Webster's Third, New International Dictionary* (Springfield, MA: Merriam-Webster, 1993).

2. Simon Ottenberg, "Ibo Receptivity to Change," in *Continuity and Change in African Culture*, ed. William Bascom and Melville Herskovits (Chicago, IL: University of Chicago Press, 1970), 130–43.

3. Achebe has made this view known on several occasions and emphasized it again during his discussion with this writer at the Inaugural World Conference of the Black Expressive Culture Studies Association held at Kent State University, Ohio, November 19–21, 1998.

Works Cited

Achebe, Chinua. *Things Fall Apart*. In *World Masterpieces*, edited by Maynard Mack, 2498–2597. New York: Norton, 1995.

Achebe, Chinua. *Morning Yet on Creation Day*. New York: Anchor/Doubleday, 1975.

Basden, G. T. *The Niger Ibos*. London: Seely, 1938.

Equiano, Olaudah. *Narrative of the Life of Olaudah Equiano*. In *African-American Literature*, edited by Henry Louis Gates, Jr., and Nellie Y. McKay. New York: Norton, 1977.

Green, Margaret M. *Ibo Village Affairs*. London: Cass, 1964.

Ottenberg, Simon. "Ibo Receptivity to Change." In *Continuity and Change in African Culture*, edited by William Bascom and Melville Herskovits, 130–43. Chicago, IL: University of Chicago Press, 1970.

Webster's Third New International Dictionary. Springfield, MA: Merriam-Webster, 1993.

Eternal Sacred Order versus
Conventional Wisdom

A Consideration of Moral Culpability in the Killing
of Ikemefuna in Things Fall Apart

DAMIAN U. OPATA

◆ ◆ ◆

> As the man who had cleared his throat drew up
> and raised his matchet, Okonkwo looked away.
> He heard the blow. The pot fell and broke in the
> sand. He heard Ikemefuna cry, "My father, they
> have killed me!" as he ran towards him. Dazed
> with fear, Okonkwo drew his matchet and cut
> him down. He was afraid of being thought weak.
> —Chinua Achebe, *Things Fall Apart*, 43

OKONKWO'S KILLING OF IKEMEFUNA—his knottiest moral dilemma in the novel—has generally been seen by critics as an unconscionable act that is tantamount to an offense against the gods of the land. After Ikemefuna's death, Okonkwo's closest friend, Obierika, tells him that what he did "will not please the Earth" because "it is the kind of action for which the goddess wipes out whole families" (46). Earlier, Ezeudu, "the oldest man" in Okonkwo's own quarter of Umuofia, had told Okonkwo not to have anything to do with the killing of Ikemefuna. He said, "That boy calls you father. Do not bear a hand in his death" (40). The authorial voice which follows after the killing of Ikemefuna ascribes a psychological motive of fear to Okonkwo's actions.

Following these tips from the text, many critics have been

unequivocal in alleging that Okonkwo committed an offense by having a hand in the killing of Ikemefuna. David Carroll (42–43), Charles Nnolim (58), Oladele Taiwo (118), G. D. Killam (20), and Robert Wren (44) share this view that Okonkwo committed an offense by taking part in the killing of Ikemefuna. Solomon Iyasere (102) sympathizes with Okonkwo for the humane qualities that he showed by looking away as Ikemefuna was about to be killed, but Iyasere neither exonerates Okonkwo nor holds him culpable for the death of Ikemefuna. From the available critical literature I have examined regarding Okonkwo's role in the killing of Ikemefuna, no critic has seen fit to exonerate Okonkwo for killing Ikemefuna. The attempt of this essay shall be to establish that, although Okonkwo felt some temporal sense of moral revulsion after he had killed Ikemefuna, he cannot thereby be said to have committed any offense against Earth. This defense of Okonkwo shall be looked at from two levels: from internal evidence in *Things Fall Apart* and from what critics have made of some of the evidence available in the text.

Ikemefuna—a sacrificial lamb—is first introduced to us as "a doomed lad," "an ill-fated lad" (6). The young virgin, with whom he is brought to Umuofia as appeasement from the people of Mbaino who had killed a daughter of Umuofia, is not even mentioned by name. All we are told about her is that she belongs to Ogbuefi Udo, the man whose wife was murdered by the people of Mbaino. Ikemefuna, on the other hand, is a communal property, but Okonkwo is asked to look after him as "there was no hurry to decide his fate" (9). Because he was regarded as a sacrificial lamb, Ikemefuna's death was already a fait accompli, at least in the eyes of Mbaino people. Under Okonkwo's roof, Ikemefuna is treated as any other member of Okonkwo's family, and he soon starts to address Okonkwo as his father. Had Okonkwo not extended the same fatherly love he has for all his children to Ikemefuna, but treated him as a captive and an object of sacrifice—which he actually was—he would probably not have endeared himself to Okonkwo to the extent of calling him "Father." Indeed, if he lost memories of his own home, it was because of the humane way in which he was integrated into Okonkwo's household. But at the end of three years, the people of Umuofia decide to kill him. As Ogbuefi Ezeudu says:

> "Yes, Umuofia has decided to kill him. The Oracle of the Hills and the Caves has pronounced it. They will take him outside Umuofia as is the custom, and kill him there. But I want [you] to have nothing to do with it. He calls you father." (40)

Ogbuefi Ezeudu's warning is significant because he is the oldest man in Okonkwo's quarter of Umuofia, and he is, by tradition, a representative of the collective spiritual conscience of the people as well as a mediator between the living and the dead. His advice should be seen as authoritative and well-intentioned. His injunction is, on a general plane, premised on the conventional wisdom that a man should not kill another who is his father, or who calls him father. Here, conventional wisdom is in agreement with the traditional sacred order. All this is well under normal circumstances. In the case under consideration, Umuofia is asked to carry out a divine command. We are not told much about the people whose function it is to carry out this type of command, but from the description on page 40 ("a group of elders from all the nine villages of Umuofia") and from the reference to this group on page 41 ("The next day, the men returned with a pot of wine"), we may conclude that it is the duty of the elders. Earlier we had been told that because of Okonkwo's personal achievements, he had already joined the group of elders (6). If Ikemefuna had been kept in a household other than Okonkwo's, Okonkwo would probably have been one of the elders to go to that household to convey the decision of Umuofia to kill Ikemefuna in accordance with the wish of the Oracle of the Hills and the Caves.

What options were open to Okonkwo after Ezeudu had spoken to him? Is it possible for us to find out his reaction to Ezeudu's warning? We shall take the latter question first. Ezeudu's advice is delivered like a command: "That boy calls you father. Do not bear a hand in his death"; later on, the warning is restated thus: "I want [you] to have nothing to do with it. He calls you father." Okonkwo's opinion is not sought; he is given an injunction. Since

Ezeudu is the oldest man in Okonkwo's own quarter of Umuofia, he can be seen as the direct representative of the ancestors of that particular quarter. His words, therefore, have the force of law. Because Okonkwo did not protest or even argue with Ezeudu, we may feel safe to assume that he accepted Ezeudu's advice. This assumption is borne out later in the novel. When the people set out to kill Ikemefuna, Okonkwo was walking directly behind him (42), but by the time they arrived at the outskirts of Umuofia, where Ikemefuna would be killed, Okonkwo had withdrawn to the rear. The passage reads:

> One of the men behind him cleared his throat. Ikemefuna looked back, and the man growled at him to go on and not stand looking back. The way he said it sent cold fear down Ikemefuna's back. His hands trembled vaguely on the black pot he carried. Why had Okonkwo withdrawn to the rear? Ikemefuna felt his legs melting under him. And he was afraid to look back. (43)

What is the proper interpretation of Okonkwo's decision to withdraw to the rear? It is plausible to believe that he did so in order not to "bear a hand in the death" of Ikemefuna (40). His decision to withdraw to the back can be seen as willingness on his part to listen to the advice of Ezeudu. If we also add to this the fact that he "looked away" when the man who had earlier growled "drew up" to kill Ikemefuna (43), we can say that Okonkwo neither wanted to "bear a hand" in Ikemefuna's death nor see him cut down (43). It may be that Okonkwo would have taken this decision if Ezeudu had not spoken to him, but since he did, we can assume that it was a way of reacting positively to Ezeudu's advice.

We now return to the first question: What were the options open to Okonkwo when Ezeudu came to warn him that he should have nothing to do with the killing of Ikemefuna? We shall consider the choice open to Okonkwo at two levels. When "the men returned" the following day to take Ikemefuna to the place where he would be killed (41), what were the things he could have elected to do? He could have chosen to do one of two things: either accompany the elders or stay behind. The latter will eventually turn out to be Obierika's counsel. Okonkwo, however, did not stay behind. Are we then to condemn him for not staying behind? Before we answer yes or no to this question, we should be reminded that Okonkwo is one of the elders of Umuofia. It was the elders who came to convey the message of the decision of Umuofia to kill Ikemefuna. The same group of elders returned the following day to take Ikemefuna away. It is possible that one of Okonkwo's reasons for deciding to accompany them is that he is one of them. But there is a more important reason: it might have simply been a question of strategy. After Okonkwo had been informed of the decision to kill Ikemefuna, he had told Ikemefuna that he was to be taken home the following day. After all, even pious Abraham in a somewhat related situation had to pretend to Isaac. Moreover, Okonkwo is the person who went to Mbaino "as the proud and imperious emissary of war" (9) to ask for "a young man and a virgin as compensation" (8) for the murder of Ogbuefi Udo's wife. In addition, Okonkwo had acted as guardian and foster father to Ikemefuna for three years. It is then proper that if Ikemefuna were to be taken home, Okonkwo should be one of those to accompany him on the journey.

From all this, Okonkwo's decision to follow the elders can be seen to be predicated on role and strategy: as a member of the elders he was supposed to go, and he also had to be there in order to let it seem to Ikemefuna that he was really being taken home. From Okonkwo's later actions when they reached the outskirts of Umuofia, where Ikemefuna would be killed, we can speculate that after Ezeudu's advice, Okonkwo, while leaving with the other elders, was thinking along these lines: "I accept Ezeudu's advice, but since I am one of the elders and since I was the person who went to Mbaino to bring Ikemefuna here and have lived with him for three years, I must accompany the elders in order to create the impression that he is actually being taken home. However, when we reach the place where he is to be killed, I shall withdraw to the rear and let the others kill him."

When they arrive at the place where Ikemefuna is to be killed, what is the turn of events? Again, what options are open to Okonkwo? We have already seen how he withdrew to the rear when they reached Ikemefuna's Golgotha, thereby leaving the others to kill the boy. The events of Ikemefuna's death are described in the following way:

> As the man who had cleared his throat drew up and raised his matchet, Okonkwo looked away. He heard the blow. The pot fell and broke in the sand. He heard Ikemefuna cry, "My father, they have killed me!" as he ran towards him. Dazed with fear, Okonkwo drew his matchet and cut him down. He was afraid of being thought weak. (43)

We have already established that the men who returned the following day to take Ikemefuna away are "elders from all the nine villages of Umuofia" (40). Given this fact, we then have at our hands a minimum of nine elders who were to see to the killing of Ikemefuna. When it was time to kill Ikemefuna, the man who we may assume was chosen for the deed either delivered a weak blow or missed his aim entirely. As Ikemefuna "ran towards" (43) Okonkwo for help and protection, none of the other men did anything: neither those immediately behind him nor the two who earlier had gone in front of him. It is clear that Okonkwo was not immediately behind Ikemefuna, for otherwise the author would not have used the phrase "ran towards." During the brief interval that he was running toward Okonkwo, none of the other elders did anything. They simply failed to do their duty.

When Ikemefuna ran to Okonkwo for protection, what choices had Okonkwo? He could have done any of the following things: (1) give Ikemefuna the desired protection, (2) take him and like Pilate wash his hands of the matter and hand him back to be killed, or (3) kill him himself. The first option is ruled out, as adopting it would have amounted to an open defiance of the Oracle of the Hills and the Caves. It would also have been an affront to all the people of Umuofia. Regarding the second option, one may argue that Okonkwo should have followed the example of Pilate, for this would have been a more humane line of action. Okonkwo's position, however, is quite unlike Pilate's. Pilate was operating within the world of human order. In Okonkwo's case, the oracle had commanded that Ikemefuna should die. Okonkwo was not excluded from bringing about the death of Ikemefuna. It would undoubtedly have been very humane of Okonkwo to behave like Pilate, but the consequence would have been different. To take Ikemefuna and to hand him back to be killed would be as if Okonkwo said to the Oracle of the Hills and the Caves, "I don't dispute what you have said, but I refuse to be the instrument that will bring about what you have decreed." This too would have amounted to a defiance of the oracle. The situation is comparable to that of citizens who feel that a particular law is morally revolting; although they would not prevent others from obeying the law, they themselves would not obey it. We are then left with the third option. Okonkwo killed Ikemefuna.

After Okonkwo had killed Ikemefuna, the authorial voice tells us that Okonkwo's reason for killing Ikemefuna is his fear of being thought weak. The authorial voice is always final, but one doubts whether it is equally always masterful. Okonkwo's killing of Ikemefuna is instinctive. No time was left for him to consider his action. In other words, his killing of Ikemefuna was not premeditated. The immediate circumstances under which he had to kill Ikemefuna seem to have been forced on him by capricious fates. He was not in control of the situation. Rather, the situation was controlling him, and we should not apply the principles of morality to a situation in which he was inexorably led by uncanny fate. Thus far, we can conclude from the evidence before us that by the beginning of the novel, Ikemefuna's death was already a fait accompli, that Okonkwo's action in killing him was not premeditated, and that the circumstances which led to his killing of Ikemefuna forced the act on him.

We now turn our attention to our second level of analysis, namely, what critics have made out of the evidence available in the text. After the killing of Ikemefuna, Okonkwo's closest friend, Obierika, blames Okonkwo for taking part in the killing of Ikemefuna. When Okonkwo accuses him of not coming along with them when they went to kill Ikemefuna, the following conversation ensues between the two of them:

> "You know very well, Okonkwo, that I am not afraid of blood; and if anyone tells you that I am, he is telling a lie. And let me tell you one thing, my friend. If I were you I would have stayed at home. What you have done will not please the Earth. It is the kind of action for which the goddess wipes out whole families."
>
> "The Earth cannot punish me for obeying her messenger," Okonkwo said. "A child's fingers are not scalded by a piece of hot yam which its mother puts into its palm."
>
> "That is true," Obierika agreed. "But if the Oracle said that my son should be killed I would neither dispute it nor be the one to do it." (46–47)

Many critics have taken a clue from this and blamed Okonkwo for killing Ikemefuna. For them, Okonkwo committed an offense by killing Ikemefuna. Okonkwo sees his action differently. The difference between Okonkwo's view and Obierika's (and, by implication, the view of Okonkwo's critics) can be summarized as the difference between rigid adherence to a sacred order and the questioning of this sacred order by bringing in considerations of conventional morality or wisdom. Obierika and Okonkwo's critics are applying the standards of conventional wisdom to a situation which entirely transcends it. But for Okonkwo, strict adherence to the eternal sacred order takes precedence and allows of no human rationalization. Hence he tells Obierika that the Earth cannot punish him for obeying her messenger. Obierika concedes this point to Okonkwo. His later statement: "If the Oracle said that my son should be killed, I would neither dispute it nor be the one to do it" (47) is then no more than sheer conventional sentimentality and hypocrisy. Did he not throw away his own twin children because tradition commanded him to? (87). Of course, the tradition which sees twin children as abominable does not state that it is the father of the twin children that must throw them away. Was Obierika not going to take part in razing Okonkwo's house and demolishing everything there? (87). Here again, custom simply demands that the house of any person who commits a *female ochu* ("inadvertent murder") should be destroyed. It does not compel every person to take part in such demolitions. In taking part in these two activities, Obierika commits the same offense (if offense it may be called) for which he holds Okonkwo guilty.

Furthermore, we need to consider whether a person who kills a condemned man can be said to have committed an offense and also to consider under what circumstances the person may or may not be exonerated. The oracle said that Ikemefuna should be killed. It did not say that Okonkwo should not take part in carrying out its wish. In the context under consideration, there is no traditional hangman whose role it is to kill people in Ikemefuna's predicament. By killing Ikemefuna, therefore, Okonkwo has not usurped any person's role. He is included in the possible list of those who can kill Ikemefuna. He kills Ikemefuna. The oracle's wish has been obeyed; by whom is of no material significance. The application of conventional practical wisdom to a transcendent, eternal, sacred order is again seen to be inappropriate. We do not apply the same normative rules with which we deal with ourselves to our dealings with our gods and ancestors, except where there is no conflict in the application of such rules to both spheres. And where a conflict exists, the gods take precedence. This is exactly the situation in which Okonkwo kills Ikemefuna.

Critics are also quick to point out that Okonkwo begins to suffer many reverses after his killing of Ikemefuna. They see these reverses as a type of punishment from the gods. Carroll, Nnolim, and Killam, in the references already cited, appear to share this view. At this stage it is sufficient to point out that there is no logical implication between Okonkwo's reversal of fortunes and his killing of Ikemefuna. They are two different entities separated in space and time, and no causal link can be established between them. More confounding and illogical is Oladele Taiwo's claim:

When one considers the trend of events, and it turns out later that it is in the funeral ceremony of Ezeudu (who had warned Okonkwo to have no part in Ikemefuna's death) that Okonkwo is invoved in an accidental killing that exiles him from Umu-ofia, one begins to wonder whether Obierika's has not been the voice of reason; whether in fact, Okonkwo has not mis-interpreted the will of the gods. . . . We are confronted with an ironic situation in which Okonkwo, in his attempt to uphold "the authority and decision of the Oracle" displeases the earth goddess. (119)

The chasing of literary motifs is as interesting as it is complex, but sometimes it backfires. The curious logic which links Okonkwo's subsequent tragedies with the killing of Ikemefuna fails to link the death of Ezeudu and his son with his part in warning Okonkwo not to have anything to do with the killing of Ikemefuna. It may well be argued that Ezeudu's death was not unexpected, since he was the oldest man in that quarter of Umu-ofia; however, we should not lose sight of the fact that we do not die in time sequence according to our chronological age. It may be pertinent for us to know why it is not long after he warned Okonkwo that Ezeudu dies. It is also significant to remark that in traditional belief such an accident as befell Ezeudu's son does not just happen. Traditionally, such deaths are associated with some type of offense against the gods of the land. Why is it that when Okonkwo's gun explodes, it is Ezeudu's son who is killed, not some other person? Why must it be at Ezeudu's funeral that his own son gets killed?

We may never have a final answer to these questions because here we are confronted with causation at a supernatural level. Nevertheless, it is certainly tragic that Ezeudu's son should be killed during the funeral of his own father. For Ezeudu, it is not indicative that the gods are pleased with him. It is equally tragic for Okonkwo that his gun should explode and kill a person, but it may or may not be the case that the gods are pleased with him. Okonkwo's type of accident is usually, at least in traditional belief, attributed to *ajo chi* ("capricious fates"). It may well be that if the gods are displeased with Okonkwo, it is for a different reason. He claims that he was simply obeying the messenger of the Earth, but his hubris would not allow him to let the matter rest at that. After experiencing a momentary sting of conscience, he seems to have taken an uncanny pleasure in his action. He even boasts of it before his friend Obierika by declaring, "If we were all afraid of blood, it would not be done. And what do you think the Oracle would do then?" (46). Because of his peculiar psychological disposition, he introduces the consideration of courage and manly valor into a situation where Obierika is considering the propriety of his (Okonkwo's) action. Earlier in the novel, he had mused thus:

> "When did you become a shivering old woman," Okonkwo asked himself, "you are known in all the nine villages for your valour in war? How can a man who has killed five men in battle fall to pieces because he has added a boy to their number? Okonkwo, you have become a woman indeed." (45)

Here again, Okonkwo is not considering his action within an eternal sacred-order paradigm; instead, his pride and psychological disposition must be brought into a situation where he should be considering the propriety of his action. If Okonkwo is to be held guilty of any offense, it is not that of killing Ikemefuna (i.e., carrying out the wish of the Oracle of the Hills and the Caves) but that of taking an uncanny pride in his action, thereby removing the act from its proper domain or locale. His offense is that of hubris.

Finally, it can be argued that if Okonkwo had committed an offense by killing Ikemefuna, he would have been reprimanded or punished according to established rules. For an offense like the breaking of the Week of Peace, he was reprimanded. For the involuntary killing of Ezeudu's son, he suffers the appropriate punishment: the demolition of his entire compound and a seven-year exile for him and his entire family. If by traditional ethos, he committed an offense by killing Ikemefuna, then he would have been punished. He is not told to perform any cleansing rites. He is not told to offer sacrifices to the Earth goddess or to any other goddess for that matter. He is not deprived of his exalted position among the elders. Undoubtedly, within the level of private morality, his action is unconscionable, but that does not *necessarily* mean that he has committed an offense. Actions could be unconscionable without ipso facto being offenses, and in the near-fatalistic world view with which we are dealing, we have unconscionable acts that our failure to execute could constitute an offense against the gods. A classic example in African literature is the fate of Shanka in Gabre-Medhin's *Oda-Oak Oracle*. Okonkwo's killing of Ikemefuna is an unconscionable act, but we cannot logically go beyond that to establish that by killing Ikemefuna he committed an offense.

Works Cited

Achebe, Chinua. *Things Fall Apart*. London: Heinemann, 1962.

Carroll, David. *Chinua Achebe*. London: Macmillan, 1980.

Iyasere, Solomon. "Narrative Technique in *Things Fall Apart*." In *Critical Perspectives on Chinua Achebe*, edited by C. L. Innes and Bernth Lindfors, 92–110. London: Heinemann, 1978.

Killam, G. D. *The Writings of Chinua Achebe*. Rev. ed. London: Heinemann, 1977.

Nnolim, Charles E. "Achebe's *Things Fall Apart*: An Igbo National Epic." In *Modern Black Literature*, edited by S. Okechukwu Mezu, 56–60. New York: Black Academy, 1977.

Taiwo, Oladele. *Culture and the Nigerian Novel*. London: Macmillan, 1976.

Wren, Robert W. *Achebe's World: The Historical and Culture Contexts of the Novels of Chinua Achebe*. Washington, DC: Three Continents, 1980.

"When a Man Fails Alone"

A Man and His Chi in Chinua Achebe's Things Fall Apart

HAROLD SCHEUB

◆　◆　◆

THERE IS A TEMPTATION, upon reaching the final pages of *Things Fall Apart*, Chinua Achebe's tale of a man and his *chi*,[1] to accept Obierika's assessment of the hero's unhappy fate. That this temptation should be avoided is evident in a study of that central character. Okonkwo does not lend himself to facile analysis. Of the various approaches to his character and fate, the first and most obvious is also the least acceptable when considered within the context of the total novel and not simply the final pages of the work. That evident conclusion is angrily expressed by the hero's close friend who, turning vehemently on the white district commissioner as they stand at the foot of the tree from which hangs the limp body of the brash Okonkwo, spits out the words that, in their simplicity, obscure rather than edify: "That man was one of the greatest men in Umuofia. You drove him to kill himself" (147). So neat, so readily apparent—and yet so disturbingly inadequate an explanation—perforce leads one to a closer investigation of the character of Okonkwo, and significant aspects of that character warn against the obvious.

I

The attempt to shroud the corpse of Okonkwo in symbols suggesting the disintegration of the Igbo society in the face of an alien encroachment must confront the fact that Okonkwo, far from being a symbol of his society and its presumed fate, can pay only lip service to that society: he is, almost from the beginning, not an integral part of it, but is rather a threat to the social tradition that rivals in corrosiveness the threat posed by the white world.

This is not to question the very real intimidation embodied in the aggressive institutions of the whites—but there is, in this novel, no certainty of Igbo social destruction. The life and fortunes of Okonkwo are played out against the dynamic background of social change, change both within Igbo tradition and within a wider framework. But Okonkwo stands alone, outside his society, just as he stands outside the world of the white man—always peripheral, opportunistically grasping those elements in his society that will guarantee his prestige and assure his ascendancy. Okonkwo dances his fierce dance of death on the outer hem of society, a product of his tradition and yet self-alienated from it, as much an outsider in some respects as is the white man. Umuofian tradition is important to him only as it aids his quest or as it infringes upon the free thrust of his surging ego. For Okonkwo, the white institutions must be destroyed not simply because they are exotic, but more urgently because they are decided obstacles to his own upward movement.

There have been obstacles before, but Okonkwo, through the exercise of his enormous will, has overcome them; it is when he recognizes the futility of his quest that he commits in desperation and pathos the final act. It is, to be sure, an Umuofian world in which Okonkwo moves, but increasingly it becomes a world that he himself has created, not the same world that is peopled by his contemporaries. All events and characters come to be seen by Okonkwo within the context that he has created. Ikemefuna, Nwoye, Ezinma, his wives, Unoka, Agbala, Igbo traditions, and the institutions of the white man—all are seen as either threats or as means to his fulfillment. He uses in a manipulatory sense Igbo society and its traditions to achieve the substance of his dream, and he accepts with important reservations the framework of the society simply because it is against those selected standards of the society that his greatness will be judged. In his mind, he molds the existing society until it matches his image of an Igbo society; with keen selectivity, he includes in that image those aspects that he considers paramount and ignores the rest. His personal social image finally consists of the muscle of the real society without the heart. When the traditional frame becomes too narrow for him, he seeks through brute force to widen it, and he must often answer for such actions; simultaneously, his own conception of the society progressively narrows until few but Okonkwo himself can measure up to his precise standards. He attempts to mythologize the past of Umuofia—highly selectively—until that too supports his notion of greatness.

Okonkwo is a man driven to fury by a dream, a self-image that he will fulfill with every means he commands. He does not loyally defend the traditions of Umuofia; he uses the people and their customs and thereby feeds a pride that balloons until finally, perhaps inevitably, he sees himself as the savior of a society that, in his eyes, has gone awry, that has fallen victim to enemy forces. His seven years of exile have further distorted his view of himself, and so far has he traveled from the realities of life in Umuofia, so idealized has his conception of that life become, so certain is he of his own strength and of the power and traits of a society that does not in fact exist, that it is not startling to hear him lament, upon his homecoming, "Perhaps I have been away too long. . . . What is it that has happened to our people?" (124) A messianic Okonkwo returns to a society that has its existence only in his imagination, and it is this image, with Okonkwo in the representative position, that is destroyed by the force of the white world. This is not the same thing as saying that Umuofian society contains within itself this flaw. Igbo society gives evidence that it will survive. Okonkwo understands force, and it is because "he knew that Umuofia would not go to war" (144) (as close as he

er comes to recognizing the realities of the world outside him),
is because he now senses the finality of his own position, that
he bows to the district commissioner. His world, unlike that of
Umuofia, contains nothing that will provide him with the traditional adaptability of his people, which enables them to survive
and prosper.

> There were many men and women in Umuofia who did
> not feel as strongly as Okonkwo about the new dispensation.
> The white man had indeed brought a lunatic religion, but he
> had also built a trading store and for the first time palm-oil
> and kernel became things of great price, and much money
> flowed into Umuofia.
>
> And even in the matter of religion there was a growing
> feeling that there might be something in it after all, something
> vaguely akin to method in the overwhelming madness. (126)

We do not, in this novel, witness the death throes of a society.
It may well be asked if this Umuofian people were so delicately
balanced in their traditions that the intrusion of a new and vital
force from the outside would destroy it. Rather, there seems to
be an almost immediate adaptation to it. Change there will be,
but Umuofian society seems not unaccustomed to change.
Okonkwo's vision and Obierika's confusion and sorrow often obscure the genuine tenaciousness of the society; they become
Umuofia's spokesmen, and in their pronouncements they distort
the values and ignore the resilience and toughness of their people.
In fact, the flexibility of this Igbo society suggests strongly its
ability to avert disintegration.

It is precisely because Okonkwo is so adamantly opposed to
many traditions of the society (rather than embodying them) that
he must die. Clutching his image of the society, he is incapable
of change; his selfishness and his perverted ideals, his own fuming
drive toward fulfillment destroy him. These combine and become
his personal god, his *chi*, and he will fall not because of forces
external to him, but rather because of flaws that are integral parts

of his character. One need only add that these are Okonkwo's problems, not those of the society.

II

If one accepts the conclusion that derives from Obierika's comments and accusations, there is little to be said about Okonkwo except that he reflects the interests and represents the values of Umuofian society and that he therefore heralds the destruction of the society through his own inability to adapt to the institutions of an alien culture that, because of its superior might, is irresistibly imposing itself on the social structures. The death of Okonkwo may therefore be seen as a symbol of the imminent decline and disintegration of the society. It is Obierika who sums up the cause and effect of Okonkwo's death, and it is Obierika, too, who earlier prophesies Umuofia's demise. In answer to Okonkwo's question "Does the white man understand our custom about land?" Obierika responds:

> How can he when he does not even speak our tongue? But he says that our customs are bad; and our own brothers who have taken up his religion also say that our customs are bad. How do you think we can fight when our own brothers have turned against us? The white man is very clever. He came quietly and peaceably with his religion. We were amused at his foolishness and allowed him to stay. Now he has won our brothers, and our clan can no longer act like one. He has put a knife on the things that held us together, and we have fallen apart. (124)

From whence the title of the work. But while it may or may not be true that Umuofian society is in fact falling apart, the application of the title to the society is one thing, its association with Okonkwo quite another.

Obierika's concern for the society and his arguments about its dissolution are vitiated by two things. First, not only does he fail to consider the demonstrated ability of the society to adjust itself to change, he also ignores—as does Okonkwo—the wide limits of tolerance that characterize the people and the traditions of Umuofia. It is not as if an alien culture can so easily violate and subvert existing traditions; it is not as if the social structure of Umuofia, upon being pricked by exotic institutions, will perish with a dusty echo. The society is not so fragile, its institutions not so vulnerable, as to support any such argument for impending and precipitous dissolution.[2]

The second consideration that militates against Obierika's comments is his own confusion. He accuses his brothers of turning against the society, thereby collaborating in the injurious intrigue. But if this be treason, then it assumes divers guises, one of which the rather muddled Obierika himself dons at times. Like Okonkwo, Obierika seems to be valiantly upholding the traditions of Umuofia, yet on the basis of their own definitions of loyalty they are not as faithful as their words make them appear. The fact is that, with the exception of the hero who wrestles with social traditions for reasons of his own, Obierika, above all others, is a consistent critic of tradition. He early questions the "will of the goddess" in excluding Okonkwo from the society because of an accidental killing, and he also queries the society's policy of destroying twin children at birth. He further challenges customs relating to the responsibilities of titled men in Umuofia, and only the arrogance of Okonkwo forces him to suggest that he was jesting. On the basis of his own arguments, Obierika is guilty of turning, if warily, against his own traditions. Nwoye is considered an outcast because he joins the Christian church, yet Obierika can match Nwoye, reservation for reservation, in everything but action.[3]

Obierika's function seems to be akin to that of the classical chorus, commenting on and explaining the actions of the story's characters. Because he plays such a role, his statements are given added weight by the reader. If his conclusions are not to be taken as those of the novelist himself, they are at least those of a cultural elder, wise and aware; because he is not generally a part of the actions of which he speaks, he apparently gains a perspective not granted to those who are emotionally involved. Yet, as prophet, teacher, and apologist, he is a failure, and his inclusion in the story complicates matters even as he attempts to make them clear and uncomplicated. An initial task in analyzing the novel, therefore, is to examine closely the significance of Obierika's statements, for what he says, accepted without debate, will lead the reader to conclusions not sustained by the novel itself.

He is, it is true, "a man who thought about things" (87), a skeptic on the one hand, an apologist on the other. He is given the opportunity to provide comments and explanations, which are tempting in their simplicity but inadequate. Since such observations appear at major climaxes in the story, Obierika is in a position to shape the reader's conception of the entire work. Because he is hasty in forming conclusions and because he does not seem to truly understand the strengths of the society, he is untrustworthy; yet, so important is his position in the novel that he cannot be ignored. One must finally ascribe to his comments D. H. Lawrence's admonition, "Never trust the teller, trust the tale." A consideration of this tale, *Things Fall Apart*, underscores this necessary suspicion of the teller, Obierika, who is a fascinating and complex part of the Umuofian world limned by Achebe.

Aside from his questionable didactic function in the novel, aside from his deceptive role as messenger and chorus, Obierika foreshadows major events and suggests weaknesses in the social armor, weaknesses that seem to give credence to the theory that things are falling apart. But just as it is well that the society generally disregards his hand wringing, so it is important that the reader not take him too literally. If the author conceived of him as a chorus, then he is a failure and represents a flaw in the novel. Seen not as a chorus but as an integral part of the story, he is simply a rather inept old man whose wisdom is proved to be foolishness by events; who, when he thinks, is "merely led into greater complexities"; and who, ironically, through his own contradictions, emphasizes not the title of the novel but rather the society's ability to question itself and, finally, to change.

III

When one first confronts the villagers of Umuofia, one is struck by the fact that they appear to be, in Gerald Moore's words, "a tense and somewhat pessimistic people, the area of light within which they could live in confidence" being "a somewhat narrow one."[4] Indeed, Umuofia does appear to be tradition-bound, characterized by fear and a preoccupation with prestige and power.

"I kill a man," chants the *egwugwu*, Evil Forest,[5] "on the day that his life is sweetest to him" (66). Death is such a constant threat that life itself seems at times to be little more than a brief rite of passage: "The land of the living was not far removed from the domain of the ancestors. There was coming and going between them, especially at festivals and also when an old man died, because an old man was very close to the ancestors. A man's life from birth to death was a series of transition rites which brought him nearer and nearer to his ancestors" (85). A sense of fear laces the entire society of Umuofia, and evil seems to be everywhere present: "Darkness held a vague terror for these people, even the bravest among them. Children were warned not to whistle at night for fear of evil spirits. Dangerous animals became even more sinister and uncanny in the dark. A snake was never called by its name at night, because it would hear" (7).

The people believe that they should never answer in the affirmative when called, "for fear it might be an evil spirit calling" (29). There is the "fear of evil and capricious gods and of magic, the fear of the forest, and of the forces of nature, malevolent, red in tooth and claw." If anyone is "so foolhardy as to pass by the shrine" where the society's war medicine is kept, medicine that is called "old woman," "he was sure to see the old woman hopping about" (69). And always hovering about is Agbala, "the owner of the future, the messenger of earth, the god who cut a man down when his life was sweetest to him" (75). Chielo, a good and generous neighbor, becomes a fearful person when she assumes the role of Agbala's priestess; indeed, there is "no humanity there."

The society is heavily dependent on nature for its subsistence, and Ani, "the earth goddess and the source of all fertility," is a major figure in the Umuofian pantheon and a central pillar of social traditions; she is also the "ultimate judge of morality and conduct," and she is "in close communion with the departed fathers of the clan" (26). The coming of the new year is celebrated with a festival dedicated to her; sacrifices are made, and the first yams of the season are offered to Ani and to the ancestral spirits. This is also a time of purification—cleaning the houses and compounds, washing utensils, a general cleansing process in preparation for the new year. Similarly, if one transgresses in any way against the earth goddess, purification rites have to be undertaken. When Okonkwo breaks the sanctity of the Week of Peace by punishing a wife, Ezeani, the priest of the earth goddess, warns him that his action could have disastrous results for the entire society: "The evil you have done can ruin the whole clan. The earth goddess whom you have insulted may refuse to give us her increase, and we shall all perish" (22). He provides instructions as to how Okonkwo can cleanse himself and the community of his crime. Again, when Okonkwo accidentally kills an Umuofian, he has to go into exile, and his fellows destroy his compound, not because they hate Okonkwo: "They were merely cleansing the land Okonkwo had polluted with the blood of a clansman" (87). Finally, when Okonkwo destroys himself, Obierika tells the district commissioner that the people of the village will "make sacrifices to cleanse the desecrated land" (147).

It seems that anything that threatens the security of the society has to be cast out: twins are thrown into the Evil Forest; Christians are told to build their church in the Evil Forest; the *osu* are castoffs, as are Umuofians dying of a sickness that is "an abomination to the earth" (13). Okonkwo, because he has committed a crime, is ostracized. The village, always aware and fearful of evil in its midst, attempts to purge itself of malevolence by expelling it. Okika, speaking of the Christians, tells his fellows, "We must root out this evil. And if our brothers take the side of evil we must root them out too" (144). Twins are discarded because "the Earth had decreed that they were an offence on the land and must be destroyed." There is a readiness to execute the orders of the goddess; if they do not, "her wrath [is] loosed on all the land and not just on the offender" (87).

The greatest fear is scarcity of food, hence the homage paid to the earth goddess. Tales told of men in Umuofian history who were blessed with plenty testify to this preoccupation with food. Indeed, a man's wealth is predicated on the amount of food he has. Citizens of Umuofia reveal their wealth through acts of generosity; during the festival, "every man whose arm was strong, as the Igbo people say, was expected to invite large numbers of guests from far and wide" (26). When locusts come in great numbers to a locust-hungry Umuofia, the event is described as a "tremendous sight, full of power and beauty" (39). Obierika, presenting his daughter to her future in-laws, is, with his fellow elders, impressed by the many pots of palm wine that the prospective in-laws brought along, and they express their surprise and satisfaction with their highest compliment: "Now they are behaving like men" (81). The insecurities that wracked the village because of the need for food seem to have led to this close affiliation between food and manhood. "Yam stood for manliness," and those who do not cultivate, those who are idle, are loathed: "he who could feed his family on yams from one harvest to another was a very great man indeed" (23). The man who is lazy, who takes no titles, is called *agbala*, which is another name for woman.

The value that is placed on strength, industry, and manliness is expressed in a number of ways in Umuofia. "No clan," exclaims Okika, "can boast of . . . greater valor" (143). And it is a fact that "Umuofia was feared by all its neighbors. It was powerful in war and in magic, and its priests and medicine men were feared in all the surrounding country" (8). The village is called "the land of the brave," and it gives high recognition to its warriors. When Ezeudu dies, he is buried with esteem, "a great funeral, such as befitted a noble warrior" (85). And when Okonkwo represents the society during a dispute with Mbaino "as the proud and imperious emissary of war, he was treated with great honor and respect" (9).

It is a masculine society, and the premium placed on manliness has become a standard of judgment. "It is not bravery when a man fights a woman" (66), says Evil Forest, and, during the journey that culminates in the execution of Ikemefuna, those men undertaking the task speak of "some effeminate men who had refused to come with them" (41).

IV

If the description of the society of Umuofia were to end at this point, it might indeed be considered a tense and pessimistic place. And it would be an easy matter to imagine the development of an Okonkwo from such origins, since those traits that best characterize Okonkwo—manliness and fear—are without question important attributes of the society itself.

But this description of Umuofia—severe, strident, apprehensive—is only a part of the story, and to characterize the society as being merely pessimistic and tense is to be as inaccurate in one's view of the novel as to conclude that Okonkwo is typical of the Umuofian people. The apparent dreariness and anxiety are relieved and balanced by a generosity and a joy of life, counterparts to a hope for food and a fear of death. The society, moreover, provides a framework which encourages the development of individual potential, and there is a constant affirmation of life.

Umuofia is, it is true, a courageous and militarily successful society, and when the community considers that it has been wronged, as it does when people from Mbaino murder the wife of Ogbuefi Udo, it does not take much exhortation to fill the people "with anger and thirst for blood." Still, it is not an aggressively warlike society: "it never went to war unless its case was clear and just and was accepted as such by its Oracle," and it "would never fight what the Igbo call a fight of blame" (9). War is not in any case a prevalent disposition in Umuofia; the attitude toward it seems rather to be reflected in Nwakibie's prayer as he breaks the kola nut: "We shall all live. We pray for life, children, a good harvest and happiness. You will have what is good for you and I will have what is good for me" (14).

While each of the details in the brief catalog that follows may be, in itself, relatively insignificant, taken together they suggest a society that is not necessarily writhing in the grips of fear and gloom. Umuofia is not an insensitive society: "On a moonlight night. . . . The happy voices of children playing in open fields would then be heard. And perhaps those not so young would be playing in pairs in less open places, and old men and women would remember their youth. As the Igbo say, 'When the moon is shining the cripple becomes hungry for a walk' " (7). It is a society marked by generosity: "I shall give you twice four hundred yams," says Nwakibie to a desperately poor Okonkwo. "Go and prepare your farm" (16).

Nor are Umuofians devoid of love. Ekwefi leaves her husband and comes to live with Okonkwo because she loves him, and, later in her life, her belief that Ezinma "had come to stay" was "that faith alone that gave her own life any kind of meaning." Okonkwo himself has to fight down feelings of affection for Ezinma and also for Ikemefuna. And the vaunting boasts of Umuofia's men are subdued by a concomitant respect for humility: "Everybody at the kindred meeting took sides with Osugo when Okonkwo called him a woman. The oldest man present said sternly that those whose palm-kernels were cracked for them by a benevolent spirit should not forget to be humble" (19). There are wrestling matches that "filled the village with excitement"; there are dances, "quick, light and gay"; and there are feasts that are "celebrated with great joy."

Change was evident in Umuofia before the coming of the white men, and its traces were apparent not only in the predictable laments of village elders about "the softness of today's youth" and "the good old days." There was a permissiveness in the social structure that allowed, even encouraged, the questioning of existing traditions. An atmosphere of change and skepticism is hinted at and revealed throughout the novel. Certainly, traditions are important, many of them inviolate. But they are not immune to human curiosity and questioning, two precursors of change. To be sure, the women, who never saw the interior of "the *egwugwu* house," kept "their imagination to themselves," but there are suggestions that even some of the most sacred customs were being questioned:

> Okonkwo's wives, and perhaps other women as well, might have noticed that the second *egwugwu* had the springy walk of Okonkwo. And they might also have noticed that Okonkwo was not among the titled men and elders who sat behind the row of *egwugwu*. But if they thought these things they kept them within themselves. The *egwugwu* with the springy walk was one of the dead fathers of the clan. (63)

Even the great Agbala was not above question and resistance. Ekwefi swore an oath "that if she heard Ezinma cry she would rush into the cave to defend her against all the gods in the world" (76), and Nwakibie told the story of Obiako who, when the oracle told him that his dead father "wants you to sacrifice a goat to him," answered smartly, "Ask my father if he ever had a fowl when he was alive" (15), a rather bold rejoinder to a god so widely feared and revered. Chielo makes this god sound formidable: "Beware of exchanging words with Agbala. Does a man speak when a god speaks? Beware . . . lest he strike you in his anger" (71). But this stern warning does not keep Ekwefi and Okonkwo from transgressing the commandment of the god.

While there is a tendency to be somewhat provincial regarding Umuofian customs (speaking of a rival group, Ogbuefi Ezeudu observes, "It is a bad custom which these people observe because they lack understanding" [23]), still there is an understanding that laws and traditions are in no sense universally applicable. Obierika's brother suggests that "what is good in one place is bad in another," and even the conservative Okonkwo allows that "the world is large." Uchendu notes that "there is no story that is not true. . . . The world has no end, and what is good among one people is an abomination with others" (99). Ajofia, the leading *egwugwu* of the community and "the head and spokesman of the nine ancestors who administered justice in the clan," says, at the height of a crisis involving the whites, "We cannot leave the matter in his [Mr. Smith's] hands because he does not know our ways, and perhaps he says we are foolish because we do not know his" (134).

All of this is to suggest that the society of Umuofia is not a tight, tradition-shackled community, that there is both an understanding and a tolerance that, when combined with a freedom to question and a broad social framework, reveal an adaptability and a resilience that will be of considerable value to Umuofia when it finally confronts the challenges posed by the whites.

When Okoye visits Unoka in Umuofia, the latter "prayed to their ancestors for life and health, and for protection against their enemies" (5). When the kola nut is broken at the home of Obierika, his eldest brother says, "Life to all of us . . . and let there be friendship between your family and ours" (82). And at the ceremony honoring Ezeudu, the one-handed spirit speaks to the spirit of the deceased: "If you had been poor in your last life I would have asked you to be rich when you come again. But you were rich. If you had been a coward, I would have asked you to bring courage. But you were a fearless warrior. If you had died young, I would have asked you to get life. But you lived long. So I shall ask you to come again the way you came before" (86).

Health and friendship, protection against enemies, wealth, courage, long life—these are basic values, as much a part of life in Umuofia as fear and a blustering masculinity.

More important than anything else, in Umuofia, "a man was judged according to his worth and not according to the worth of his father," so that the achievements of individual persons as opposed to the collective accomplishments of the group are emphasized. "Age was respected among his people, but achievement was revered" (6). The social structure of Umuofia is neither narrow nor rigid, then; there is ample room for individual endeavor, achievement, aspiration, idiosyncrasy. It is a framework that not only invites questions and tolerates change, it encourages dreams and enables a desperately ambitious youth like Okonkwo to become, despite his father's singular lack of success, an important, wealthy person; "his fame rested on solid personal achievements" (3). The citizen of the community is not reduced in circumstances because of caste or birth or status; he can become wealthy and famous through the effective and resourceful use of his wit and his hands: "As the elders said, if a child washed his hands he could eat with kings" (6).

Is Okonkwo symbolic of his people and their traditions? For the people of Umuofia, there are two faces, at least: its fears and insecurities balanced by hopes and joys. They do not live in a confined ideological world closeted tightly with their traditions and fears.

But Okonkwo does live in such a closet.

V

Okonkwo is a man drawn by a dream and driven by fear, the latter providing much of the substance of the dream.

Obierika is incorrect when he speaks of Okonkwo's fate. It is not that the whites "drove him to kill himself" (147)—fear and the dream remain the motivating factors throughout. Nor is the hero's fate in any substantive way symbolic of the destiny of the society. More to the point, as far as the character and fortunes of the central character are concerned, is the Umuofian saying (which is quoted in the novel in another context but which better than anything else serves as an apt introduction to this complex being), "As a man danced so the drums were beaten for him" (130–31).

This is the tale of a man and his *chi*, and if the title of the novel cannot be applied to the traditions and society of Umuofia, it can be employed without reservation when considering Okonkwo and his dream. The profoundly personal nature of his fate and the distance he has traveled from his people and their customs are summed up in the bewilderment with which the Umuofians greet Okonkwo's murder of the head messenger: "Why did he do it?" (145). They do not know. Early in the novel, the drift begins as Okonkwo moves away from the society and its traditions into his own world.

Before the dream, there was fear, and when the dream vanished, only the fear remained. The dream was founded on fear, was heavily shot through with fear, and the two became, almost inextricably, one. The genesis of the dream was the father. Okonkwo's birthright was fear, fear that he would become like his father: "his whole life was dominated by fear, the fear of failure and of weakness. It was deeper and more intimate than the fear of evil and capricious gods. . . . Okonkwo's fear was greater than these. It was not external but lay deep within himself. It was the fear of himself, lest he should be found to resemble his father" (9–10). The fear festered and infected his soul. Initially, it was given raw form in his revulsion against his father, the old man who "wore a haggard and mournful look except when he was drinking or playing on his flute." It was when he was drinking or playing on his flute that Unoka came to life, "his face beaming with blessedness and peace." He would play in other villages, relishing "the good fare and the good fellowship, and he loved this season of the year, when the rains had stopped and the sun rose every morning with dazzling beauty." He was a poet, sensitive and alone:

> Unoka loved it all, and he loved the first kites that returned with the dry season, and the children who sang songs of welcome to them. He would remember his own childhood, how he had often wandered around looking for a kite sailing leisurely against the blue sky. As soon as he found one he would sing with his whole being, welcoming it back from its long, long journey. (4)

But that was in his youth: "Unoka, the grown-up, was a failure." He was a poor man, "and his wife and children had barely enough to eat" (4). He was also a debtor, borrowing heavily and seldom paying back what he owed. When he "talked about music, . . . his face beamed," but he "was never happy when it came to wars" (5). When he went to the priestess of Agbala to ask why his crops continually failed, he was told to "go home and work like a man." And when he died, "he died of the swelling which was an abomination to the earth goddess" and "was carried to the Evil Forest and left there to die" (13). It was characteristic of him that "when they carried him away, he took with him his flute." It was in music and beauty that Unoka's character blossomed and in which he sought meaning: "He could hear in his mind's ear the blood stirring and intricate rhythms of the *ekwe* and the *udu* and the *ogene*,[6] decorating them with a colorful and plaintive tune. The total effect was gay and brisk, but if one picked out the flute as it went up and down and then broke up into short snatches, one saw that there was sorrow and grief there" (5). This, then, was Okonkwo's father: a lover of beauty and a connoisseur of joy, well acquainted with sorrow and the scorn of his fellows.

Fear of becoming another Unoka led Okonkwo to loathe those things that his father loved; the revulsion shifted and was given new form, and a second step was taken in the quest for fulfillment:

> Even as a little boy he had resented his father's failure and weakness, and even now he still remembered how he had suffered when a playmate had told him that his father was *agbala*. That was how Okonkwo first came to know that *agbala* was not only another name for a woman, it could also mean a man who had taken no title. And so Okonkwo was ruled by one passion—to hate everything that his father Unoka had loved. One of those things was gentleness and another was idleness. (10)

As the village attempted to root out anything that added to its feelings of insecurity, so Okonkwo set about balancing those fears that made him insecure. He despised idleness because his father was idle, and "during the planting season Okonkwo worked daily on his farms from cock-crow until the chickens went to roost" (10); even when the work was completed and the harvest gathered, when the time for celebration was at hand, "somehow Okonkwo could never become as enthusiastic over feasts as most people. . . . He would be very much happier working on his farm." And when he detected "incipient laziness" in his first son, Nwoye, "he sought to correct him by constant nagging and beating" (10).

Hard work would mitigate Okonkwo's fear of resembling his father: "... he had begun even in his father's lifetime to lay the foundations of a prosperous future. It was slow and painful. But he threw himself into it like one possessed. And indeed he was possessed by the fear of his father's contemptible life and shameful death" (13).

But Unoka was also a gentle man; he loved easily, and Okonkwo had to conquer this characteristic as well: "Okonkwo never showed any emotion openly, unless it be the emotion of anger. To show affection was a sign of weakness; the only thing worth demonstrating was strength" (20). Fear of resembling his father thus led to a fear and concomitant dislike of what he perceived as weakness and femininity. A purely negative attitude, an aversion to gentleness and idleness, laid the foundations for the positive thrust of Okonkwo's ambitions. He began to see how he could most successfully fight back the specter of his father. Fears were slowly giving birth to hopes and to a dream. Okonkwo was able to discover in the traditions and values of Umuofia the blessings necessary to his efforts to erase the anxieties that were his birthright. The greatest of the village's concerns was a lack of food; consequently, there was an emphasis on work, production, and cultivation, and the people reserved some of their highest honors for those men who were the most productive. Through hard work, Okonkwo would be able to accomplish two things: he would exorcise, to some extent at least, the spirit of his father, and he would simultaneously gain the approbation of his peers.

The community of Umuofia cherished courage and manliness; its warriors were among its most revered citizens. Unoka feared blood; his son did not. Okonkwo had, in fact, "shown incredible prowess" during two wars. The gentleness that he disdained in his father was displaced by an intense emphasis on machismo and valor. Once again, he was able to diminish his anxiety—regarding effeminacy, this time—and thereby gain the plaudits of his village. This abhorrence of gentleness robbed Okonkwo of a sensitivity that would have humanized him, that would have muted his strident championing of virility. When the drums beat, signaling the commencement of wrestling matches, there was occasion for merriment and exhilaration in Umuofia, but for Okonkwo there was more: he "trembled with the desire to conquer and subdue" (30). Conquest and the fear from which that need grew now marked his actions as nothing else did. He killed Ikemefuna, a boy for whom he had much affection, because "he was afraid of being thought weak" (43). There were times, such as this one, when he had to work energetically against sentiment; after executing Ikemefuna, he was unable to sleep and eat. An act that was carried out because of his concern that he might be thought spineless resulted in weakness nonetheless, and Okonkwo combated that frailty in the only way he could: " 'When did you become a shivering old woman,' Okonkwo asked himself, 'you, who are known in all the nine villages for your valor in war? How can a man who has killed five men in battle fall to pieces because he has added a boy to their number? Okonkwo, you have become a woman indeed' " (45).

This preoccupation with masculinity informs everything Okonkwo does and thinks. The highest compliment he is able to pay to another human he gives to his beloved daughter, Ezinma: "She should have been a boy" (45). All of his actions, even his manners, are shaped by this preoccupation. When Ekwefi follows the priestess who has taken Ezinma away, Okonkwo does not immediately follow, but allows "what he regarded as a reasonable and manly interval to pass" before he goes. When the elders of Mbanta refuse to wage war against the Christians because "it is not our custom to fight for our gods," Okonkwo's reaction is characteristic:

> "Let us not reason like cowards," said Okonkwo. "If a man comes into my hut and defecates on the floor, what do I do? Do I shut my eyes? No! I take a stick and break his head. That is what a man does. These people are daily pouring filth over us, and Okeke says we should pretend not to see." Okonkwo made a sound full of disgust. This was a womanly clan, he thought. (113)

And when, after his exile, he returns to his own community and sees what has been wrought by white institutions, "he mourned for the clan, which he saw breaking up and falling apart, and he mourned for the warlike men of Umuofia, who had so unaccountably become soft like women" (129).

The obsession with masculinity and the fear of weakness are most virulently expressed when he thinks of Nwoye. He wants his son "to be a greater farmer and a great man," but he is afraid. "Nwoye is old enough to impregnate a woman. At his age I was already fending for myself. . . . A child that will grow into a cock can be spotted the very day it hatches. I have done my best to make Nwoye grow into a man, but there is too much of his mother in him." And an additional conclusion: " 'Too much of his grandfather,' Obierika thought, but he did not say it. The same thought also came to Okonkwo's mind" (46). When Nwoye becomes interested in the teachings of the Christians—"the poetry of the new religion, something felt in the marrow" (104)—Okonkwo is incredulous. "To abandon the gods of one's fathers to go about with a lot of effeminate men clucking like old hens was the very depth of abomination." And he wonders, "how . . . could he have begotten a son like Nwoye, degenerate and effeminate?" He toys with the idea that Nwoye is not really his son: "He, Okonkwo, was called a flaming fire. How could he have begotten a woman for a son?" He concludes, "Living fire begets cold, impotent ash" (108–9). Okonkwo later calls his other sons to him: "You have all seen the great abomination of your brother. Now he is no longer my son or your brother. I will only have a son who is a man, who will hold his head up among my people. If any one of you prefers to be a woman, let him follow Nwoye now while I am alive so that I can curse him" (121–22).

Okonkwo's definition of manliness has become broader and now includes not only human weakness but, in addition, anything that threatens him. He has become unable to find both strength and gentleness in the same idea or person. Obierika says to him, "It was always said that Ndulue and Ozoemena had one mind. . . . I remember when I was a young boy there was a song about them. He could not do anything without telling her."

Okonkwo responds, "I did not know that. . . . I thought he was a strong man in his youth." Ofoedu comments, "He was indeed," but "Okonkwo shook his head doubtfully" (47–48).

VI

Okonkwo's fears of idleness, gentleness, and weakness were eased through his hard work and toughness, and he became "one of the greatest men of his time" (6). The anxieties of his village were his anxieties, and in this climate of fear, he grew his own. His terrors and annoyances needed channeling, and he was finally able to direct them into areas that would bring him peace of mind and, at the same time, achieve for him the blessing of the community. The means for diminishing his fears—work and a unique view of manhood—soon develop into, and remain for a time, values for Okonkwo, and they feed his dream of greatness. His own stature will be measured against standards that grow directly out of his fears. Initially, "Okonkwo was ruled by one passion—to hate everything that his father Unoka loved" (10). Now he is "ruled by a great passion—to become one of the lords of the clan" (92), the prerequisites of such greatness being hard work and an exaggerated notion of manhood. The revulsion and anxiety have blended into the dream, a dream of eminence heavily infused with a naive sense of gender. The shift is complete; Okonkwo can now "lay the ghost" of his father: "Whenever the thought of his father's weakness and failure troubled him he expelled it by thinking about his own strength and success" (13).

What began as pure revulsion against his father and later a disgust with those things his father loved has been elevated into a personal system of values, and those values, which have become the substance of his dream, were determined not by Umuofia and its traditions but by Okonkwo's reaction of terror to his father's weakness and his espousal of those traits that the society of Umuofia would respect and that simultaneously meshed with his hatred of what he considered his father's flaws. But the society did not consider Unoka an abomination; it also values certain attributes that the old man possessed but that Okonkwo deems frailties. Okonkwo simply ignores these values, then later sees them as evidence that Umuofia is falling apart, that it has lost the strength and manliness of the good old days. By this time, so completely has he become involved in his personal image of the society, an image based on his distorted dream, that he has long since lost contact with the realities of Umuofia and the breadth and flexibility of its traditions. Okonkwo attempts to impose his image of the society on the society itself, and if Umuofia does not fit the image, then it is Umuofia that is wanting, for Okonkwo has no doubt that his image contains the only worthwhile system of values. So carefully and selectively has he come to view Umuofia and its ideals that its past has become mythologized for him and its present values are distorted—not because he has changed the system of values but because he has omitted all values that characterize, as far as he is concerned, his failure of a father. Okonkwo is left with a partial view of his society, one that he proceeds to nurture, to revere and refine, one that reflects his own dreams and slowly edges away from reality. In the end, only Okonkwo himself will be able to measure up, for he has molded the society, by selectivity and not by consciously changing its values, into his own image.

Hard work and demonstration of his strength are not ends in themselves; they are soon replaced by the larger vision, the ascendancy of Okonkwo. In exile, "work no longer had for him the pleasure it used to have" (92), because work, by itself, is unimportant. Okonkwo wants rather to climb "to the utmost heights." Since he is "not a man of thought but of action" (48), he deals with any obstacle that stands between him and that goal with an "inflexible will" and a force that is basal and impulsive. It is typical of Okonkwo that "whenever he was angry and could not get his words out quickly enough, he would use his fists." He "ruled his household with a heavy hand. His wives, especially the youngest, lived in perpetual fear of his fiery temper, and so did his little children. Perhaps down in his heart Okonkwo was not a cruel man. But his whole life was dominated by fear, the fear of failure and of weakness" (9). The greatness that he envisions is severe, devoid of generosity and love. His dream of ascendancy embraces an image of a society that exists merely to buttress his own position, and the whole is really a nightmare of brute strength that ignores the feelings of others and manipulates existing traditions as well as people and beliefs into a single-minded move toward fulfillment.

Okonkwo is successful in purging himself of those humane characteristics that he considers flaws, replacing them with a selfishness that is almost boundless. Though it "was unheard of to beat somebody during the sacred week" (21), he attacks his younger wife for little reason. In the midst of the preparations for a celebration, Okonkwo is restive, and he chooses a foolish excuse, which allows him to beat and later to shoot at Ekwefi. He uses the gods of the society for his own ends. He does so in minor ways, as when he warns Nwoye that "Amadiora will break your head for you!" leaving little doubt but that Okonkwo will carry out that divine task. He also finds the gods useful in more serious circumstances, as when he uses the oracle to rationalize his murder of Ikemefuna. One should not, he murmurs piously, "question the authority and the decision of the Oracle, who said he should die" (46). When it is to his own benefit, then, "the law of the land must be obeyed." But he is equally prepared to defy the most sacred of Umuofia's gods, and Ezeani is closer to the truth when he accuses Okonkwo of having "no respect for our gods and ancestors" (21). Okonkwo commits acts against the earth goddess that are "unheard of" in Umuofia. He beats his wife during the sacred week; he kills Ikemefuna, even though he is told that he should not participate in that activity; and, though gravely warned not to do so by Chielo, he follows her to the cave of Agbala. These are conscious acts of disobedience, and they reveal Okonkwo's childish, self-centered qualities, which characterize him throughout the novel and which make sense only when placed in the context that has been outlined here.

Okonkwo similarly manipulates the society and the freedom it offers its citizens: he uses his family, and he readily disobeys the gods when such conduct contributes to his dream. During his exile, that dream is heightened and his alienation from Umuofian society is deepened. His own prestige becomes all-important, and his family exists as a means to that end. Though Ezinma, for example, is sought after by "young men and prosperous middle-aged men of Mbanta," Okonkwo wants her to wait to marry someone from Umuofia: "with two beautiful grown-up daughters his return to Umuofia would attract considerable attention" (122). Moreover, "his future sons-in-law would be men of authority in the clan. The poor and unknown would not dare to come forth." Thus does he prepare for his return. "The first thing he would do [upon returning to Umuofia] would be to rebuild his compound on a more magnificent scale. He would build a bigger barn than he had had before and he would build huts for two new wives. Then he would show his wealth by initiating his sons into the *ozo* society" (121) The dream, like Okonkwo, is drained of all humanity, and external show displaces any serious advocacy of tradition. What was Okonkwo's goal? Why did he want to achieve all of this? Because "only the really great men in the clan were able to do this. Okonkwo saw clearly the high esteem in which he would be held, and he saw himself taking the highest title in the land" (121).

This is, in the end, all that remains for Okonkwo: this hollow dream. Since his youth, he has been pursuing it—his whole life, his *chi*, yearning to bury forever the diseased body of Unoka. Fear created the dream, and the dream contained only the external trappings of greatness, for Okonkwo thought that this would allay the persistent ghost of his father. Everything around him became a means to that goal, and he stopped at nothing: he was willing to use the society, to break its most cherished traditions, to defy its gods, to convert his family into pawns, to achieve the fulfillment of his haunting dream. There was no room in the vision for anyone else; others existed to be used or to reflect his nobility. Because he was such a strong supporter of certain aspects of social life, he considered himself a loyal Umuofian, and, propelled by his own fears of inadequacy, he embellished and developed these few traits at the expense of everything else for which Umuofia stood. So narrow did his image of the society become and so confident was he of his own dominance that he became, not a symbol of the society, but more exclusively than before, a man pathetically alone. In his solitude, he deepened his devotion to his dream and thereby alienated himself even more decisively from the society. In exile, this self-image was heightened to the point that he became the indispensable man, the savior of his people.

But he soon discovers that he is not indispensable: "Seven years was a long time to be away from one's clan. A man's place was not always there, waiting for him. As soon as he left, someone else rose and filled it. The clan was like a lizard; if it lost its tail it soon grew another" (121). The discovery is a shattering one, and Okonkwo longs for a past that never was: "Those were the days when men were men." His distance from the society is further underscored and his own dawning recognition of this remoteness suggested when he decides, in his frustration, to wage war on his own institutions in addition to the new ones brought in by the white men: "If Umuofia decided on war, all would be well. But if they chose to be cowards he would go out and avenge himself" (141). Okonkwo stands alone, still declaring that any who disagrees with him is a coward. Okonkwo against the world: he knows now that his quest is a hopeless one. He is no mirror of Umuofia; rather, he simply proves the wisdom of the Igbo saying "As a man danced, so the drums were beaten for him." For Okonkwo, then, things indeed fall apart. "I shall fight alone if I choose" (142), he snaps at the end, and in his final, empty martyrdom, there is no realization that he has been fighting alone throughout his life. Unoka, on his deathbed, unwittingly composed Okonkwo's epitaph while writing his own: "A proud heart can survive a general failure because such a failure does not prick its pride. It is more difficult and more bitter when a man fails alone" (18).

VII

The community did not despise Unoka's love of beauty and joy, and the village did not reject Okonkwo's hard work and emphasis

on things masculine. The village of Umuofia embraced both ex-
tremes, but its heart could not be found in one at the expense
of the other. Unoka had to die alone (even ignoring the fact of
his physical disease) because he existed on the outer limits of the
society in which he lived. This is why Okonkwo, too, had to die
alone. It is true that Unoka was not representative of the society,
but then neither was Okonkwo—and both for the same reason:
each represented isolated facets of a multifaceted community. The
people of Umuofia put a premium on manliness, but there were
other sides, softer dimensions and alternatives. The society was
never as one-sided, as single-minded as Okonkwo. The very resilience of Umuofia, the fact that both the father and the son
were able to exist within its framework, argues against its disintegration.

Does this novel, then, present "the collapse of a traditional
village community as a tragic defeat"?[7] Does it detail "the disin-
tegrative effects of colonial occupation"?[8] In one sense, these questions are unanswerable, because they go beyond the limits of the
work. We do not know what happened to the people of Umuofia
as they continued to deal with the institutions of the whites, but
on the basis of the details provided in the novel, we may conclude
that the society was not falling apart. More to the point, there is
little in the novel (aside from Obierika's conclusions) that suggests
"tragic defeat" and disintegration as far as the people and
traditions of Umuofia are concerned. Tragic defeat and disintegration do characterize the central character, but that is quite
another matter.

Okonkwo was, initially, a product of the community, but his
dream, after first adapting itself to the requirements of that community, took new directions. Okonkwo succeeded in the eyes of
the villagers, and his success led to excess. He became tyrannical
and selfish, narrowing his own ideal world to suit his ends and
expecting all others to meet those standards. His dream seduced
him away from Umuofian tradition, and when he died he was so
far removed from the mainstream of Umuofian life that he could
be said to represent little more than himself.

The death of Okonkwo, then, does not mean the metaphorical
destruction of the community by alien influences, as aggressive

and vicious as those influences were to become. In his complexity, Okonkwo defies such simple symbolic analysis. His is an intensely personal fate; it does not mirror the larger conflict. Never once does he see life whole. His aloneness is self-imposed, his final alienation the result not of Umuofian belligerence in the face of change, but rather the final act of his own desperately conceived fiction. He is a giant of individuality, drawn a shade bigger than life, driven by fear, buoyed by a dream, and shattered by his *chi*, the flagellating flaw in his character that would allow him neither respite nor perspective. Okonkwo is an eternal dreamer, and reality deforms his visionary grace; he is a single-minded opportunist struggling not merely for survival but for paramountcy. Disfigured by greed, striking out at anything that threatens him, scornfully assaulting those who refuse to accept his world, alone and tormented by fears of inadequacy, Okonkwo writhes in a hell created not by an alien culture; it is the hell of his *chi* that cripples him, that destroys his sight, twists his soul and feeds him with a perverted dream of greatness. Okonkwo, constantly and fiercely demonstrating his manhood, never wholly understands the value of a man, sacrificing his own dignity and threatening that of others in the name of sheer strength. It is the only manhood he comprehends, and he worships the empty dream; in the process of achieving it, he purges himself of love and is finally a shell of a man, driven to his pathetic act of self-annihilation. The Okonkwo seen hanging from the tree is an empty man, tortured and twisted by his own *chi*, motivated by his own agonizing conception of the universe and his place in it, misled by the angst of his manly ideal. He is a product not of the society but of his own inadequacies and fears, and he progressively diminishes or destroys those aspects of his character that would humanize him, until he finally destroys all that is left—the external shell.

Notes

All page references to *Things Fall Apart* are from the "African Writers Series" edition of 1962.

1. Personal god.

2. It should be emphasized too that the ultimate destiny of Umuofian society, as it confronts the white institutions, lies outside the purview of this novel. All that can reasonably be said is that evidence from the novel suggests survival rather than destruction. Since Obierika's comments have the effect of directing readers to conclusions that have little support in the novel itself, however, they must be considered and argued.

3. From another point of view—not Obierika's—his questioning simply affirms the society's ability to examine itself and, if necessary, to change. But this is not Obierika's position. He is "guilty" not by Umuofian standards but by his own, and the reliability of his prophecies and comments is considerably diminished.

4. Gerald Moore, *Seven African Writers* (London: Oxford University Press, 1962), 59.

5. An *egwugwu* is a masquerader who, during certain religious occasions, impersonates a divinity.

6. Musical instruments.

7. Janheinz Jahn, *Muntu: An Outline of the New African Culture*, trans. Marjorie Grene (New York: Grove, 1961), 215.

8. Judith Illsley Gleason, *This Africa: Novels by West Africans in English and French* (Evanston: Northwestern University Press, 1965), 81.

How the Center Is Made to Hold
in *Things Fall Apart*

NEIL TEN KORTENAAR

◆　◆　◆

A WHOLE VOLUME has been written by Emmanuel Mezie-madu Okoye on the encounter between traditional Igbo re-ligion and Christianity in the novels of Chinua Achebe, a volume which concludes that Achebe has done his research and that his depiction of the colonization of Igboland is historically accurate. Fiction, of course, cannot be judged by its verifiability; it expresses not what happened but what might have happened. Precisely because it must be plausible, however, fiction has to meet stan-dards of correspondence and be adequate as an image of the human experience of the world (Ricoeur, *Temps III*, 278). Okoye's desire to establish the accuracy of Achebe's fiction is not mis-placed. However, if we consider the novels as historiography and judge how faithful they are to the past, it is not just the details of culture and of incident that must be considered. The writing of history has two components: it depends on verifiable facts, and it arranges those facts in a narrative. How does Achebe establish his narrative authority when writing about a period more than fifty years in the past and more particularly about a world view that has lost its original integrity?

Things Fall Apart ends with the decision taken by a historian to recount the process whereby a whole world was overturned. The narrative this historian will write is not, however, the one the reader has just finished reading, but a less objective and necessarily less accurate narrative. In the final pages, the new district commissioner walks away from the site of Okonkwo's suicide and wonders whether to make Okonkwo's death a chapter or a paragraph in his projected book, *The Pacification of the Primitive Tribes of the Lower Niger*. This appeal to an obviously false authority deploys irony to establish Achebe's own credentials as a historian of Igboland.[1] We do not ask why we should trust the narrative we have just read: the district commissioner's projected history and by implication other texts on Africa stand condemned as manifestly untrustworthy, and that is enough. We deconstruct what is told us of the district commissioner and reconstruct a higher level where we join the author in seeing around the Europeans. But where exactly is this higher level?

In *Things Fall Apart*, the district commissioner's false narrative assumes the Otherness of the Africans. Humanity is not one. What the district commissioner finds of interest in Okonkwo's suicide is its mystery: its impenetrability is an example of the foreignness, the difference of supposed primitives. By fitting Okonkwo into a comprehensible narrative, the commissioner establishes both Okonkwo's essential Otherness and his own heroic character—his narrative says in effect, "I have travelled through Africa and seen such things for myself"—thus eliminating the threat of that difference. To underline the falsity of this version of events, Achebe must reestablish the humanity of his Africans, must insist that Africans live in the same world and are absolutely not Other.

The effect of Achebe's plain style—in spite of what Weinstock and Ramadan argue, it is singularly stripped of symbol—is to stress the everyday ordinariness of Igbo life. This world is comprehensible. The transition in the book from precolonization Africa to an Africa that has felt the European presence is, in terms of style, unremarkable. Indeed, because the transition is so fluid, Achebe has to draw our attention to it by means of divisions: the encroachment of the European missionaries takes place while Okonkwo is in exile during the division identified as part two.

C. L. Innes has pointed out how in *Things Fall Apart* when Mr. Brown, the missionary, and Akunna, one of the great men of the village of Umuofia, discuss God, they misunderstand each other. But more remarkable is how they can discuss and learn from each other at all, as clearly they do: their mutual tolerance and their open-mindedness are applauded by the author and contrasted with the fanaticism of Mr. Smith and of Okonkwo. The report of the discussion between Mr. Brown and Akunna sounds like the published proceedings of a modern conference on interfaith dialogue, full of a confidence that beneath the differences of language and ritual there is a common quest for God and a common view of human nature. There can only be discussion where there is an agreement more fundamental than the subjects of dissension. Argument is only possible where there are common terms. Mr. Brown does not speak of Christ; Akunna does not speak of Ani, the goddess of the land. Instead they speak in much more general terms of God and sound like nothing so much as eighteenth-century deists.

Achebe goes further in making African and European the same in a later novel, *Arrow of God*, which is generally considered a more complex, satisfying novel, with richer characterization and greater unity of plot than *Things Fall Apart*, but which is for that very reason less interesting. In that novel, the narrative moves freely and alternately into the minds of both Igbos and English people. Their thoughts, their desires, and their strategies are remarkably similar. The ease with which the narrative moves between the two communities is matched by the ease with which characters travel from one world to another. They misunderstand each other to be sure, but Europe and Africa are contiguous in time and space. By implication the story of each fits metonymically into a larger narrative, the history of modern Africa generally. Rather than a conflict between two worlds, we have a conflict between individuals who are very similar but who cannot see into each other's hearts. The unforeseen results of this mutual blindness recall similar tragedies in novels by Hardy.

The problem with seeing two cultures as occupying the same world is that they can then be measured against each other and one preferred to another as a reflection of that world. To measure them is to assume a scientific objectivity that allows the observer to stand outside both. But in this case, scientific objectivity is a mode of knowledge associated with one of the cultures to be measured. Achebe cannot appeal to the scientific model of knowledge and still be fair to the Igbos about whom he is writing. What Timothy Reiss calls the analytical-referential model of knowledge, the way of knowing associated with science and modern historiography, sees language as a tool that, placed between the observer and the world observed, allows the observer to know the world as it truly is and to manipulate it. It is inseparable from Europe's claim to know fully the world and other societies, in a way that other societies with other modes of knowing are never allowed to know Europe.

Achebe believes, with Reiss, Foucault, and Lévi-Strauss, that the West's knowledge of the world is as culture-based and time-bound as any other mode of knowledge. The title *Things Fall Apart* refers to the Yeatsian prophecy of the decline and fall of the current incarnation of the West. In using it to speak of the collapse of the Igbo world, Achebe plays with cultural equivalence. One mode of knowledge is forced to give way before another, but not because the other has a stronger claim to be able to know the world. Both are time-bound, culture-bound; either may fall apart. At one moment of history, the Igbo world view gave way before the Western analytical-referential model. The triumph of one world view does not imply its greater fitness in an evolutionary sense; given different circumstances, the encounter could have had other results. In Nadine Gordimer's *July's People*, for instance, it is the self-assured, bourgeois world of white South Africa that is falling apart, giving way before an African world it cannot comprehend.

To emphasize the exclusivity of the two worlds, Achebe often leaves Igbo words untranslated. These foreign traces in an English text refer metonymically to a whole world that cannot be adequately translated, a world that Achebe implicitly shares with the characters he writes about. The non-Igbo reader, by implication, can only achieve a mediated knowledge of that world. There is no model that will contain both worlds.

However, there is in this glorious relativity an *aporia* that Foucault, Lévi-Strauss, and Reiss only overcome by openly admitting. The analytical-referential model continues at the present moment as the dominant mode of knowledge: it includes us and we are unable to see around it. It is incontrovertible because we look at it only through the lenses that it provides. Achebe is writing of a moment of epistemic rupture, when one mode of knowledge gives way before another. But how can he do justice to both? Reiss believes that we cannot understand Greek tragedy, for instance, because the Greek epistemic mode within which the tragedies were written is not ours. How then can the Igbo world be made intelligible once it has bowed before another *episteme*?

The difficulty is signaled in chapter nine of *Things Fall Apart*, which describes how a year before the present of the novel a medicine man exorcised Ezinma, Okonkwo's daughter. Ezinma was an *ogbanje*, a malicious spirit that had been born many times to the same earthly mother, only to die and return to the world of the unborn each time the mother came to love it. Ezinma was ordered to reveal where her *iyi-uwa* was buried, the stone representing her link to the world of the unborn. This she did, and the medicine man dug it up: Ezinma would now stay in the land of the living. Achebe's narration recounts what happened without comment or irony: the reader must suspend disbelief and enter into the Igbo world view. So too, later in the book, a militant Christian who dared to kill a sacred python falls ill and dies. The traditionalists accept that the gods were protecting their own; let the reader think what he likes. However, although there is no rhetorical irony in the presentation of the *ogbanje* scene, there is an irony implicit nonetheless.

In the present of the novel, a year after the exorcism, Ezinma's mother wakes Okonkwo to tell him his daughter is suffering from *iba*. The glossary at the end of the book tells the non-Igbo reader that *iba* is fever. The word is presumably not translated because "fever" in English has the wrong connotations: it would be thought of as something to be diagnosed, then treated with medicine. Okonkwo's people see in *iba* a manifestation of a spiritual disorder: the mischief of an *ogbanje* or the perversity of one's *chi*. Ekwefi, Ezinma's mother, is terrified.

The chapter opens with the buzzing of a mosquito in the ear of Okonkwo, who recalls a story his mother told him about why Mosquito buzzes near Ear, who had once refused to marry him. The inclusion of this story can be ascribed to the encyclopedic thrust of the narrative: in *Things Fall Apart* details are relevant not because they further the plot or reveal character but because they contribute to the display of Igbo culture. However, the irrelevant on one plane may assume significance on another. Mosquitoes have a meaning for both Achebe and the reader that they do not have for Okonkwo. The chapter, by making mosquitoes and *iba* contiguous, even if not explicitly linking them as cause to effect, acknowledges a connection where the characters themselves do not see one. Achebe and his reader both know Ezinma's fever would be diagnosed as malaria by a doctor, and the recurring deaths of an *ogbanje* would be considered a superstitious explanation of a high infant mortality rate more appropriately responded to by modern medicine.

We cannot say Achebe is exchanging ironic glances with his reader over the heads of his characters. The reader, if at all involved in Okonkwo's world, is likely to miss the reference to malaria. Yet I believe my reader will agree that the mosquitoes are significant and point to a foreign *episteme* that is otherwise absent. In Wayne Booth's terms, the irony is covert but stable and finite. If reconstructed, it constitutes an invitation to the reader to join the author at a level of understanding higher than that of the literal account. When later in the novel the killer of the python is himself killed, the reader suspends disbelief: we are given only the Umuofia point of view, and though another explanation is conceivable, it is not suggested. But in the exorcism of the *ogbanje*, a second, irreconcilable way of looking at things is offered, and we are reminded that no reader of the novel, and not Achebe himself, believes entirely in the existence of *ogbanjes*. Achebe shows us Okagbue the medicine man actually finding Ezinma's *iyi-uwa* yet is careful to indicate that Okagbue is digging in the pit alone when he announces his find: the reader may think what he will.

The exorcism of the *ogbanje* is recalled in an explanatory retrospective; it is thus twice distant in time from the reader—it occurs before the present of the novel, which is already set in the past. In another novel, such distancing might make it easier to accept the inexplicable and the uncanny without question. In the homeostatic world of Umuofia, however, where nothing seems ever to change, the distance is removed. The exorcism appears related synchronically to the events of the present of the novel, specifically to the execution of Ikemefuna, Okonkwo's adopted son. When Okonkwo is woken up to respond to Ezinma's *iba*, it is the first time he has been able to fall asleep since his participation in Ikemefuna's death three nights before. It is not an *ogbanje* but guilt that haunts him.

There is, moreover, present in the account of Ezinma's exorcism a potential figure of doubt: Nwoye, Okonkwo's son. The reader has already seen Nwoye ill at ease with traditional metaphysics. When his friend was executed to fulfill the ordinance of the oracle, Nwoye felt something give way inside him "like the snapping of a tightened bow": he had experienced a similar chill when he heard the crying of infant twins abandoned in the Evil Forest. That was in chapter seven. In chapter nine, we are told that one year earlier, at the time of the digging up of Ezinma's *iyi-uwa*, Nwoye "stood near the pit because he wanted to take in all that happened" (59). Did he see Okagbue find the stone that had always been there or did he see him plant a stone? This is not an idle question. If Nwoye saw the stone found, then he would have had to deny much that he once knew when later he joined the Christians, who dismissed Igbo religion as so much superstition. If he saw the stone planted, then his crisis in faith over the death of Ikemefuna can be seen to have had its seeds in an earlier time.

In another chapter, Achebe shows us the *egwugwu* judging a

marital dispute: the glossary at the back defines these, with thoroughgoing unbelief, as masqueraders impersonating ancestral spirits. We are told that the women of Umuofia never asked questions about the *egwugwu* cult. They "might have noticed that the second *egwugwu* had the springy walk of Okonkwo," and they might have noticed "that Okonkwo was not among the titled men and elders" (63–64), but if they did, they kept these thoughts to themselves. Perhaps it was never possible that any reader of the novel should believe that the *egwugwu* were ancestral spirits returned to earth, but it is clear that the narrative itself does not believe. The reference to a possible doubt among the women spectators advertises the distance of the narration from faith in the world it describes.

Abdul JanMohamed explains the ambivalence in this scene by invoking a "double-consciousness." Achebe's characters, says JanMohamed, like all people in an oral society, make no distinction between the worlds of the secular and the sacred. However, this lack of discrimination would make the Umuofians appear "foolish" to modern readers, so Achebe makes his characters aware of the border between secular and sacred, but quick to repress what they know (33). JanMohamed's implication is that modern, Western-educated readers know more than did the traditional Umuofians and so can judge the Umuofians as "foolish" or at least ignorant. JanMohamed is right about the double consciousness in *Things Fall Apart*, but it is not limited to the characters; a double consciousness characterizes the narrative as a whole. As we saw in the *ogbanje* episode, two world views are present even when the characters are not aware of them. It is in the reader, rather than in the characters that a double consciousness is created.

This double consciousness is perhaps inevitable when writing about a society that did not itself know writing, or when using English to describe an Igbo-speaking world. Achebe's solution, as Abdul JanMohamed has detailed, was to forge a written style that as much as possible echoed oral storytelling. The abundance of proverbs and the absence of original imagery are only the most obvious features. More significant is the flatness of the style: it is repetitive and additive, and it refuses to subordinate or privilege narrative elements. Everything is thus made equal, and there is a seeming lack of direction. The flatness of character also echoes oral narration: Okonkwo's psychology goes largely unexamined, and he is a type, both larger and flatter than life. Only thus, by telling Okonkwo's story as the kind of story Okonkwo himself knew, can Achebe be fair to an oral culture. To bring to bear on Umuofia the novelistic techniques of bourgeois Europe, designed to explore the interior individual, would be unjust, because they would suggest that writer and readers know more about Umuofians than the Umuofians know about themselves.

JanMohamed describes the syncretism that results from writing about an oral culture that did not know writing, but the asymmetry involved in writing the history of a society that did not conceive of itself historically has not been sufficiently explored. An example of this asymmetry is the following passage, in which Elizabeth Isichei in her *History of the Igbo People* explains the powers ascribed to the *dibia*, the Igbo priests:

> I think that it is possible that Igboland's *dibia* were developing real skills—or sciences—in the sphere of what we would now call extra-sensory perception. The imposition of colonial rule has basically put an end to these skills, and deflected Igbo intellectual energies into such "modern" spheres as medicine or physics. It is possible that in doing so it cut off a real and original advance of the human mind, and impoverished the total development of human knowledge. (124)

Isichei is writing a history of the Igbo people in order to prove that they have a history. Igbo knowledge must therefore qualify as real knowledge by European definitions, meaning it must be a science, verifiable and replicable. Igbo science was advancing because, Isichei affirms, the human mind does not stand still but is engaged in a progressive evolution. In other words, a history could be written of Igbo experiments in extrasensory perception if the records existed. However, in portraying the *dibia* as scientists, Isichei is ignoring what the Igbo saw as true about themselves.

She denies the reality of the Igbo gods and implies that while the *dibia* thought they were praying, they were actually doing something else that only we moderns can appreciate.

The narrative voice in *Things Fall Apart*, too, occasionally lapses into the knowing tone of an anthropologist; for instance, he will explain, "Darkness held a vague terror for these people, even the bravest among them" (7). The narrator and his modern audience, presumed to be unafraid of darkness, believe they can know "these people" more fully than these people know themselves.

Chinweizu, Jemie, and Madubuike argue that since most Africans believe in spirits and the efficacy of magic, one should expect to find magic in the African novel. They further argue that there is no shame in believing in magic: Westerners are just as fervent in their belief in favorable and unfavorable omens. The Nigerian critics may be right about Westerners, but by their reasoning one would expect to find magic occupying a large role in the Western tradition of the novel. One does not, and the reason is that the realistic novel as established in the nineteenth century appeals for its authority to history writing, and modern historiography is based on the analytical-referential model of knowing. In novels we are invited to judge characters who believe in omens or in magic as superstitious.

Of course, Africans need not write realistic novels in the Western tradition. The metamorphoses in Amos Tutuola's novels belong to another world view altogether, one that eschews cause and effect and inner and outer as explanations of events. Achebe's problem is that he wants to show that Africa has a history, as Europe has a history, and so he does not want to insist on the difference of Umuofia. Instead he invokes a double consciousness.

In the *ogbanje* episode that we looked at, the analytical-referential model underlies the traditional Igbo model. But the one is not allowed to contain the other. Achebe wants his readers both to remember what we know and to forget what we know; or rather he wants his readers to suspend disbelief, not as in a fantasy that is without implications for our life in the world, but to suspend disbelief and yet continue to judge.

How we are to suspend disbelief even as we judge can be seen in a short story entitled "The Madman," in which Achebe presents a series of disputes demanding adjudication. Where one can stand outside and survey the two sides of a dispute, judgment is easy. Nwibe, an upright citizen, puts an end to the quarrel between his two wives by labeling one mad, the other one foolish for arguing with a mad woman, and bidding them both be silent. A quarrel between the local madman and the market women over the rightful possession of the market stalls where the madman sleeps is judged without difficulty by the reader: the madman is in the wrong because he is mad. However, when the madman steals Nwibe's cloth while the latter is bathing and the naked citizen chases the now-clothed madman, the townspeople judge incorrectly. They assume Nwibe, who is naked, is the mad one. The family consults two medicine men: one says Nwibe cannot be treated; the other, less famous and less strict, agrees to attempt a cure. Nwibe is cured, and the townspeople praise the successful medicine man.

Most readers will be confident they share Achebe's own judgment on the story: Nwibe was not truly insane, and the medicine man who cured him was a lucky confidence man. The humor of the story lies in the fact that while we see that Nwibe is a victim of circumstances—he is a modern figure in an absurd universe—the townspeople do not believe in chance but believe everything has significance. The author invites his readers to see around the characters.

However, as soon as we have seen around the townspeople, the validity of our stance is called into question. How can we judge sanity or insanity across cultures? The townspeople assumed Nwibe was insane when he ran into the sacred precincts of the market; we attribute the sacrilege to Nwibe's uncontrolled rage. But if he were not insane when he ran naked into the market, the townsfolk reason, the gods would certainly have taken away his wits as a punishment. Nwibe himself accepts that he was insane. And it is quite possible that Nwibe really was insane, whether driven to insanity by the gods or by the horror of what he had done. Who is to stand outside the difference of opinion between the reader and the characters and to judge?

The definition of madness is culture specific. The townspeople see a naked man and assume he is mad, nakedness being part of the code for madness. Nakedness itself is defined by cultural context. In the market, Nwibe's wife hurriedly removes her topcloth to cover her husband, behavior that would be mad in many a non-African context. One cannot stand outside and pontificate on differences between cultures; the best one can do is appreciate where the differences lie.

This double consciousness, whereby we judge and suspend judgment at the same time, leads to a certain unease. One student of mine objected that she could not even be sure the original madman in the story was really mad. True, he talked to the highway, but she could not be sure that this kind of communication with the world outside himself did not indicate a poetic sensibility the Igbo townspeople lacked. How is one to judge? Her suggestion will be felt by most readers to be a misreading, but it is a useful one, because it challenges us to justify the judgments that we have been invited to make. Achebe intends for us to judge—or the story would lose its humor—but also to doubt our judgment.

This discussion of radical doubt sounds like many another contemporary critical celebration of a postcolonial text. Abdul JanMohamed praises Achebe's "syncretism"; Homi Bhabha argues that the indeterminacy of the postcolonial text makes it more valuable than the European critical approaches that privilege representation. My discussion, however, is intended to show that this quality of instability is as much a fault as it is a virtue, and that it is neither virtue nor fault, but a necessary condition of Achebe's text.

Paul Ricoeur argues that the proper way to consider the past is not as the same nor as different, but first as the same, then as different, and then in terms of an analogy parallel to the past: as a narrative (*Temps III* 219–27). *Things Fall Apart* is about epistemic rupture, but rupture threatens to make narrative, which implies continuity and development, impossible. Yet the novel insists that the Igbo have a story. This needs to be insisted on, for in the district commissioner's eyes Okonkwo has no narrative of his own. The imperialists brought history to Africa, but, as Fanon observes of colonial settlers, it is not the history of the plundered country that they made, but the history of the mother country (40). They could not make African history, because Africa was a blankness in their imagination, a land without narrative. George Allen, as the author of *The Pacification of the Primitive Tribes* is identified in *Arrow of God*, sees in Africa an invitation to make history extend to all "who can deal with men as others deal with material" (33). Narrative is thus a product of European agents acting on raw material extracted from Africa: a literary parallel to the processes of colonialism more generally.

Edward Said argues that if non-European peoples are to be written about with justice it must be in a narrative in which they are themselves the agents (240). They would then be seen as the makers of their own world. JanMohamed, however, following Jack Goody and Walter Ong, characterizes oral societies as homeostatic; that is, oral cultures without written records testifying to the past tend to ignore the ways in which the past was different from the present and conceive of the world as always the same. Of course, people who have not built empires and did not have written records have nevertheless a past that can be unearthed by archaeologists and ethnographers. But to tell their story as history is to describe them in a way they themselves would never have recognized.

The problem with writing Igbo history is not just that the records are missing. The records are missing because the Igbo did not have writing, and, if one follows Walter Ong, it is writing that produces the self-consciousness of historical agents. Hayden White, in agreement with Hegel, argues that some periods, however event-filled, lack objective history for the very reason that people in those periods lacked the self-consciousness to produce written history (12). Ahistorical peoples may accomplish much, but no narrative can be written about the unself-conscious.

The district commissioner, George Allen, was making history. He acted always with an idea as to how he would narrate the story of his actions afterward. And the narrative of his own actions he fitted into the larger narrative of the British involvement in Africa. That in turn he saw as part of the narrative of British history, which was part of a yet larger narrative project, the unfolding of human potential. Allen has an eye on this larger narrative and the contribution he can make to it, which will be rewarded with a place when the history of his epoch comes to be written. Allen's own narrative, it is plain, is blind to others and self-deluding. Even a fellow British colonialist, twenty years later, when *Arrow of God* is set, will find Allen's narrative insufferably smug. Where Allen saw glory, Achebe and we see sordid conquest and imperialist greed. But the point is that because Allen and his contemporaries emplotted their own lives as narratives, it is possible for the historian who follows to emplot those lives as narratives. Where the Europeans in Africa saw epic, the modern historian sees irony, but the historian's configuration of events is possible at all only because the British prefigured their own lives in a narrative (Ricoeur, *Temps I*).

Is Okonkwo the hero of his own life, to use David Copperfield's words? Okonkwo does emplot his life according to a certain narrative pattern. He designs his life according to the upward curve of a romance: the hero of lowly origins overcomes great obstacles to prove his nobility. He rejects one kind of tale—the stories of animals, told by women—and delights in tales of tribal wars and military prowess (38). His faith that this is the story he is intended to live out is the guiding principle of all his actions.

The notion of emplotting one's life as a narrative is expressed by the Igbo as wrestling with one's *chi*. The term *chi*, as Achebe points out in an article on the subject, is rich in suggestive meaning. One definition seems to be that the *chi* is the writer of one's life story, and one must wrestle with one's *chi* to give the story the shape one wants. A strong man emplots his own life—when he says yes, his *chi* says yes also. Yet the narrative of one's life may not be the narrative originally emplotted—one cannot wrestle with one's *chi* and hope to win, as Okonkwo finds out. The upward curve that Okonkwo emplots takes a sharp downward turn and becomes the inverted U of tragedy. However, the reason Okonkwo has a story at all, even though not the story he intended, is because he self-consciously thinks of his life in terms of a story.

But is Okonkwo's emplotted story an example of historical narrative? Is it not more accurately an example of mythic thinking? Peter Munz distinguishes between cyclical myth, that is, myths of eternal return, and linear myth (or history), narratives that incorporates a sense of unidirectional time (119–26). *Things Fall Apart* introduces Okonkwo by relating how he gained fame by wrestling Amalinze the Cat in one of the fiercest fights Umuofia had seen since "the founder of their town engaged a spirit of the wild for seven days and seven nights" (3). Okonkwo lives in the same world as the mythical or semimythical founder of Umuofia, in the same space as spirits of the wild.

According to Lévi-Strauss, past and present are joined in myth, "because nothing has been going on since the appearance of the ancestors except events whose recurrence periodically effaces their particularity" (236). Thus every wrestling match would be a ritual repetition of the original fight between man and nature, man and spirit. At the same time, in myth the past is disjoined from the present because the original ancestors were of a nature different from contemporary people: they were creators, and their successors are imitators (236). The ancestors set the rules that moderns must follow. In *Things Fall Apart* the ancestors return in the shape of *egwugwu* to render judgment in modern disputes.

Ricoeur lists three instruments of thought that allow the writing of history. They are the calendar, the succession of generations, and, above all, the survival of archives, documents, and traces of the past (*Temps III* 153). These make possible extrapolations from the individual's story to the story of the world, to history. At least two of these connectors are not present in the Umuofia consciousness.

References to time in *Things Fall Apart* are to seasons, to moons, to weeks, and to time that has passed since memorable events occurred. There is no calendar measuring an absolute scale, for such calendars are the product of literate societies. Instead, time is cyclical, observing the recurrence of the seasons and the market

days. We can date *Things Fall Apart*, locate Okonkwo's story in
relation to events happening elsewhere, because at the end of the
book the Europeans appear. In the first two-thirds of the book,
we are shown a society such as we suppose might have existed
at any time in the last three hundred years (they have guns, but
have not met Europeans). At the end of the novel, however,
when the missionaries arrive, there are references to the queen
of the English. Since Victoria died in 1901, the narrative must be
set in the late nineteenth century. There is a slight contradiction
here. Okoye establishes that the events on which *Things Fall Apart*
is based, specifically the killing of a solitary white man on a bicycle
and the retribution exacted by British forces, occurred in 1905.
That is the year of the large-scale British expedition to subdue
Igboland. JanMohamed too assumes the novel is set in 1905. Of
course, what Achebe has written is fiction and does not have to
be faithful to the calendar in the same way as history has to be.
But in not being faithful to dates, he suggests his narrative has
come loose from history, as in a way it has. The time frame by
which these events can be dated and related to other events—
the scramble for Africa, the Boxer Rebellion in China, the Boer
War in South Africa, or the discovery in 1899 by Sir Ronald Ross
that the malaria parasite is transmitted by anopheles mosquitoes—
is unknown to Okonkwo.

In Ricoeur's opinion the dominant connector between the individual and history is the *trace*. The French means "track" or
"spoor," as well as "trace"; synonyms include "vestiges" and "remains." The *trace* is something that exists here and now and yet
points to something that exists no longer (*Temps III* 177ff.) There
are traces in *Things Fall Apart* that indicate to the reader, but not
to the Umuofians, that change has occurred in Umuofia.
Okonkwo's gun—he points it at one of his wives in a moment
of anger—indicates that European encroachment has begun. Fire-
arms were introduced into Igboland by way of the coastal trade
with Europeans only in the seventeenth century; not until the
nineteenth century did they become widespread (Isichei 75–76).
Okonkwo takes snuff from a snuff bottle with a spoon, unaware
that his ancestors did not always do so. The women in his com-

munity grow cassava and maize, products originally brought from the New World by the Portuguese (Isichei 8). These traces signal to the reader, but not to Okonkwo, that the approach of the Europeans is inevitable, has indeed already begun.

The Igbo might still have a history even if they are not aware of making history. Hayden White argues that once one people has entered history, has learned to see itself historically, then mankind as a whole has entered history; a historical consciousness implies a progressive integration of the world. It cannot be otherwise if we are one species. Those who do not enter history as makers enter as the victims of the makers (56). Eric Wolf, in *Europe and the Peoples without History*, has written of the integration of the world into a single history, not the history of progress postulated by Europe, but the history of makers and victims implied by the development of capitalism.

One could read the first two-thirds of *Things Fall Apart* as a synchronic presentation of a whole society. References to past and present events are commingled because there has been no change and thus there is no significance to time passing. The novel takes on a diachronic presentation only when the missionaries appear, bringing change and, just as important, the notion of change. Such a reading implies that the Umuofia community was an ahistorical, organic whole disrupted and set upon the path of history by the brutal entry of the Europeans. According to this reading, traditional Igbo society has an end, but no beginning or middle, and therefore cannot be fitted into a proper narrative. Indeed the end is better seen as the beginning, as the Igbos' entry into history.

This reading stresses that Umuofians are not proper individuals, not true narrative agents but rather they fulfill defined roles in a community structure. James Olney finds in Okonkwo "the generalized portrait of a man whose character is deliberately and significantly without individualizing traits" (167). He concludes, "Thus one must read Okonkwo's fate, he being representative and typical, as nothing less than the symbolic fate of the traditional Ibo society with the advent of the white man" (171). Olney, eager to prove his thesis that African narrative stresses the type rather than the individual, summarizes Okonkwo as follows: "We learn of Okonkwo, and this is really about all, that he is physically powerful, ambitious, generous and honest, proud, quick to anger, hard-working, a great wrestler" (167).

Okonkwo is all those things and not much more than those things. Nor, as Olney points out, does Okonkwo change in the course of the narrative (169). However, there is something that Olney leaves out because it does not fit his thesis, a detail that does not fit with Okonkwo's representative status and that makes him an individual in time, and that is his relationship with his father.

The succession of generations is the third of Ricoeur's connectors between the life of the individual and history. Okonkwo is not the quintessential African of Olney's and George Allen's imagination, fulfilling the role of dutiful son, honoring the ancestors, and maintaining their common wisdom. It is true that Okonkwo identifies with the ancestors to the point of donning a masquerade costume and becoming one of the *egwugwu*. On the other hand, Okonkwo has made rejection of his father the principle of his life. He is a self-made man. Because Unoka, his father, was a failure, always in debt and without status, Okonkwo has had to forge his own career. Okonkwo, the mainstay of tradition, has inherited nothing but has, as it were, engendered himself.

The contradiction is signaled in the text when Nwoye, Okonkwo's son, abandons the traditional ways and joins the Christians. Okonkwo is enraged: why, he cries in his heart, should he be cursed with such a son (108)? If all male descendants were to follow Nwoye, who would there be to offer sacrifices to the ancestors? "He saw himself and his fathers crowding round their ancestral shrine waiting in vain for worship and sacrifice and finding nothing but ashes of bygone days, and his children the while praying to the white man's god" (108). Okonkwo forgets that, even if Nwoye were to prove completely loyal, Okonkwo would never join his father around an ancestral shrine. Unoka died of a noxious swelling disease that made it impossible for him to receive the necessary burial. Instead he was put out in the Evil Forest to die. Unoka's spirit cannot join the ancestors and cannot be reborn; he is doomed to wander the world as a ghost. Okonkwo, upstanding titled man that he is, has an altar to the ancestors in his compound, but his father is not among the ancestors worshiped there. Okonkwo, who imagines himself and his father haunting the cold ashes of an abandoned altar, is not really as concerned with the fate of tradition as he is with the flouting of his own will; it is not the rights of ancestors that he cares about, but his *own* rights as a father to dictate to his son.

Okonkwo the wrestler patterns his life on the model of the founder—he proves his own greatness by reenacting the achievements of the founder. We have here a notion of time that stresses repetition, the return of the same: wrestling is a ritual that repeats the founding of the village. But Okonkwo's motivation is not merely obedience to the universal law; it is the restoration of what has been lost and what in every generation has always been lost. He is himself a would-be founder. The established pattern has been flouted by Unoka and is only reasserted by Okonkwo. The narrative of his life both follows the model of the successful man laid down by tradition and establishes that model. It sets down the law: if Nwoye follows it, all shall be well; if he does not, there will be trouble. To establish his own authority as lawmaker, Okonkwo appeals to the divine origins of the law, declares he is merely following traditional custom. But in this case, traditional custom is an assertion of Okonkwo's own will.

Okonkwo wants the narrative of his life to correspond to the truth of traditional wisdom and at the same time to guarantee that truth. But what his narrative shows is that the search for absolute and fixed truth is itself the product of Okonkwo's upbringing, and must be understood in its context. Okonkwo, who sets himself up as defender of community values, totalizes those values and in so doing betrays them. When Okonkwo's adopted son, Ikemufuna, is sentenced to death by the oracle, Okonkwo accompanies the executioners. He does this to prove his fidelity to the oracle. He sets divine authority above personal sentiment. But this is the loyalty of the doubter who must prove to himself his uncompromising faith. In participating in the execution, Okonkwo flouts the advice of the elder Ezeudu. The law is not universal and absolute but made by men operating in historical circumstances. This Ezeudu understands. The law will be obeyed, but it need not be carried out by Okonkwo personally. Okonkwo, however, misunderstands the law. He wants it to be universal and to govern all situations. It does not.

The oral world of Umuofia is not wholly based on repetition and stability; there is an instability implicit, the instability of narrative. The succession of generations marks change, and this is most evident in the rejection of Okonkwo's law by his son, Nwoye, who converts to Christianity. Christianity is brought by the Europeans, as history itself appears to be. But Christianity is portrayed as a fulfillment of historic trends among the Igbo; Nwoye has sought something other and thinks he has found it in Christianity. He has had doubts about the religion of his fathers; the songs of the Christians fill his soul with sweetness and peace; they answer a need in his soul. Similar doubts are expressed by Obierika, who comes to destroy Okonkwo's compound after his friend has been exiled for an offense that was purely accidental. Achebe is anxious to show that the Igbo make their own choices, are not victims of history, but makers of history. There is continuity and development, not just repetition and rupture. The Igbo chose Christianity, as Nwoye did, or rejected it, as Okonkwo did, because they were aware of themselves making their own world in time.

The title of the novel establishes that Okonkwo's whole life will be seen from the perspective of his end. But that end is not gratuitous; it is of a piece with his life. To appropriate what Louis O. Mink has written of the narrative unity of Oedipus's life: Okonkwo who hangs from the tree at the end is the son of a man who could not be properly buried, the warrior who must forever prove his own courage, the wealthy man who has taken the second highest title in the land, the short-tempered husband quick to suspect insubordination and to beat his wives, the wearer of a spirit mask, the father who is rejected in his turn by his son, the man who wrestles with his *chi*, and the killer of the white man's messenger. He is alive and he is dead, and he could not be anywhere else than hanging on that tree.

The coming of the Europeans is not portrayed by Achebe as

arbitrary, a *deus ex machina* dropped from another realm. It fulfills in inevitable fashion the tragic narrative he has been telling. The narrative of traditional Igbo society can only now be told with an eye to the end, the coming of the colonizers. But that does not mean Igbo history is derivative. It is no different from the history of eighteenth-century France, which is always written and can only be written with 1789 in mind, even though those who lived at the time may have not seen the revolution coming. Umuofia's responses to the coming of the Europeans are the responses of self-conscious narrative agents to the circumstances in which they find themselves.

Ricoeur makes a useful distinction between seeing history as a totality and seeing it as a totalization. We can no longer, with Hegel, see history as a totality that can be expressed as the development of the spirit, or as any other single concept. Universal history can mean tyranny if it means the hegemony of a particular society, and that is what seeing history as a totality is likely to mean (*Temps III* 312). Not only is it wrong to see history as a totality, but it is no longer even possible. We must make do, not with a totality, but with a totalization, an imperfect mediation of a horizon of expectation (the future) and an area of experience (the past and the present) (*Temps III* 359ff.). It is with such a totalization that Achebe is concerned.

In *Things Fall Apart* the author disappears behind an omniscient narrator who claims to know all sides. We should be suspicious of such objectivity; suspicious but not wholly skeptical. The objectivity can be justified if we keep in mind the writer who writes about the past with one eye on the present. *Things Fall Apart* is the work of a young Igbo in pre-independence Nigeria who must establish the common humanity of Africans and the difference of traditional African culture, and who must show history made by Africans in order to inspire them to make history. The needs of the present determine how the history is written, but that does not make the history false. An aphorism of John William Miller puts it well:

There can be only one point of view from which history can be written, and further, there is such a point of view. Obviously something of this sort is necessary if history is to avoid dogmatic assertions of what really happened or skeptical refusal to say what really happened. Whatever the one point of view may be through which history needs to be written if it is to escape subjectivity, it seems that it, too, is a historical resultant. Thus the one necessary point of view from which history is to be written is itself the outcome of history. (188)

Note

1. Among the difficulties involved in writing *Igboland* is orthography. Achebe's first novel betrays the time of its writing because it still uses the orthography bestowed on the name of his people by the British: *Ibo*. But the *b* of *Ibo* is but an approximation of a sound not found in English. In orthography as it has been standardized since the writing of *Things Fall Apart*, this sound is represented by the letters *gb* in combination. This is not two consonants but one; using two letters to represent one sound (approximately β, a voiced bilabial fricative) is a tactic that makes possible the writing of the Igbo language on a typewriter. The name of the ethnic group is thus written *Igbo* in the group's own language. English has adopted this revised spelling, in spite of the problem of pronunciation for English speakers, as part of the larger movement that considers it proper that a people name themselves.

Works Cited

Achebe, Chinua. *Arrow of God*, 1964. Reprint. London: Heinemann, 1974.
———. "Chi in Igbo Cosmology." In Achebe, *Morning Yet on Creation Day*, 93–103. Garden City, NY: Anchor, 1975.
———. "The Madman." In Achebe, *Girls at War and Other Stories*, 1–10. London: Heinemann, 1972.
———. *Things Fall Apart* [1958]. Reprint. London: Heinemann, 1962.
Bhabha, Homi K. "Representation and the Colonial Text: Some Forms of Mimeticism." In *The Theory of Reading*, edited by Frank Glover-smith, 93–122. Brighton, England: Harvester, 1984.
Booth, Wayne. *A Rhetoric of Irony*. Chicago, IL: University of Chicago Press, 1974.

Chinweizu, Onwuchekwa Jemie, and Ibechukwu Madubuike. *Towards the Decolonization of African Literature*. Washington, DC: Howard University Press, 1983.

Fanon, Frantz. *The Wretched of the Earth*, trans. Constance Farrington. Harmondsworth, England: Penguin, 1967.

Goody, Jack. *The Domestication of the Savage Mind*. Cambridge: Cambridge University Press, 1977.

Gordimer, Nadine. *July's People*. New York: Viking, 1981.

Innes, C. L. "Language, Poetry, and Doctrine in *Things Fall Apart*." In *Critical Perspectives on Chinua Achebe*, edited by C. L. Innes and Bernth Lindfors, 111–25. Washington, DC: Three Continents, 1978.

Isichei, Elizabeth. *A History of the Igbo People*. London: Macmillan, 1976.

JanMohamed, Abdul. "Sophisticated Primitivism: The Syncretism of Oral and Literate Modes in Achebe's *Things Fall Apart*." *Ariel* 15, no. 4 (1984): 19–39.

Lévi-Strauss, Claude. *The Savage Mind*. London: Weidenfeld, 1986.

Miller, John William. *The Philosophy of History*. New York: Norton 1982.

Mink, Louis O. "History and Fiction as Modes of Comprehension." In *New Directions in Literary History*, edited by Ralph Cohen, 107–24. Baltimore, MD: Johns Hopkins University Press, 1974.

Munz, Peter. *The Shapes of Time*. Middletown, CT: Wesleyan University Press, 1977.

Okoye, Emmanuel Meziemadu. *The Traditional Religion and Its Encounter with Christianity in Achebe's Novels*. Berne, Germany: Lang, 1987.

Olney, James. *Tell Me Africa*. Princeton, NJ: Princeton University Press, 1973.

Ong, Walter J. *Orality and Literacy*. London: Methuen, 1982.

Reiss, Timothy J. *The Discourse of Modernism*. Ithaca, NY: Cornell University Press, 1982.

Ricoeur, Paul. *Temps et récit*, vol. 1. Paris: Seuil, 1983.

———. *Temps et récit*, vol. 3, *Le temps raconté*. Paris: Seuil, 1985.

Said, Edward. *Orientalism*. New York: Pantheon, 1978.

Weinstock, Donald J., and Cathy Ramadan. "Symbol and Structure in *Things Fall Apart*." In *Critical Perspectives on Chinua Achebe*, edited by C. L. Innes and Bernth Lindfors, 126–34. Washington, DC: Three Continents, 1978.

White, Hayden. *The Content of the Form*. Baltimore, MD: Johns Hopkins University Press, 1987.

Wolf, Eric. *Europe and the Peoples without History*. Berkeley: University of California Press, 1982.

The Metamorphosis of Piety in Chinua Achebe's *Things Fall Apart*

CLAYTON G. MACKENZIE

◆　◆　◆

M ATTERS OF RELIGION are thematically central to *Things Fall Apart* and *Arrow of God*. Both novels reflect revisions in the nature of traditional worship, and both attest to the demise of traditional mores in the face of an aggressive and alien proselytizing religion. The disparities between the two novels are equally significant. Possibly for reasons of historical setting, *Things Fall Apart* differs from *Arrow of God* in its presentation of the status of indigenous beliefs and in its precise delineation of the evolutionary process of those beliefs—a process not articulated in any detail in the later novel. The shifts of belief in *Things Fall Apart* are marked by the pragmatic transference of old pieties for new, a metamorphosis demanded by the realities of a revised socioeconomic hierarchy.

THE FIRST MENTION of the religious beliefs of Umuofia in *Things Fall Apart* is a reference to the Oracle of the Hills and the Caves. It is a decisive allusion, correlating the will of the oracle with the life and direction of the clan and leaving no doubt as to the significance of the divine agency and of the necessity of obedience to it:

> In fairness to Umuofia it should be recorded that it never went to war unless its case was clear and just and was accepted as such by its Oracle—the Oracle of the Hills and the Caves. And there were indeed occasions when the Oracle had forbidden Umuofia to wage a war. If the clan had disobeyed the Oracle they would surely have been beaten, because their dreaded *agadi-nwayi* would never fight what the Ibo call *a fight of blame.* (9)

That the oracle is perceived as supreme there can be no doubt. The sacrifice of the boy Ikemefuna is undertaken expressly because the "Oracle of the Hills and the Caves has pronounced it" (40). Though the execution may run counter to clan feelings of attachment to the youngster, a profound sense of individual and collective religious belief lends to the sacrifice an inexorable determination. It is a mysterious decision, but the Umuofia, for the maintenance of the universal well-being, must comply with it. Not even the most powerful paternal feelings of Okonkwo can stand in the way of the expression of religious duty and faith.

Opposition of a sort comes only from Obierika, who asserts a defiant passivity in response to Okonkwo's charge that he appears to be questioning the authority of the oracle: "[I]f the Oracle said that my son should be killed I would neither dispute it nor be the one to do it" (47). Lekan Oyeleye suggests this indicates that "Obierika's loyalty to the community gods is not as over-zealous and thoughtless as Okonkwo's brand of loyalty" (22). But the issue of Obierika's exceptionalism is stronger than this. Achebe's narrative characterizes Obierika's inaction as being not only at variance with Okonkwo's view of things but with the received canon of traditional deific lore. Obierika claims that "the Oracle did not ask me to carry out its decision" (46), but this is a spurious absolution since, as a member of the clan, he is as responsible as the next clansperson for the execution of the oracle's instructions.

His impiety is further censured by the source of the rebuke, since even the iron-willed Okonkwo, who has by this time himself transgressed against the earth goddess, Ani, in the beating of his wife, has duly and humbly atoned for his crime.[1] Had Obierika's unapologetic misgivings found any sympathetic ear, one might have thought it would have been that of his friend—but not so. True, part of Okonkwo's interrogative tone stems from his own inner turmoil about the death of Ikemefuna but, on a more significant level, as a penitent transgressor he speaks for the devotional mores of the clan in asserting the preeminence of collective obedience and action.

Okonkwo has been mentioned and, since he tends to dominate most critical deliberations on *Things Fall Apart*, it is worth offering an explanation of his diminished role here. Undoubtedly, Okonkwo's relation to the deific system is important, but it may not be as pivotal as some critics have contended. Bonnie Barthold, for example, believes that the "narrative structure of *Things Fall Apart* is defined by Okonkwo's relationship with the earth goddess, Ani, and the ever-increasing seriousness of the offenses he commits against her" (56).[2] The Ani-Okonkwo colloquy is intriguing but in fact most of the novel's allusions to deities come from persons other than Okonkwo and, as shall be argued, Achebe goes to some lengths to construct a religious pantheon that ranges beyond any single god or goddess. It is significant, too, that the initial religious allusions of the novel locate themselves firmly in the territory of an oracle-clan discourse, and that, subsequently, the spiritual experiences of individuals are repeatedly referenced to that all-pervading dialogue.

Elsewhere in the novel, the strength of other oracles is attested. A group of fugitives who have found sanctuary in Umuofia recount the story of the arrival of the first white man in their village. The elders of the village consulted their oracle. It foretold the demise of the clan and the arrival of more strangers: "It said that other white men were on their way. They were locusts, it said, and that first man was their harbinger sent to explore the terrain. And so they killed him" (97–98). All true, of course, and all the more reason for the clan to believe in the efficacy of oracular worship and counsel. The role of the oracle in Umuofia at the outset of *Things Fall Apart* is unambiguous, unequivocal, certain.

In Achebe's other novels, there is little reference to oracles. *Arrow of God*, the most religious of these, is steeped in traditional belief but focuses essentially on the chief priest, Ezeulu. He is given some oracular functions; for instance, it is for him to name the day of the Festival of Pumpkin Leaves (3)—but for the most part, there is articulated no elaborate ritual of oracular consultation. The world of *Arrow of God* has the feel of a monotheistic world, as its title suggests. Personal chi are mentioned, but Ulu stands firmly as the tutelary god; and Ezeulu is, essentially, the agent of Ulu rather than an intermediary priest who brings back divine messages from places of holy conference.

This may seem a minor, even insignificant, distinction between the two novels but it is important. After all, it is made clear in *Things Fall Apart* that Chielo, who at first dominates belief and worship in Umuofia, is the priestess of Agbala. Yet, the religious pantheon of *Things Fall Apart* is essentially polytheistic. Agbala is divine, but the novel explicitly styles him as only one of many divinities who are material to the life of the clan. Achebe, in fact, goes to some lengths to reveal a cosmology of deities in the novel. The notion of personal gods, or chi, is established early (10); the narrator offers an account of the dispute between the sky and earth (38); their presence and that of Amadiora, the divine thunderbolt, is forcefully reiterated (102–3); the gods and goddesses of the traditional system are a source of disparagement on the part of the Christian intruders (103); a group of converts derisively repudiates the clan's worship of more than one god (110); and the clansman Okika reminds the clan of its constellation of gods and goddesses: Idemili, Ogwugwu, Agbala, "and all the others" (143).

This is not necessarily to infer that the setting of *Things Fall Apart* is a more "traditional" setting or a more authentic religious setting than that of *Arrow of God*. But it does indicate differences in the indigenous theistic designs of the two works. These may be traced further. In *Arrow of God*, the powers of the chief priest of Ulu, Ezeulu, are considerably less than his equivalent in *Things*

Fall Apart—the priestess of Agbala Chielo. On the question of going to war, an option expressly raised in both novels, the oracular authority of the priest in *Arrow of God* is notably less secure than it is in the earlier work. Here, for example, is how Nwaka advocates war against the Okperi (a course of action opposed by Ezeulu):

> Nwaka began by telling the assembly that Umuaro must not allow itself to be led by the Chief Priest of Ulu. "My father did not tell me that before Umuaro went to war it took leave from the priest of Ulu," he said. "The man who carries a deity is not a king. He is there to perform his god's ritual and to carry sacrifice to him." (27)

In *Things Fall Apart* we are told that there can be no war without validation from the Oracle of the Hills and the Caves. This, as Cook rightly maintains, "is not a rationalisation of weakness but takes its stand from a position of strength" (72). In *Arrow of God*, the oracular right of Ezeulu to forbid war is diminished by personal slanders as to his true earthly intentions. Obligations of divine belief have been weakened by the doubts and meanderings of mortal integrity. That Nwaka is at least partially successful in his argument is evidenced by the narrator's assertion that "Umuaro was divided in two" (27) on the matter.

The disparities between the two novels may be partially explained by the variant time frame that separates the events they describe. *Things Fall Apart* is located at points immediately before and after the arrival of the colonists. The work is a third over before white people are even mentioned (51), and even there the allusion is merely a trivial speculation about whether they have toes or not. The novel is more than two-thirds over before a white person actually appears in Umuofia—an occasion that brings out every man and woman in the village (101). *Arrow of God*, on the other hand presents not simply a single white missionary but an entire colonial community within the opening three chapters. Here, white people are not fantastical rumors but a familiar and integral part of the social landscape. Their leader,

Captain T. K. Winterbottom, has already spent fifteen years in the African colonial service and is now firmly entrenched in his bungalow atop "Government Hill" (29).

Clan attitudes toward the indigenous religion in *Arrow of God* have been tempered, before the novel has even started, by contact with a dominant, monotheistic creed—and one which, though regarded with hostility by many clanspeople, has not yet seriously challenged the supposedly inviolate nature of indigenous belief and worship. By way of contrast, *Things Fall Apart* presents the process of attitudinal beliefs in relation to the indigenous religion prior to the sociohistorical point at which *Arrow of God* begins. It appears that the arrival of Christianity not only secures native converts but also distorts, even among hostile clan nonconverts, responses to and perceptions of indigenous beliefs. This goes beyond what some critics have called a simple "hybridization of culture" (Ashcroft, Griffiths, and Tiffin 129). Hybridization implies a compromise of differences, a common meeting ground. It cannot of itself encapsulate the spirit and movement of Achebe's representation. Homi Bhabha has written incisively of "the cultural and historical hybridity of the postcolonial world . . . as the paradigmatic *place of departure*" (21; emphasis added). It is that point of "departure" in which Achebe seems acutely interested. He seeks to move beyond espousal of a dualist model of cultural attrition and interadaptation, to a delineation of the metamorphosis of faith-oriented traditional pieties into economically driven "New World" pieties.

ONCE THE FIRST white person has arrived in Umuofia (101), a repudiation of indigenous clan religious beliefs follows almost immediately:

> At this point an old man said he had a question [for the white man]. "Which is this god of yours," he asked, "the goddess of the earth, the god of the sky, Amadiora of the thunderbolt, or what?" . . .
>
> "All the gods you have named are not gods at all. They are gods of deceit who tell you to kill your fellows and destroy

innocent children. There is only one true God and He has the earth, the sky, you and me and all of us." (102–3)

After this, the notion of the traditional oracle, so strong hitherto, disappears without a trace from the novel. It is never again mentioned or even intimated. There are many opportunities when it could have been. The killing of the royal python is one. Achebe makes clear to us that the python is "the emanation of the god of water" (12) and therefore sacred. Accidental killing of such an animal could be atoned through sacrifices and an expensive burial ceremony. But because no one has ever imagined that someone would knowingly kill a python, there is no statutory sanction for the crime. A decision about action, even if it is to be that no action should be taken, is required by the clan. What is interesting is the nature of the consultative process leading to that decision, and what does not happen rather than what does.

Chielo, the priestess, is not consulted. In fact, after she has called the clan's Christian converts "the excrement of the clan" (101), we hear nothing more from or about her in the novel. A priestess, the high priestess of Agbala, who has hitherto played a central role in the process of traditional life, takes no further part in the story or the events it describes. No one suggests that the Oracle of the Hills and the Caves should be consulted over the killing of the python. The clan's first instinct is to resolve the issue through human discussion:

> The rulers and elders of Mbanta assembled to decide on their action. Many of them spoke at great length and in fury. The spirit of war was upon them. (112)

We know from the first chapter of the novel that the clan never went to war unless its cause was confirmed as just by the oracle (9). Why is it that consultation of the oracle is now not even mooted as an option? Indeed, divine conference with the oracle, once so integral a part of clan life, is suddenly abandoned to a new order of things—to a secular consultative context in which those wishing to go to war are opposed by those who do not wish to go to war. The reasons put forward by the latter are interesting:

> "It is not our custom to fight for our gods," said one of them. "Let us not presume to do so now. If a man kills the sacred python in the secrecy of his hut, the matter lies between him and the god. We did not see it." (113)

In other words, the gods can look after themselves, why should we do their fighting for them? A fascinating modification of devotion has occurred here. The cosmology of deities, the very cornerstone of clan being, has suddenly become distanced from the actuality of the existence of Umuofia. At one time an integral weave in the fabric of clan life, the indigenous religious order has abruptly become remote and distant. It is now located in a schemata of parallel activities in which the divinities of an ordered universe and the mortals of an ordered world function independently, avoiding interference in each other's affairs and linked only by a respectful cordiality of verbal oblation on the part of the traditional worshiper.

The transformation is dramatic and arresting. But is the new equation of relation plausible? In a sense and for a time, yes. It looks as if it is working in the case of the slaying of the royal python, an act which has apparently precipitate consequences. Okoli, a prime suspect in the crime, falls ill and dies: "His death showed that the gods were still able to fight their own battles. The clan saw no reason then for molesting the Christians" (114). Perhaps Obierika's thesis of godly acceptance and human inertia, of belief and oblation without enactment, is a credible modus vivendi after all?

The assumption is false. The narrative rapidly and subtly undermines any thoughts that divine sanction comes without a reciprocation of mortal action. Okoli had in fact denied the crime, and Achebe is careful to present no evidence against him. Not long after, we learn that Enoch was most likely the real offender (131). What is significant is not whether Okoli is guilty or innocent but that his death enables the clanspeople to seize upon a bogus exemplar of divine self-help in order to reassert the new order of things—to withdraw to the sanctuary of a piety that is passive, undemanding, and removed, one which places no burden of sacrifice or atonement or forceful action upon the celebrant.

To the chagrin of Okonkwo, the spokesperson of the old faith now as he had been earlier in the face of Obierika's heretical passivity, the most the clan can offer against the Christians for the slaying of the emanation of the god of water is ostracization. It is an action calculated not to avenge the outrage against the god, but rather to distance the village from the crime that has been committed: "We should do something. But let us ostracise these men. We would then not be held accountable for their abominations" (113). And the death of Okoli, be it fortuitous or not, removes from a grateful clan even that necessity.

This sense of wily self-preservation which now characterizes the clan may be usefully compared, for example, to its response earlier in the novel to Okonkwo's beating of his youngest wife. During the beating, his first two wives and a host of neighbors beg him to stop since this is a sacred week—and "it was unheard of to beat somebody during the sacred week" (21). Ezeani, the priest of the earth goddess, Ani, visits Okonkwo to rebuke him and refuses to eat "in the house of a man who has no respect for our gods and ancestors" (21). His is not a humanitarian concern but a religious one:

> "The evil you have done can ruin the whole clan. The earth goddess whom you have insulted may refuse to give us her increase, and we shall all perish." His tone now changed from anger to command. "You will bring to the shrine of Ani tomorrow one she-goat, one hen, a length of cloth and a hundred cowries." (22)

The whole episode is marked by certainties of transgression, of censure, of atonement. At the center of this process stands the priest, the intermediary between deity and mortal. There is no questioning of his position, no doubt about his authority, no possibility of his denial. Just as in the killing of Ikemefuna, there is no ambiguity or blurring of responsibilities and significances. The progress of the clan, divinely guided and humanly effected through the collective obedience of the clanspeople, is distinct and emphatic.

How rapidly things change. The only decisive communal action that occurs in the last third of the book is the burning of Mr. Smith's church (130–35). This act, in revenge for the unmasking of an egwugwu (131), an ancestral spirit and therefore part of the indigenous religious cosmology, fills Okonkwo with something approaching happiness (136). We are told:

> When the egwugwu went away the red-earth church which Mr Brown had built was a pile of earth and ashes. And for the moment the spirit of the clan was pacified. (135)

The destruction of the church is framed in terms of a human victory. Immediately after the burning of the building, we learn that Okonkwo's clan "which had turned false on him appeared to be making amends" (136); Okonkwo himself rejoices that it was "like the good old days again, when a warrior was a warrior" (136); and a few lines later we learn that "[e]very man in Umuofia went about armed with a gun or a matchet" (136). There is a sense of the clan's human destiny having been reasserted as the prerogative of the clan itself. No one thanks the gods for the building's destruction; no one even credits them with a hand in it.

Yet, why should this be? It is, after all, the egwugwu who have burned down the church. The egwugwu are explicitly linked, through their patronizing deity, with the world of the godly immortals:

> "All our gods are weeping. Idemili is weeping. Ogwugwu is weeping, Agbala is weeping, and all the others." (143)

Technically, it is not the living clanspeople at all who have been responsible for the action. Though the egwugwu masks are worn by living beings, according to traditional doctrine a transmigration of flesh and spirit occurs in which the human impersonators become unearthly spirits. If the victory over the church is a victory of the deific world (and we are told, after all, that "the spirit of the clan was pacified"), how is it that the clan itself interprets the destruction of the church as a human act and never alludes to it in terms of divine intervention?

One explanation may be that they are no longer convinced of the divinity of the egwugwu, regarding the ritual of the nine spirits as no more than a historic reenactment of people and actions from times past. Whether this is the case or not, the clanspeople appear not to covet further the idea that the path to community survival is traceable irrevocably to the cosmology of indigenous gods. If they did, they would surely have left the issue of the egwugwu unmasking to the gods. Instead, they take up arms, apparently without any kind of oracular consultation, and steel themselves for the worst.

ADEWALE MAJA-PEARCE has speculated that one of Achebe's purposes in *Things Fall Apart* is to assert that "the spiritual values of pre-colonial Africa were in no way inferior to those of Europe, merely different" (10). That difference became a source of vulnerability. The religious codes and practices of Umuofia, unchallenged for centuries and perhaps millennia, had not evolved strategies for adaptation or confrontation. Like the sacred python, no one ever thought their sacredness would or could be challenged. The real power of missionary proselytization lay in the breaking down of community norms. The Evil Forest became no longer evil; the outcasts became no longer outcasts; the objects and rituals of traditional sacrament were destroyed.

Despite this, some Umuofians yet seek an accommodation, a hybridization, perhaps, with the new theology. As he struggles to find a compromise between the religion he has always known and that which has suddenly arrived, the village elder Akunna debates the issue of the gods with the missionary Mr. Brown:

"You say that there is one supreme God who made heaven and earth," said Akunna on one of Mr Brown's visits. "We also

believe in Him and call Him Chukwu. He made all the world
and the other gods."

"There are no other gods," said Mr Brown. "Chukwu is the
only God and all others are false." (126–27)

Mr. Brown is no intercessor, no hybridizer. He spurns the idea
that he is the earthly representative of his God, leading Akunna
to exclaim, aghast, "but there must be a head in this world among
men" (127). There is no compromise offered. Mr. Brown rejects
not only the central indigenous notion of a multideity system
but also the pivotal function of a high priest or priestess within
a religious framework.

It may be possible to see in *Arrow of God* how both of these
crucial tenets of traditional worship—polytheism and priestly in-
tercession—have been corrupted in the revised perception of traditional lore. As noted earlier, not only is Ulu a rather "singu-
larized" god, but his earthly messenger, Ezeulu, is emphatically
disrobed of the trappings of infallible or absolute authority by the
clanspeople. Further, the clan's attitude toward Ulu becomes less
than coherent in the later stages of the novel. When Ezeulu says
he cannot enact a ritual that will enable new yams to be planted
because Ulu has not sanctioned it, a clan delegation urges him
to perform the rite anyway and to lay the blame on them (208).
When he refuses, a new choice is mooted:

> So the news spread that anyone who did not want to wait and
> see all his harvest ruined could take his offering to the god of
> the Christians who claimed to have power of protection from
> the anger of Ulu. (216)

The contest is styled as a battle of singularities, one god versus
another. It is an essentially biblical construct: a binary contest
between feast and famine, between protection and threat, between
the knight and the dragon—and, implicitly, between good and
evil. Traditional theology has been undermined by Christian mythology and subsumed into a biblical schemata of loss and salvation. Gone are the ordinances of seasonal and festive celebra-

tion, gone the multiplicities of divine representation, of elemental hierarchies, of ancestral phantasms and conferences. The shape and detail of traditional beliefs have evaporated. Ulu, disconnected from his deific order, must battle for authority in the pavilion of his foe. Of course Ulu will lose. He may offer only the mysterious piety of suffering; Christianity, as it is unfolded and displayed in *Arrow of God*, offers the clear piety of economics, a simple exchange of spiritual faith for material prosperity.

Joseph Swann speculates that the demise of Ulu may have been self-willed, "not for any reason of cultural dissatisfaction, but as a simple historical necessity, to safeguard the bare existence of the clan" (194). But what is existence without faith? In the clan's ancient frame of things, it should be as nothing. The fact that it is now feasible attests to a shift in the devotional perspective of the clan members. Knowingly or otherwise, they are trapped into a revisionist interpretation—in effect, a Christianization—of their traditional beliefs. Where once they might have accepted the ruling of the divinity, and starved in the certainty of a mysterious but painful purpose, now an alien creed offers an alluring alternative.

Things Fall Apart reveals a time when this was not so and goes on to present the temporal nexus point between the ways of the old religion and the ways of a new world order. On the face of it, the new order seems more logical and democratic and, to contemporary sensibilities, humane. The clanspeople meet and discuss their tactics; the imperatives of action are no longer handed down to them by unseen deities who communicate imperiously through their human emissaries. It is, of course, a superficial freedom. In truth, they now act under a new and equally powerful imperative, a colonial imperative. This new relationship, however, is not founded on mystical ordination or divine machination. It is a relationship of pragmatism and commodity.

That point is made abundantly clear in the abduction of the six clanspeople by the district commissioner's officers (137–39). This may be compared with the abduction of Okonkwo's child Ezinma by Agbala's priestess, Chielo (70–76). After a bizarre odyssey, the child is returned unharmed and without explanation

(77). The six men, on the other hand, are ransomed. Either the clan pays the requisite cowrie fine or the six will be hanged. Just as no one questions the motives of Chielo, so no one questions the motives of the district commissioner. But the reasons for the silences are quite different. Chielo is not challenged because the ways of the gods are beyond mortal comprehension; the district commissioner is not challenged because, by contrast, his position is abundantly comprehensible. He goes to some lengths to explain the readily discernible economics of commodity transfer: the freedom of six human beings for two hundred bags of cowrie shells. It is a logical, business transaction, and the clan finds it as compelling as it did obedience to the Oracle of the Hills and the Caves.

There is no talk of gods or goddesses or holy wars. The clan's financial penance is part of the new order that has enveloped their traditional life. An egwugwu has been unmasked; their six leaders have been captured through false promises of parley; an extortionate ransom demand has been made—yet the response of the clan is pragmatic. The men of the clan meet at the marketplace and agree to raise the fine without delay (139). The matter is settled on a commodity basis. Faith in oracular arbitration has been replaced by faith in a new kind of fiscal logic. This eclipse is signed by the fact that the night preceding their decision is a night of the full moon. Normally a time of sacred and secretive communal ritual, it is on this occasion presented as a time of desolation and emptiness (139).

The economics of religious school education provide momenta no less forceful than the exchange of prisoners for money. This is how the novel describes the impact of Mr. Brown, a missionary educator, on the life and times of the village:

> Mr Brown's school produced quick results. A few months in it were enough to make one a court messenger or even a court clerk. Those who stayed longer became teachers; and from Umuofia labourers went forth into the Lord's vineyard. New churches were established in the surrounding villages and a

few schools with them. From the very beginning religion and education went hand in hand. (128)

Mr. Brown's school offers advantages to its students and to the work of the missionary himself. For the local participants it promises advancement within the prevailing socioeconomic system; for Mr. Brown it affords the opportunity to convert to Christianity those who have entrusted their education to his care. But the benefits come at a price. The need for court messengers or court clerks, or indeed for people who can read and write, is one generated by the demands of a colonial hegemony, not by the requirements of clan administration. The knowledge and understanding that Mr. Brown's school seeks to promulgate is openly abrasive to the organization and culture of the clan.

Eustace Palmer argues that "[a]s long as a reasonable person like Mr Brown is in charge of the mission station, co-existence is possible between the new religion and traditional society" (58). In fact, the interrelations between the two can never be characterized in terms of coexistence, because the economics of Mr. Brown's religion demand ideological substitution, not concurrence or hybridization. In *Things Fall Apart*, Christianity, like colonialism in general, is depicted as offering a clear rationale of "exchange" for Umuofia. In return for adherence to Christian doctrine, the church offers explicit routes for individual economic advancement.

As the meaning and decisiveness of that interaction dawns on the clan, it corrupts the ancient way of things. What use is there in praying to Agbala for the white people to go away when the new order presents so persuasively the dimensions of its power that only cooperation and attempted advancement within its structure seem practicable? Achebe's irony, of course, is that the Umuofia come to believe in the supremacy of the missionary colonizers as devoutly as they once had in their own theater of gods. But these are devotions engendered by quite different experiences: the former, through the compulsion of physical aggression and economic inducement; the latter, through the magnificence and munificence of faith. In the end, the metamorphosis of piety is not a change from belief in one religious system to belief in another religious system but rather a switch from faith in a world where life is given, to commitment to one where security and achievement are measured and earned very differently.

AUTHORS WRITE NOVELS for a multiplicity of reasons, not all of them obvious or cogent. It is possible, as Theo D'haen has suggested, that some postcolonial literatures seek to "take revenge upon the mother country, among other things by means of their shared post-colonial literatures" (16). But *Things Fall Apart* is not about revenge—though Achebe misses few opportunities to satirize the colonial presence. The Nigerian poet Tanure Ojaide offers another possibility:

> Literature might be devoted to leisure in other cultures, but for us Africans who are experiencing the second half of the twentieth century, literature must serve a purpose: to expose, embarrass, and fight corruption and authoritarianism. . . . It is understandable why the African artist is utilitarian. We do not have the luxury of some Western writers, who are apolitical and can afford to write art for art's sake and be confessional (a euphemism for self-therapy). (17)

While no one may accuse Achebe of complacency, Ojaide's premise of utilitarianism is more difficult to decipher in *Things Fall Apart*. The problem is that once things have irrevocably fallen apart, once a unique and intricate construct of a matured civilization has been irreversibly dismantled, then rehearsing the indiscretions of the past can easily be regarded as motiveless reminiscence. Yet, there is clearly a purpose to *Things Fall Apart*, and it may be discernible as much in the need for personal therapy as in the quest for historical truth. Achebe perceives a gap between how things were and how things are. The intercessionary phase has been typically fashioned as the sublimation of one culture by another. This is a neat enough postcolonial aphorism, but without the detail and minutiae of human circumstance, its veracity can remain only intuitive.

Things Fall Apart and *Arrow of God* after it provide the detail, the historical glimpses, of a traditional and colonial past. These are not concurrent glimpses and not even consecutive. But, in a sense, their temporal dislocations are all the more informative. In particular, the shifting time frame of Umuofia in *Things Fall Apart* delineates not only how things fell apart but theorizes on why they fell apart. It bestows no ebullient credit; it lays no absolute onus of blame. As Aijaz Ahmad has written, history cannot decisively resolve theoretical debate because "[t]he difficulty with theoretical debate . . . is that it can neither ignore the facts nor be simply settled by them; thought . . . tends always to exceed the facts" (287). Obscurities of absolution and blame are of themselves the ironically definitive truths of history. The decline of Umuofia was a decline effected by a concatenation of unfortunate, calamitous, and mysterious circumstances. It cannot be argued that the learning of this past is overtly utilitarian for what has been lost will not exist again and therefore cannot be lost again. What can be said is that the novel reconstructs the detail of grand and momentous events, rejecting nineteenth-century ahistorical polarities of Africa and Occident and asserting a process of metamorphosing piety against a backdrop of seemingly irresistible social and economic imperatives.

Notes

1. For a discussion of Okonkwo's transgressions against the earth goddess, see Maja-Pearce 10–16 and Barthold 56–58.

2. See as well, Lindfors, who explores Okonkwo's relationship with his chi (78–79).

Works Cited

Achebe, Chinua. *Arrow of God.* London: Heinemann, 1974.
———. *Things Fall Apart.* London: Heinemann, 1962.

Ahmad, Aijaz. *In Theory*. London: Verso, 1992.

Ashcroft, Bill, Gareth Griffiths, and Helen Tiffin. *The Empire Writes Back*. London: Routledge, 1989.

Barthold, Bonnie J. *Black Time: Fiction of Africa, the Caribbean and the United States*. New Haven, CT: Yale University Press, 1981.

Bhabha, Homi. K. *The Location of Culture*. London: Routledge, 1994.

Cook, David. *African Literature: A Critical View*. London: Longman, 1977.

D'haen, Theo. "Shades of Empire in Colonial and Post-Colonial Literatures." In *Shades of Empire in Colonial and Post-Colonial Literatures*, edited by C. C. Barfoot and Theo D'haen, 9–16. Amsterdam: Rodopi, 1993.

Lindfors, Bernth. *Folklore in Nigerian Literature*. New York: Africana, 1973.

Maja-Pearce, Adewale. *A Mask Dancing: Nigerian Novelists of the Eighties*. London: Hans Zell, 1992.

Ojaide, Tanure. "I Want to Be an Oracle: My Poetry and My Generation." *World Literature Today* 68 (1994): 15–21.

Oyeleye, A. Lekan. "*Things Fall Apart* Revisited: A Semantic and Stylistic Study of Character in Achebe." In *The Question of Language in African Literature Today*, edited by Eldred Durosimi Jones, 15–23. Trenton, NJ: Africa World, 1991.

Palmer, Eustace. *An Introduction to the African Novel*. London: Heinemann, 1972.

Swann, Joseph. "From *Things Fall Apart* to *Anthills of the Savannah*: The Changing Face of History in Chinua Achebe's Novels." In *Crisis and Creativity in the New Literatures in English*, edited by Geoffrey V. Davis and Hena Maes-Jelinek, 191–203. Amsterdam: Rodopi, 1990.

Problems of Gender and History in the Teaching of *Things Fall Apart*

RHONDA COBHAM

◆   ◆   ◆

T HIS IS A SEXIST NOVEL!" the (female, white) student
declared. Her ethnic earnings jangled in angry assent as she
stabbed the pages of her Heinemann paperback for emphasis. As
if to distance itself from the offending object, her red-checked
imitation Palestine Liberation Organization scarf slipped backward
off her shoulders. It was clear that she spoke on behalf of all
oppressed humanity.

In a voice tinged with long-suffering, her teacher (also white,
but male) attempted to explain that not to write about wife beating in a story about a society where it was practiced would be
aesthetically inauthentic. He tried to shift the discussion back to
an appreciation of the critical distance between the author and
his main character before the jocks at the back of the class got
wind of what was going on, but it was too late. Within seconds
the high school class had degenerated into a slanging match between those who felt texts like *Things Fall Apart* should be expur-
gated from the syllabus and those who wanted to tell the cen-
sorship group what they would like Okonkwo to do to them if

he were a member of the class. The teacher held his head in his hands and fantasized about reintroducing corporal punishment.

Change the bracketed terms of ascription and this in modified form becomes a scenario that all teachers of Achebe's novel must recognize. I encountered it in a more subtle, inverted form when a Nigerian university student (female) during a discussion of Buchi Emecheta's *Joys of Motherhood* suggested tentatively that though she could appreciate how Nnu Ego felt about her husband in the Emecheta novel, she thought that the writer was being polemical because "traditional Igbo women did not feel that way about these kinds of things," and it became apparent that her point of reference for the psychological responses appropriate for traditional Igbo women was the vision of early Igbo society presented in *Things Fall Apart*.

In an age where violence and the demand for women's rights are constant features of our public rhetoric, there may be something instructive about the way in which these representative student responses insist on conflating all kinds of textual and political issues. In the response of the wearer of ethnic earrings, several issues have been conflated. In the first place, there is no concept of historical time in her reading of the novel. For all she probably knew, the Igbo society Achebe was describing was contemporaneous with both the author and herself. Achebe, through his pseudo-autobiographical character, Okonkwo, was merely describing and rationalizing the attitude toward women which he himself shared with the contemporary Igbo society. For her, this (mis)reading is borne out by Obierika's closing eulogy for his dishonored friend which she reads simplistically as overt endorsement of all that Okonkwo stood for. Her sense of dis-ease is compounded by the total identification of the most brutal elements within her own society with Okonkwo's attitudes and actions. PLO scarf notwithstanding, she cannot imagine what it must feel like for an entire culture to have its customs, values, and idiosyncrasies not merely challenged but made totally irrelevant by a simple equation of moral authority with superior military strength.

Where Western student readers of *Things Fall Apart* complain that the novel is "sexist," meaning usually that they find Okonkwo misogynist, African student readers are more likely to praise Achebe and chastise a writer like Buchi Emecheta for not being as authentic as Achebe in portraying traditional Igbo women. Okonkwo's physical abuse of his wives is evaluated precisely within the novel on a scale of values that has at its highest point the devotion of the old couple Ndulue and Ozoemena, who remain devoted to each other even in death, and at its lowest point the cruelty of wife batterer Uzowulu, whom the egwugwu themselves must discipline. But for the student reader in a Western culture, Okonkwo's petty viciousness remains a more vivid travesty of human rights than the action of the district commissioner in the novel, when he enjoins the jailers to treat with dignity the elders whom he has just tricked, humiliated, and imprisoned.

In the case of the African student reader, the issues that are conflated are somewhat different. Speaking from within modern Nigerian society, she cannot help but be aware of the differences between the world she inhabits and the one Achebe describes. She is a product of the Africanized Nigerian education system and has been taught to respect the world of tradition by her parents as well as by books like *Things Fall Apart* on her school examination syllabus. She fully expects to be married in church as well as in some modified form of a traditional ceremony and to be the only legal wife of her modern, educated husband. The polygamously married senior sisters of her father belong to a world to which she pays her respects but which she assumes is as remote to her reality as the Igbo village Achebe describes at the turn of the century—at least for the present. Because her interaction with traditional culture is indirect, and because she considers her emancipated notions of a woman's role a product of her Westernized/Nigerianized education, she cannot conceive of women in traditional Igbo society sharing her notions of selfhood. For her, the world that Achebe brings to life is a beautiful tableau that exists to reinforce her sense of belonging to a noble tradition. And this is true, whether her ethnic origins are Igbo, Yoruba, or East African Kikuyu.

Both the readers of the novel described above imply by their conflation of lived and imagined realities that there is some truly objective, unbiased version of traditional life which it is the writer's duty to deliver to the reader in such a way that our sympathies are engaged for the "right" causes and our imaginations are stimulated in the "right" directions. Neither seems concerned that the imaginative point of departure for the writer could have incorporated different preoccupations and perspectives from the ones they bring to their reading of his work.

Achebe probably had an agenda in writing his novel quite different from either of these readers in studying it. As the son of a village catechist and a scholarship winner, first to secondary school and then to the newly established Ibadan College, Achebe was one of the first generation of African writers to be familiar from early childhood with Western and indigenous traditions. Both the eloquent oral traditions of the Igbo community and the compelling prose of the King James Bible would have imbued him with a love of beautiful language and an appreciation of the timing and perfect cadence of a well-wrought sentence. The texts which formed his vision of Africa, however, were novels like Joyce Cary's *Mr. Johnson* and Conrad's *Heart of Darkness*, texts in relation to which Achebe has described himself as a resisting reader.[1] Like his modern African readers, he would have been aware of the ways in which the values of his Christian family differed from or coincided with those of more traditional Igbo families. Like his Western readers, he must have been uncomfortably aware that many of the traditions which still influenced his life would have been considered brutal or misogynist from the perspective of the fictive author of *The Pacification of the Primitive Tribes of the Lower Niger*.

Unlike both groups of readers, however, and indeed, unlike either of the cultures to which they had access, Achebe's generation of African intellectuals had no readily available symbolic discourse through which they could represent and ascribe value simultaneously to the various cultural influences that had formed them. To be sure, they could quote Yeats and Eliot at will to each other in one breath and spar with traditional proverbs in the next, but who besides them would get the joke? Who in their community who had come before them or was likely to come after them would understand and give full value to all aspects of their accomplishments and ways of seeing? Okonkwo voices a similar angst in a rare moment of filial solidarity with his father in *Things Fall Apart* as he contemplates the defection of his eldest son, Nwoye, to join the Christians:

> Suppose when he died all his male children decided to follow Nwoye's steps and abandon their ancestors? Okonkwo felt a cold shudder run through him at the terrible prospect, like the prospect of annihilation. He saw himself and his father crowding round their ancestral shrine waiting in vain for worship and sacrifice and finding nothing but ashes of bygone days and his children the while praying to the white man's god. (108)

In the rhetoric of our age, we would say that both Okonkwo and his creator are concerned with the construction of a personal, in this case masculine, identity through which to mediate their connections to past, present, and future communities. Okonkwo's quest is easily charted. Deprived by his father's anomalous lifestyle of an inheritance of land, yam seed, or junior wives, he has access to no material objects that can provide him with a reference for who he is or what he may become. In fact his most immediate point of male reference, his father, is described by the society as *agbala*, a word that "could . . . mean a man who had taken no title," but which also means "woman" (10). Like Shelley's monster in *Frankenstein*, Okonkwo must fabricate a social context for his identity and values rather than simply assuming a system of references in relation to which he can define himself. He does so by isolating and responding to specific symbols of masculinity within his culture as if they, in the abstract, could constitute all that a man needed to construct his social self.

The pivotal example of this process in the novel is Okonkwo's understanding of the concept of courage. At the outset it is the masculine attribute most immediately accessible to him, as it seems wholly contingent upon his performance as an individual.

In the opening paragraphs of the novel, Okonkwo is defined for us in terms of his courage when he throws Amalinze the Cat in wrestling. Later we discover that Okonkwo's courage on this occasion is immediately translated into affirmation of his social identity since it wins him the love of a woman whom, in terms of material wealth, he is not yet "man enough" to marry.

Such early instances of social recognition for his courage are compounded over the years as Okonkwo struggles manfully against bad weather and harvests to acquire his own yam seed and as he takes lives in battle. Gradually, for Okonkwo, prestige and manliness become synonymous with the ability to do difficult, even distasteful jobs without flinching. When the oracle demands the life of his ward, Ikemefuna, Okonkwo finds himself without access to a system of values which would allow him to distance himself from the killing of the child who "calls [him] father" (40) and remain a man. He strikes the blow that kills the child, offending the earth goddess, Ani, and setting in motion a chain of events which ultimately leads to his downfall.

Okonkwo's limited personal understanding of physical ascendancy as courage and his equation of courage with masculinity are set against a much richer and more complex set of values available to his clan as a whole. In the novel, Okonkwo's friend Obierika is the main spokesman for this greater tradition. His words are reinforced structurally by the narrative's juxtaposition of Okonkwo's actions and those of other members of the society in a way which invites us to consider the complexity of the clan's values. Thus, Okonkwo sees tenderness as incompatible with masculinity, viewing marriage as yet another social situation in which a man's worth is measured by his ability to control others through superior physical strength. Yet the reader is made aware of the ways in which such notions of male prerogative are qualified by the community. Okonkwo's response to the almost simultaneous deaths of Ndulue and his wife, Ozoemena, dramatizes the gap between his personal code and that of the clan as a whole:

"It was always said that Ndulue and Ozoemena had one mind," said Obierika. "I remember when I was a young boy there was a song about them. He could not do anything without telling her."

"I did not know that," said Okonkwo. "I thought he was a strong man in his youth."

"He was indeed," said Ofoedu.

Okonkwo shook his head doubtfully.

"He led Umuofia to war in those days," said Obierika. (47–48)

Okonkwo himself is punished when he breaks the Week of Peace and beats his wife, a judgment which reflects a symbolic recognition of wife beating as violence even though it may also be associated with legitimate masculine privilege. Finally there is the unequivocal censure of the *egwugwu*, who are called forth to reprimand the chronic batterer, Uzowulu. Their judgment shows where the community draws the line between physical prowess and bullying, courage and cowardice.

Okonkwo's most complex conflation of brute force with the "masculine" virtue of courage occurs in the final pages of the story where he cuts off the head of the court messenger and then hangs himself. Here courage is dissociated from those other manly attributes: caution, diplomacy, and the ability to weigh both sides of an argument. The irony is that none of these higher values in his society will have any effect on the superior military might of the colonizers. Thus, in a twisted sense, Okonkwo and the district commissioner share the same world view: that ultimately physical strength and the ability to inflict one's will on another human being, be it one's wife, one's son, or one's natives, are the only significant forms of social differentiation in establishing a masculine identity.

The act of suicide marks symbolically the parting of the ways between Okonkwo and his clan. Until now he has accepted the censure of his community for his unpremeditated acts of violence, because at heart he accepts that their universe encompasses his. Faced now with the whispered comment "why did he do it" (145) after he kills the messenger, Okonkwo finally decides that his clanspeople no longer share his values and that to be a man on their terms would be a form of living death. His community reciprocates his final act of distancing, to the extent that it denies him a man's burial. Yet, ultimately, Okonkwo characteristically underestimates the flexibility and comprehensiveness of the clan's values. When Obierika declares, "[t]hat man was one of the greatest men in Umuofia" (147), he extends to Okonkwo the same complex and qualified acceptance accorded to Ndulue, who was great and/but who could not do anything without telling his wife. Thus the accolade of manhood is conferred on Okonkwo even in default, both in the words of his friend and in the act of narration which constitutes Achebe's novel.

Okonkwo's final solution brings us back full circle to the dilemma of his creator. Like Okonkwo, who attempts to carve out a relationship with his clan in the absence of an inherited sense of identity, Achebe must renegotiate a relationship to traditional Igbo society, which his education, religious training, and internalized moral standards have made tenuous. Like Okonkwo, he often proceeds by isolating specific aspects of the societies to which he has access and allowing these to stand for many other possible readings of a given social situation. Achebe has described his mission in writing *Things Fall Apart* as being to teach other Africans that their past was neither as savage nor as benighted as the colonizers represented it to be. Another way of stating this goal could conceivably be that Achebe needed to prove to himself that the best of the values he associated with his Christian upbringing were compatible with the values of traditional Igbo society.

There are many examples of selective incorporation of supposedly Western/Christian values into the celebration of the traditional way of life in *Things Fall Apart*. I would like to discuss briefly three: the killing of Ikemefuna, the presentation of marriage, and the selective elaboration of women's roles within traditional Igbo society.

In presenting Ikemefuna's death, Achebe, like Okonkwo, must find a way of synchronizing the qualities he wishes to represent with the values he has internalized. While sharing the mission-school horror at the idea of human sacrifice that he attributes to the converts in *Things Fall Apart*, Achebe must find ways of addressing this issue while keeping the reader's sympathy for the community as a whole. He does so by structuring the story of Ikemefuna's death so that it parallels the biblical story of Abraham's near-sacrifice of his son, Isaac. The journey out of the confines of the village, the boy's carrying of the vessels associated with the sacrifice, and his last disarming words, "[m]y father, they have killed me" (43), all resonate with the Bible story. Isaac performed each of the roles attributed to Ikemefuna, including the utterance of a last disarming remark: "My father . . . behold the fire and the wood: but where is the lamb" (Genesis 22:7). The major difference, of course, is that no ram is provided to be a substitute for Ikemefuna. Yet we feel sure that, just as Abraham would have killed his son had the ram not been caught in the thicket, Okonkwo would have spared his, had a ram materialized for him. Both fathers act in strict obedience to their gods, and both contemplate the deed they must perform with horror as well as fortitude.

There are further parallels between Okonkwo's situation and the New Testament story about God's sacrifice of his son, Jesus, for the greater good of all humanity (itself a version of the Abraham/Isaac motif). What is important here, however, is that Achebe has picked the form of human sacrifice most compatible with Judeo-Christian myth as the centerpiece of his examination of human sacrifice in Igbo culture. The more ubiquitous forms, such as the "throwing away" of twins in the bad bush or the killing of slaves on the death of their masters, are mentioned only in passing, as evils already under fire within the traditional society, whose eradication is hastened by the coming of the missionaries. For the tragedy of Ikemefuna's death to be shared by his readers as a moment of pathos rather than of revulsion, the parallel with Abraham must function as a shared archetype. The object of sacrifice must be a sentient individual, bound to the person who makes the sacrifice by familial affection. In this way the act of sacrifice becomes a symbol of devotion to a principle higher than earthly love, rather than the brute machinations of a culture incapable of elevated sentiments. Though Okonkwo's personal intervention in Ikemefuna's death remains tragically wrongheaded, the context in which he acts retains its dignity.

Achebe's technical manipulations of such parallels within his story are reinforced as thematic strategies in the conversations between the enlightened missionary, Mr. Brown, and the enlightened Igbo, Akunna. Their conversations may be read as a metaphor for Achebe's own search for a point of convergence between the two codes which have informed his ethics. Similarly, his description of what it is that attracts Nwoye to the Christians mirrors his own strategies with the reader in using biblical myth to reinforce Igbo values. As he points out: "It was not the mad logic of the Trinity that captivated [Nwoye]. He did not understand it. It was the poetry of the new religion, something felt in the marrow" (104).

On the personal and political levels, Achebe's presentation of women within Igbo society can be seen to follow a similar pattern. Although we are told of Okonkwo's many wives and children, the male-female relationships in Okonkwo's family which Achebe isolates for our scrutiny are almost indistinguishable from those of monogamous couples within Western tradition. Okonkwo has three wives but we come to know only one: Ekwefi, the mother of Ezinma. She has married Okonkwo for love, having run away from her first husband. Her relationship with her husband, for better or worse, has all the passion, violence, and shared trauma we associate with the Western romantic tradition. Achebe's point clearly is that all of these emotions existed in traditional Igbo society but, as with his choice of situation in dealing with the issue of human sacrifice, the relationship he describes between Okonkwo and Ekwefi is by no means normative. We never really see the wives in Okonkwo's compound interacting with each other the way we are shown the men interacting among themselves or even Okonkwo interacting with his children. From a Western perspective the omission is hardly experienced as a loss, as the reader can identify effortlessly with the structure if not the content of the relationship between Okonkwo and Ekwefi. Indeed, its similarity to versions of marriage with which Western students are familiar may help explain why empathy with Ekwefi's mistreatment is so spontaneous and a reading of the text as misogynist can take place so easily. By contrast students seem to have much more difficulty dealing with friendly alliances between senior and junior wives in the work of other African writers. Many of them reject outright the idea in Ama Ata Aidoo's *Anowa* that a wife could actively seek out a junior wife for her husband as a way of marking her own material consequence, of asserting her own identity. Such relationships are important in the constructing of female identity, and that is clearly not what Achebe's novel is about.

A similar selective process occurs in the presentation of women's public roles. Achebe names one of the two groupings within the clan which endowed women with specific political authority: the *umuada* (93), or daughters of the clan. Since Igbo marriage ties were usually exogamous, a woman also belonged to another group in her husband's village consisting of the wives of the clan. Directly or indirectly, these groups controlled between them many aspects of civic and familial spheres of influence. In *Things Fall Apart* these range from the policing of stray animals (80) to the solemnizing of certain stages within marriage and betrothal rituals (92–93) and the preservation of a maternal line of land entitlement (91, 94–95). Indeed, Okonkwo's survival in exile hinges on his right to exercise his entitlement to land in his mother's village via the connections vested in her as a wife in Okonkwo's father's clan and a daughter in her father's clan.

Achebe does not tell us, however, that the *umuada* also regulated the markets in each town and that their intervention or threatened intervention was crucial in civic as well as marital disputes. When Uzowulu is brought to judgment for chronic abuse of his wife, one of the elders asks why such a minor matter has been brought to the attention of the *egwugwu* and is told: "Don't you know what kind of man Uzowulu is? He will not listen to any other decision" (66). It is clear that Achebe introduces the *egwugwu* here to underline for his audience in terms they can appreciate how seriously the community looks upon violence against women. But in fact it would seem from the anthropological accounts that a more likely scenario in a case such as this would have been the intervention of the wives of the clan, who would have enforced the judgment by "sitting" on the man in question: that is by so shaming him publicly through rude songs and obscene gestures that he would be forced to mend his ways. Alternatively, the kinswomen of the battered woman who had married into the clan of the offending male could have threatened to enforce a sexual strike if their husbands did not see to it that Uzowulu mended his ways.[2]

Clearly Achebe would have been hard put to imbue such scenarios with the decorum expected of women within Western tradition. And indeed, he may have internalized a Western view of legal authority, which defines male courts of law as the ultimate seat of power in any society, to such an extent that alternative ways of dramatizing Uzowulu's ostracism through female intervention may have seemed ineffective by comparison. In any event, their omission from the narrative leaves us with no example of female authority within the Igbo social structure that is not compatible with traditional Western ideals of femininity as nurturing, ornamental, or in need of protection. Indeed, a truly jaundiced eye would have also to note that the women in the novel are described cooking, plaiting their hair, decorating their bodies, dancing, running from *egwugwu*, and being given in marriage. We do not see them planting their farms, bartering their goods in the marketplace, sitting in judgment on members of their community, or taking action alongside or against their men. The only woman we see acting with any authority is the priestess, Chielo, and she is presented, in terms consistent with Western practice, as a witch—a force for good or evil separated from the regular run of womenfolk rather than part of a chain of ritual and social female authority.

Such omissions become all the more difficult to reconcile when one remembers that it was precisely the outbreak of the Women's War in Aba in 1929, organized by the wives and daughters of a number of clans, that had delivered one of the most sweeping challenges to colonial authority in living memory among the Igbo at the time when Achebe was writing. In fact, it was this event which motivated the British government to give research grants to several "amateur" colonial anthropologists to study Igbo society specifically. These studies produced the spate of early anthropological accounts Achebe satirizes in his reference to the district commissioner's projected book, *The Pacification of the Primitive Tribes of the Lower Niger.*[3]

One sees the consequence of this selective process in one situation in the novel which in my opinion would have been richer had Achebe paid closer attention to women's political structures within Igbo society. When Okonkwo is forced to flee to his motherland after committing the female crime of manslaughter, he is given a lecture by his maternal uncle on the importance of the feminine principle in Igbo culture. Okonkwo, who can only define masculinity in relation to what his father was not, is understandably out of his depth when asked to accept a notion that his identity may also be formed by qualities represented by his mother. But because we as readers have no sense of the full range of qualities, both protective and assertive, that are associated with the feminine principle in Igbo society, we are given as few options as Okonkwo in interpreting the scene. We know that he should be patient and dependent and grateful for the protection of his motherland. We also know that in spiritual terms the earth goddess, Ani, is the deity Okonkwo has most often offended and that she is responsible for his exile. However, we have no way of knowing that female power symbolized by Ani is represented in the clan by a system of legal codes and practices controlled by the women in Okonkwo's society, that, in a sense, Okonkwo's refusal to be comforted by his motherland is also a rejection of aspects of the very civic culture by which his access to the privileges of manhood is partially regulated. Much of this would seem to be implied in Achebe's presentation of this scene but there is none of the rich working out of all the implications that occurs elsewhere in the unfolding of masculine systems of values and authority.

Achebe's selective use of those aspects of Igbo traditional society which best coincide with Western/Christian social values speak ably to his own need to establish a view of a world, both modern and traditional, of which he can be a part. To call this treatment of the formation of a masculine sense of identity sexist is a facile and not very accurate reading of a gendered response to a specific cultural dilemma. That Achebe's narrative is indeed a selective, gendered one which partakes of both traditional and Judeo-Christian patriarchal values only becomes a problem in the light of the history of *Things Fall Apart*'s reception as the definitive, "objective" account of the Igbo, not to say African, traditional past. In expanding a hypothetical paragraph in a district commissioner's text into the saga of a lost civilization, Achebe was able to address imaginatively the nostalgia, social insecurity, and nationalist sentiments of an entire continent. The problem is that he succeeded so well that his representation of the past has become a substitute for the reality which, inevitably, is far more complex than one novel could hope to make it. The result is that, like the institutions it helped debunk, Achebe's text has itself become the object of deconstructive exercises in the work of more recent Nigerian writers. In the work of Buchi Emecheta, Achebe's chapters (or, perhaps, extended paragraphs?) on the position of women in Igbo society have been revised to offer a complete alternative vision of the attitudes of traditional women to their status in the society. It is a partisan and revisionist picture, committed to challenging Igbo and Judeo-Christian values from the perspective of an upwardly mobile fellow traveler in the women's movement. However it, too, must resist the temptation to limit the roles it ascribes to women in traditional society to those "invented" by Achebe. Indeed, for the modern woman writer in Africa, Achebe's authority must seem as compelling and as difficult to challenge as the district commissioner's voice must have been for Achebe in his time.

This irony serves to remind us that literature, like anthropology or history, is a form of selective representation, replete with its inherent assumptions about authenticity and objectivity. For those of us who teach *Things Fall Apart* as an appendix to anthropological and sociological documents, or as a way of bringing history to life, it is important to keep in mind that this particular fiction is a response to history which mimics the structure and claims to objectivity of science without for a moment abdicating its right as fiction to be selective, subjective, or unrealistic. Those of us who teach *Things Fall Apart* as literature in the hope of reaffirming traditional values may do well to bear in mind that the values we discover in the text will be most likely our own.

Achebe's novel is a brilliant resolution of the conflict experienced by his generation between traditional and Western notions of manhood, courage, and the construction of communal values. Such resolution is seldom if ever about choosing between two clearly defined alternatives and inevitably involves a process of selection. When our students accuse Achebe of sexism or Emecheta of historical inaccuracy, what their statements really attest is the creation for better or worse of an African literary canon based on a highly selective system of values shared by Achebe and his cohort of African intellectuals that has come to be used as a way of reading history: a touchstone for the literature as well as for the society of the postcolonial age. Time, perhaps, to rename *Things Fall Apart—Things Are Consolidated?*

Notes

I am indebted to Bernth Lindfors, editor of the MLA *Handbook on Critical Approaches to the Teaching of "Things Fall Apart"* for permission to reproduce in this article a modified version of my essay for that volume: "Making Men and History: Achebe and the Politics of Revisionism in *Things Fall Apart*." All page numbers in the text refer to the edition in the African Writers Series (1962).

1. Achebe's comments on Western writers' views of Africa are well known. His most sustained critique of Conrad is the essay "An Image of Africa," first published as part of the Chancellor's Lecture Series, 1974–1975, pp. 31–43, at the University of Massachusetts at Amherst.

2. M. E. N. Njaka lists *umuada* as one of the names for daughters "in their capacity as a women's council. Their duty is to guard against anything that may disturb the orderly nature of Igbo cultural life, particularly when things are not normal and there are violations of the constitution (*Igbo Political Culture* [Evanston: Northwestern University Press, 1974], p. 158). Njaka lists the Women's Rebellion of 1929 and the Women's Riots of 1957 as two well-known instances of violent political action taken by *umuada* in a range of eastern communities, but cites also the intervention of one *umuada* as late as 1961 to discipline corrupt politicians in the 1961 elections. Njaka sees the *umuada* as "potentially the most powerful organ in the state. Despite this power, however, the Umuada are said to be like mothers—always lenient and not so fierce

as they sound" (124). It is this dual aspect of their political character—as both tender and terrifying—which seems to be obscured by Achebe's selective portrayal of women's roles.

3. Sylvia Leith-Ross's *African Women: A Study of the Ibo of Nigeria* (London: Faber and Faber, 1939) is the best known of these anthropological studies. It contains an extensive preface explaining how both government and private research foundations came to take a specific interest in Igbo women after the Aba riots of 1929. Other studies of the region undertaken in the wake of the riots include Margery Perham's *Native Administration in Nigeria* (London: Oxford University Press, 1937), C. K. Meek's *Law and Authority in a Nigerian Tribe* (London: Oxford University Press, 1937), G. T. Basden's *Niger Ibos* (London: Seely, 1938), and M. M. Green's *Igbo Village Affairs: Chiefly with Reference to the Village of Umueke Agbaja* (1947; reprint, London: Cass, 1964).

Okonkwo and His Mother

Things Fall Apart *and Issues of Gender in the Constitution of African Postcolonial Discourse*

BIODUN JEYIFO

◆　◆　◆

In the oral tradition, we often do not know
whether the storyteller who thought up a particular story was a man or a woman. Of course
when one examines the recorded texts, one might
wonder whether a myth or story doesn't serve
particular interests in a given society.

—Mineke Schipper

The Chielo-Ezinma episode is an important subplot of the novel and actually reads like a suppressed larger story circumscribed by the exploration of Okonkwo's/man's struggle with and for
his people. In the troubled world of *Things Fall
Apart*, motherhood and femininity are the unifying, mitigating principles, the lessons for Africa
and the world.

—Carole Boyce Davies

So Okonkwo encouraged the boys to sit with him
in his *obi*, and he told them stories of the land—
masculine stories of violence and bloodshed.
Nwoye knew that it was right to be masculine
and to be violent, but somehow he still preferred
the stories that his mother used to tell him, and
which she no doubt still told to her younger children—stories of tortoise and his wily ways, and
of the bird *eneke-nti-oba* who challenged the
whole world to a wrestling contest and was finally thrown by the cat. . . . That was the kind

of story that Nwoye loved. But he now knew that
they were for foolish women and children, and
he knew that his father wanted him to be a man.
And so he *feigned* that he no longer cared for
women's stories.

—Chinua Achebe, *Things Fall Apart*
(my emphasis)

O KONKWO'S *mother?* Within the total narrative space of *Things Fall Apart*,[1] there is only one direct, substantive mention of our hero's mother. As far as I know, this has never been formally registered in the extensive discussions and commentaries on the novel, let alone critically explored, and this seems quite consistent with the author's more evident interest in the complex, tortured relationship of Okonkwo with his father and, later in the concluding sections of the novel, with his son Nwoye. As Carole Boyce Davies remarks in the article from which the second epigraph to this essay was extrapolated, in *Things Fall Apart* Achebe's "primary concern is woman's place within larger social and political forces" (247) which are, in the order of things, the spheres of male initiative and control.

And yet the single, brief mention of Okonkwo's mother is extraordinarily suggestive both for reading Okonkwo's particular brand of misogyny and neurotic masculinist personality and for analyzing larger questions of the author's construction of male subjectivity and identity in the novel. This "new" reading would indeed be a *rereading* whose condition of possibility derives from the manifold feminist project that is such a decisive, perhaps the most decisive, current of postcolonial critical discourse at the present time.[2] In this short essay, I shall examine this one substantive reference to Okonkwo's mother in fairly close detail, hoping to deploy this close textual exegesis as a bridgehead to a more general discussion of gender-related issues in the constitution of a postcolonial African critical discourse. I shall be arguing in effect that between Achebe's "undertextualization" of Okonkwo's mother and a feminist rereading of the novel, which would foreground her and relocate the "motherlore" she represents in the intense gender politics of the novel, we encounter an instance of the fundamental challenge posed by issues of gender in postcolonial criticism and scholarship. The point has been repeatedly made that the *nationalist* "master texts" of African postcolonial literature, *needed*, as the basis of their self-constitution as *representative*, canonical works, to subsume gender difference under the putatively more primary racial and cultural difference of a resisting Africa from a colonizing Europe.[3] By this occlusion of gender difference, Okonkwo's mother, his wives, and daughters recede into the *ground* which enables the *figure* of Okonkwo and his father and son to achieve their representational prominence. But beyond this "programmatic" undertextualization of Okonkwo's mother, *Things Fall Apart*, as a powerful work of realistic fiction, could not fail to inscribe the effects of sexual difference and gender politics within the very "overtextualization" of "men's affairs" in the novel, this being the social totality of the precolonial order as it comes into contact with the invading colonial capitalism. This has an important *political* lesson: national liberation in Africa, as long as it remains a historic agenda enforced by neocolonial dependency and arrested decolonization,[4] and as it is profoundly inflected by new postnationalist discourses and cultural production, must reconfigure its founding moment as not irredeemably marked by an inevitable, *natural* sexism.

THE ALLUSION TO OKONKWO'S MOTHER occurs in chapter nine of the novel; significantly, she is not named. The precise narrative moment seems, on the surface, of no particular thematic noteworthiness: three days after his participation in the ritual murder of the youth Ikemefuna, his "adopted" son, Okonkwo is just beginning to emerge from the emotional and spiritual trauma of that event. Characteristically, it irks him that he has indeed been weak and "unmanly" enough to have succumbed to the trauma. Indeed the whole episode lasts one short paragraph and can thus be quoted entirely:

For the first time in three nights, Okonkwo slept. He woke up once in the middle of the night and his mind went back to the past three days without making him feel uneasy. He began to wonder why he felt uneasy at all. It was like a man wondering in broad daylight why a dream had appeared so terrible to him at night. He stretched himself and scratched his thigh where a mosquito had bitten him as he slept. Another one was wailing near his right ear. He slapped the ear and hoped he had killed it. Why do they always go for one's ears? When he was a child his mother had told him a story about it. *But it was as silly as all women's stories.* Mosquito, she had said, had asked Ear to marry him, whereupon she fell on the floor in uncontrollable laughter. "How much longer do you think you will live?" she asked. "You are already a skeleton." Mosquito went away humiliated, and anytime he passed her way he told Ear that he was still alive. (53; my emphasis)

It is significant that in the very next sentence after this recalled story we are told: "Okonkwo turned on his side and went back to sleep." Like the mosquito bite which presumably worried his brief wakeful moment within a restful sleep only as a very minor irritation, Okonkwo's memory of his mother's stories in his childhood is very easily suppressed, and it is easily consigned to the domain of "silly women's stories." This seems quite consistent with the larger pattern of intrafamilial and intergenerational conflicts elaborated in the novel: Okonkwo's relationship with his father, and later his relationship with his son, Nwoye, are foregrounded over relationships with his nameless mother, his wives, and his daughters. From a feminist perspective, this, more than anything else, reveals the male-centeredness of Achebe in this novel. While this is incontrovertible, it is only part of the story, and it barely scratches the surface of the complex and ambiguous gender politics of the text of *Things Fall Apart*. This point needs some elaboration.

As the third of the epigraphs to this essay indicates, Okonkwo's son, Nwoye, unlike his father, does not succeed in completely repressing either the memory of *his* mother's stories or their pow-

erful, subliminal hold on his imagination and psyche. Consequently, he has to *feign* a "manly" indifference to this motherlore.
Okonkwo, by contrast, seems to have succeeded completely in a
willed amnesia of his mother's creative role in the formation of
his personhood, his sensibility. Indeed the precise nature of this
willed amnesia is awesome: while his father, Unoka, perpetually
figures in both his psyche and his vigilant, conscious mind as an
active, powerful (if negative) presence, Okonkwo's mother is assimilated into the neutral, abstract function of "mothers in general." For Okonkwo, his mother's stories and their significations
evaporate into the generalized phallogocentric rubric of the "sil-
liness" of motherlore. The catch in all of this is that neither this
particular story, nor the many other women's stories given in
Things Fall Apart, is silly; rather, in almost every instance, these
stories are only deceptively simple and are usually of extraordi-
nary emblematic, subversive resonance to the central narrative of
Okonkwo's obsession with his father and his sons.[5] A close look
at Okonkwo's mother's story and its narrative of the fractious,
bitter liaison between Ear and Mosquito illustrates this point well.

Perhaps the most arresting detail in this story is the structure
of reversals of gender hierarchy between the respective female
and male personas in the tale. Thus Ear, the female persona, is
the dominant, supercilious agent in the conflict. Mosquito, the
male suitor, not only figures as an atrophied, diminished, "inadequate" phallus; the very manner and terms of his rejection strike
deep: loss of vital powers unto death ("You are already a skeleton"!). Since this tale is told by Okonkwo's mother and thus
belongs in *motherlore*, we can surmise that Mosquito here encodes
the male's neurotic fear of female power as the nemesis of male
potency and life force. Putative female superiority in this vertical
structure is compounded by Ear's additional figuration in traditional mythological anthropomorphism of the body and its organs as *both* male and female, as Trinh T. Minh-ha tells us in her
book *Woman, Native, Other*:

> As a wise Dogon elder [Ogotemmeli] pointed out, "issuing from
> a woman's sexual part, the Word enters another sexual part,

namely the ear" (the ear is considered to be bisexual, the auricle being male and the auditory aperture, female). (127)

The embodiment of abstract female power in this system of significations is particularly noteworthy in the way that it combines both "male" and "female" principles and their elaborated attributes and values. This, however, is a structure unperceived by Okonkwo and is indeed alien to his rigid, overliteral conceptions of the "masculine" ideals.

Is it of little or no consequence to the gender politics in the text of *Things Fall Apart* that abstract female power represented by the Ear and abstract male identity represented by the Mosquito are so vastly unequal in suppleness, vitality, and resonance? In other words, is this story, told by Okonkwo's mother and with all its powerfully resonating meanings, a mere narrative detail, a figural embellishment of the text bearing little relevance to the central conflict of Okonkwo's masculinist personhood, which is lodged elsewhere, that is, with the father and the Law of the Father?

There is absolutely no question that this tale of Okonkwo's mother, obviously drawn from the vast repository of motherlore, is centrally linked to Achebe's critical construction of Okonkwo's masculinist personality as this is conflictually played out, first with his father, then with his son. And this is all of one piece with the overabundant inscription in the novel of its protagonist's obsession with *maleness*. and his corresponding fear of and suppression of *femaleness*. However, the major interpretive problem that we confront here seems to be that while *femaleness* as we encounter it in Okonkwo's mother's tale is a superior, stronger entity, which confronts male identity with belittlement and insecurity, femaleness, as Okonkwo encodes it is the exact opposite: weakness, fecklessness, cowardice, irresoluteness, sentimentality. In effect this means that in the light of Okonkwo's peculiar construction of "female" attributes, the pesonas of his mother's tale would be reversed: Ear would represent male superiority and Mosquito would represent female shrewishness. But this hardly resolves this issue, as long as Okonkwo operates as an isolated figure removed from the social context of his Umofia community. Moreover, given Okonkwo's excessively literal phallocratic imagination, it would be as much of an absurdity to represent "maleness" by an orifice in the body as it would be to represent "femaleness" by the mosquito with its broomstick figure. Nothing reveals this crude, physical phallicism more than the fact that the gun, the machete, and the cudgel (for wife beating and child beating), three overliteral extensions of an aggressive, neurotic, masculinist identity, are Okonkwo's ultimate answers to any and all crises. We see this in several incidents in the novel: the beating of his second wife during Peace Week; the severe beating of his son, Nwoye, when the unhappy youth was spotted among the new community of Christian converts; and the climactic moment of the novel, which results in Okonkwo's beheading of the first in the line of the advancing party of the hirelings of the colonial administration who have come to break up the village assembly at the end of the novel. 7

This problem of Okonkwo's negative transvaluation of female strength and superiority in his mother's tale to weakness and inferiority, however, disappears once we place Okonkwo in the context and nexus of his society's moral economy and symbolic codes.[6] This is a historically and culturally constructed context; it is a precapitalist, prefeudal social formation in which, as amply demonstrated in Ifi Amadiume's *Male Daughters, Female Husbands*, "maleness" or "femaleness," the categories "man" or "woman," do not operate as rigidly divided, biologically literal, or ontological entities.[7] And Achebe's realist integrity renders this structure felicitously. Indeed *Things Fall Apart* not only has one of the most extensive and dense novelistic inscriptions of the *genderization* of subjectivity, signification, and social space in postcolonial African fiction; the novel's overcoded inscription of the processes of engendering is massively fractured and ambiguous and cannot be read as a simple, unambiguous inscription of phallocratic dominance. Let me cite only one composite group of these ambiguous inscriptions of gender and gender relations in the present context. Thus, on the one hand, Okonkwo's representation of "femaleness" as weakness and irresoluteness seems to have validation in the division of cognitive and perceptual categories in his society, which ascribes the designation "female" to smaller crops like the cocoyam and the designation "male" to bigger crops like the yam, a system which also describes an "ochu" (abomination) as either "female" or "male," depending on the degree of threat or destabilization to the social order that it poses. But on the other hand, the same panoply of symbolic values and cognitive codes describes as "female" the most important deity in the religion and sacred lore of the community (Ani), making her priest *male* (Ezeani); conversely, the important deity of the Oracle of the Hills and the Caves is male while his highest functionary is the *priestess* Chielo.

On a different but related note, it is important to stress the limits of a psychologistic reading of the relationship of Okonkwo to his parents and his sons and daughters, which might fasten one-sidedly on his relations with his father and later with his son. It is indeed tempting to read an Oedipalization in the fact that almost everything that we are told about Unoka, Okonkwo's father, can be symbolically assimilated to the figure of Mosquito in the mother's story. By this reading, the driving fear of "femaleness" in Okonkwo's psyche is thus really both "guilt" for the father's fate of "mosquito" vitiation and eventual "death," and strong identification with and "possession" of the mother. But this is purely speculative and a rather sterile and fanciful, if fascinating, line of critical inquiry. Okonkwo both loathes the memory of his father and represses the lore of his mother; in the process he distorts both the "masculine" and the "feminine," by keeping them rigidly apart and by the ferocity of his war on the "feminine." His son, on the other hand, only *feigns* acceptance of this rigid masculinist code, but keeps alive the memory of motherlore in his conflicted, sorrowing consciousness. One crucial difference between father and son takes us beyond the purely psychologistic. This is the fact that the driving, all-consuming ambition of Okonkwo to be one of "the lords of the land," to take the highest title which only few men (and no women) ever manage to achieve within the course of several generations, this ambition in the service of material interests and social recognition of the highest kind is absent in the son. Throughout the course

of the novel, the evolving moral and spiritual sympathi-
Nwoye move him away from such worldly sights to identifica
with the unprotected and "unprotectable" of his culture, th
immiserated by the contradictory codes and practices of his society. We can indeed say that within the gendered scale of valu-
ations and representations by which Okonkwo seeks to establish
the greatest possible distance between himself and his father's
"effeminacy," his son Nwoye is "feminized": he refuses Okonkwo's
interpellative call to be a "man" contemptuous of "female" attributes. This important distance between father and son is elo-
quently but succinctly captured in the economy of the following
short passage:

> The missionary ignored him and went on to talk about the
> Holy Trinity. At the end of it Okonkwo was fully convinced
> that the man was mad. He shrugged his shoulders and went
> away to tap his afternoon palm-wine. But there was a young
> lad who had been captivated. His name was Nwoye, Okonkwo's
> first son. It was not the mad logic of the Trinity that captivated
> him. He did not understand it. It was the poetry of the new
> religion, something felt in the marrow. The hymn about broth-
> ers who sat in darkness and fear seemed to answer a vague
> and persistent question that haunted his young soul in the
> question of twins crying in the bush and the question of Ike-
> mefuna who was killed. He felt a relief within as the hymn
> poured into his parched soul. The words of the hymn were
> like the drops of frozen rain melting on the dry plate of the
> panting earth. Nwoye's callow mind was greatly puzzled. (103)

In the first epigraph to this essay, Mineke Schipper raises the
important question of the gendered provenience of stories and
fictions in the precolonial oral traditions and the particular interests which such gender origins might serve. This question is
at the heart of one of the major issues in African critical discourse
at the present time: the project of reclaiming a separate, distinct
tradition of African female writing and criticism which is not
easily, indeed, *will not be* subsumed within the male-dominant tra-

dition which, to date, has claimed to speak for the *whole* of African literary and critical traditions. It is impossible to take a full measure of this project without realizing that its objective is not merely to "correct" the stereotypes and misconceptions of the male-centered writers and critics, and not merely, in the words of the editor in the *African Literature Today* issue on "Women," that African women now seek "to take their stand by their men,"[8] but rather to reclaim "women's stories" (herstory) from the void or repressed zones into which men and male-centeredness had consigned them. For just as the nationalist anticolonial counterdiscourse in literature and criticism once had to rewrite and reinvent a *presence* that colonialist discourse, in its arrogance, imposture, and triumphalism, had theorized as absence, so also women writers and critics have to recover the submerged female tradition. What contemporary African feminist criticism at this level of self-authorization adumbrates is a return to *female* sources within Cabral's famous call for a return to "the source," or more radically, female sources as *the* source. In other words, the identification of creative female precursors or foremothers, and of discrete intertextual revision and influence between female and female-centered writers and critics, defines the most radical autonomization of gender difference in feminist African criticism at the present time. Particularly powerful instances of this expression are Chikwenye Ogunyemi's "The Dynamics of the Contemporary Black Female Novel in English" and an important essay by Florence Stratton, which I now examine in the context of our reflections in this essay.

In "Periodic Embodiments: A Ubiquitous Trope in African Men's Writing," a trenchant critique of the male-dominant tradition of postcolonial African writing, Florence Stratton has uncovered, as few other feminist critical writings have, the depth of the male-centeredness or phallocentrism of this tradition. According to Stratton, this male-dominant, male-centered tradition, given the fact and consequences of historic colonization, has been largely constructed around woman as the "embodiment" of the male writers' vision of the new African nation in all its changing historical experience, from colonial humiliations and anticolonial struggles to the postcolonial agony of neocolonialism and virtual recolonization. Furthermore, Stratton avers that in making these "periodic embodiments" of woman as ideal symbol and representation of the nation, male writers have basically assumed that man is the visionary, the artist, the maker of the history of the nation, and woman the sign (of national or racial integrity, resistance, and sovereignty) mobilized by male creativity, initiative, and revolutionary will. Perhaps the most telling point of Stratton's forceful argument in this article is the view that this deeply phallocratic assumption goes beyond its usual identification with the conservative current of the anticolonial and postcolonial African male writer's idealization of woman as the repository of cultural "essence" (what Stratton calls "the pot of culture" syndrome). Beyond this mostly Negritudist romantic nostalgic idealization, Stratton also assimilates male writers of a more radical anti-imperialist, even antisexist vision and sensibility, like Sembene or Ngugi, to this whole tradition of "periodic embodiment." This critique in effect implicates virtually *all* male African writers and critics.

What this line of polemic and projection indicates is, I believe, that feminist criticism, even when it critically engages and contests both imperialist domination and post-independence misrule in the context of the postcolonial state, will not be content with how women are positively depicted by certain "progressive" male writers, that is, with regard to "accuracy," "sympathy," or "solidarity" with female oppression and resistance to it. The stakes, it seems, are much higher: women are no less visionary and creative, and no less makers of history and shapers of experience than men; "women's issues" will no longer be subsumed into a supposed "broader" framework of national or racial collectivity defined and legitimized by men. And perhaps Stratton's most provocative thesis in this article is the implicit, subtextual *uterocentrism* of her suggestion that men's denial or erasure of women's initiative and power is a product, and a projection, of a fundamental male anxiety and insecurity about femaleness and its putative *primal* connection to creativity.[9] By the light of this particular uterocentric critique of *all* male writers and critics, we have to look

beyond the so-called strategic, programmatic suspension of gender difference in the name of a unified resistance to foreign *racial*
domination for the deeper causes of the marginalization of
women, as characters, writers, and critics, which enabled the constitution of postcolonial African literature and critical discourse
as an engendered tradition. We also have to go beyond the excuse
that colonial educational policies being what they were, women
simply weren't there in that great moment of "awakening" when
modern African literatures and critical discourses began to stake
their claims against outright European colonialist disavowals and
"post-imperial," neoliberal condescending universalism.[10] The
deeper, more daunting cause, Stratton suggests, is perennial male
anxiety and fear of femaleness as *the* source of creation and creativity. While I think we should ultimately reject this uterocentrism and the considerable obfuscations and mystifications to which
it could give rise, I suggest that there are eminent political and
hermeneutic considerations which demand that we do not simply
dismiss it out of hand. Again let us turn to our rereading of
Okonkwo and his mother for a brief elaboration of this point.

Okonkwo's repression of motherlore and the significations embedded in his mother's tale of the Ear and the Mosquito would
seem to support this thesis of deep-rooted male insecurity about
and fear of female power and creativity, with the corresponding
need or will to tame it, domesticate it, marginalize it, and project
it as the gift and vocation of a few "exceptional" women who are
thus, like Chielo in *Things Fall Apart*, "honorary men." It would
thus seem that the need and impulse for men to "colonize"
women, to identify with the "master" subject position elaborated
in Hegel's famous master-slave dialectic, runs very very deep and
is reproducible across different social formations. It is in connection with this problem that the discourses of African feminist
writing and criticism on a "double yoke" and a "double colonization," where African women's creativity is concerned, poses a
great challenge to male writers and critics. We must remember
that no colonization is ever given up easily, voluntarily, in "a fit
of absent-mindedness."

It remains to state that for this radical feminist critique to be an effective intervention in postcolonial African critical discourse, it is important to disentangle biological, literal *maleness* from male-centeredness or phallocentrism as this involves elaborate signifying, perceptual, and representational orders which make man the center and ground of reason, intellect, and will. One is born *into* and not *with* these codes already in place in the genes, and one has a choice either to, on the one hand, enter unproblematically, willingly, or opportunistically into them or, on the other hand, begin to study them, understand them ever more fully and consciously, and help to destabilize or overthrow them. What Molara Ogundipe-Leslie once said about women and biology applies equally to men:

> True, the biological identity of a woman counts and is real. But woman, contrary to what some men [and most] think, is more than "a biological aperture," as Anaïs Nin said. Woman's biology is indeed an important and necessary aspect of her, but it is not all she is and it should not be used to limit her. (5)

The distinction that Lacan makes, as Gayle Rubin informs us, between the "function of the father" and a particular man who embodies that function is useful here: particular men may refuse to embody and actualize this function as phallocratic values define and consecrate that function.[11] If, as Nancy Chodorow has argued, "mothering" is reproduced by technologies of gender erected by patriarchy as it combines with different modes of production, no less is "fatherhood" so produced and reproduced, even if as the more privileged term of a patriarchal relational structure. Nwoye's memory of his mother's stories, his preference for "women's stories," and his merely feigned and not actual acceptance of a phallocratic erasure of motherlore all reveal the possibility of a breach between maleness as biology and maleness as either a consenting or a resisting response to the interpellations of neocolonial, patriarchal neocapitalism.

This last point opens up for critical inquiry and research priorities the overdetermined spaces in which both female creativity and transformative initiative, and the divergent male responses to them, are played out. Okonkwo, as we have seen, struggles against colonial conquest and a nascent imperialist domination, but with an aggressively masculinist personality and its deep alienations. Largely on account of this contradiction, his resistance is futile. This point has an emblematic pertinence to present antinomies of postcolonial critical discourse, for what Okonkwo could not have perceived, we have inherited: colonial definitions and codifications of rights, duties, and responsibilities not only divided colonizers from the colonized, but they also separated surrogate "native" rulers from their "native" subjects and "native men in general" from "native women in general." African male-centered writers and critics should take this lesson to heart as they create a "national" literature which, if not a mere appendage, a mere extension of metropolitan European traditions, is nonetheless imbricated in deeply gendered alienations and reifications whose genealogical roots go back to colonialism.

This lesson applies equally to Okonkwo's son, Nwoye, who, although he symbolically disavows the nationalist-masculine ethic that is embodied in his father's personality and doomed resistance, nevertheless goes over to the colonizers and more or less embraces the colonialist ideology of the "civilizing mission." It is not overstating the case to observe that his "feminization" does not lead him to an adequate, critical comprehension of the invading colonial project. The historic separations consummated by colonial capitalism divided fathers and sons and "native" men from "native" women, but it also separated arriviste "*assimiles*" from the rest of the "native" population and a small but structurally significant group of middle-class women from their subaltern, disenfranchised "sisters."[12]

EVEN THOUGH ITS MOST IMPORTANT project lies elsewhere—in constructing a tradition of women's creativity in orature and literature with roots going back to precolonial society—it is a permanent task of feminist literary criticism and scholarship to contest and delegitimize the "undertextualization" of women and "women's affairs" in the mostly male-authored writings which claim to speak on behalf of the "nation," the continent, the "Black world." An ancillary task in this respect is the interrogation of the appropriation of "woman" as idealized "embodiment" of male-authored and male-centered myths and fictions of national resistance or racial pride: women's bodies will no longer passively bear the marks of opportunistic, mystifying idealizations which help to obscure the oppressions and wrongs done to real women. In this essay, I have argued, rather self-consciously as a male, leftist critic, for a task to complement, not "complete," these projects of contemporary African literary-critical feminism(s): the uncovering of such divergent, conflicting constructions of "maleness" as we have identified in Okonkwo and his son, Nwoye, in *Things Fall Apart*. The motivation behind this enterprise bears restating: to reconfigure the nationalist silencing and repressing of gender difference as deeply fractured, bearing the very marks of this repression in the failures and contradictions of national liberation in the post-independence epoch in Africa. This reconfiguration allows us to rewrite national liberation as a historic phenomenon with a greater complexity in issues of gender and gender politics than a benighted, categorical phallocentrism.[13] This is underscored by Carole Boyce Davies's words in the second epigraph to this essay: "In the troubled world of *Things Fall Apart*, motherhood and femininity are the unifying, mitigating principles, the lessons for Africa and the world."

This "lesson" apparently eluded Fanon's otherwise penetrating critique of the ideology of the national liberation movement in Africa as evidenced in the celebrated text titled "The Pitfalls of National Consciousness," the most widely debated chapter of *The Wretched of the Earth*. In that text, Fanon's desperate and prophetic warnings mostly addressed class and ethnic contradictions of nationalism and registered a deafening silence on questions of gender. But Fanon's critique does not exhaust the intellectual legacy of radical, insightful criticism of national liberation in Africa. We have also, among others, the legacy of Cabral and the liberation movements of the Portuguese ex-colonies. Lars Rudebeck, in his seminal work on Cabral and the PAIGC, *Guinea-Bissau: A Study in Political Mobilization*, has written:

In the final analysis, Cabral seems to have viewed the anti-imperialist struggle very much as a cultural struggle—as a people's struggle to reconquer its right to a place in history. ... The most important specific example of cultural struggle possible to discern within the total struggle and distinguishable from the school system is probably the systematic emphasis given by the PAIGC to the problem of female emancipation. This does not mean that the struggle for female emancipation is not integrated with the total struggle, nor does it mean that it is not an important part of the general educational task of the schools. It only means that this problem has been considered important enough in its own right to be singled out for specific attention in the concrete political practice of the PAIGC. (225)

Things Fall Apart occupies, if only in a fractured, ambiguous manner, a similar conceptual, ideological space of radical nationalist ideology in Africa. And it is a space which has been considerably expanded in postcolonial African fiction, by Achebe himself in *Anthills of the Savannah*, and by other male writers like Ousmane Sembene, Nuruddin Farah, Femi Osofisan, and Ngugi wa Thiong'o. Indeed, it is the accumulated energy of this entire tradition that powers the savage satirical indictment of the sexual exploitation of women as a fundamentally constitutive part of the callow, boastful, collective masculinist identity of the arriviste, compradorial bourgeoisie of neocolonial Kenya in Ngugi's *Devil on the Cross*. Male critics and theorists who wish to seriously engage feminism must critically reclaim this tradition.

Notes

1. *Things Fall Apart* (London: Heinemann, 1958). All subsequent citations are from this edition and appear parenthetically in the text.

2. This is to be measured primarily in the number and quality of critical interventions by women in postcolonial debates of the last decade and a half. This "feminization" of the discipline, however, exceeds mere body count; its major effect has been to make us rethink some of the ruling concepts and paradigms of the field of postcoloniality: "nation"

and "canon," representation and subjectivity. This essay is an initial attempt to productively engage aspects of these interventions.

3. On this point it is instructive to reexamine the documents of the two historic Negro Writers Conferences, Paris 1956 and Rome 1959. Present at these conferences were the most prominent African, African-American, and Afro-Caribbean writers and intellectuals, predominantly male, many of whom were later to become the core of the political and intellectual elites of Africa, the Caribbean, and post–Civil Rights Afro-America. It is now widely accepted that the perspectives authorized and the agenda defined by these two conferences were decisive in the constitution of nationalist and Pan-Africanist postcolonial discourses, but with scant recognition of how deeply gendered and male-dominant these were. In the *Proceedings* of the Paris Conference there is a photograph of the participants; out of some fifty-five persons, only one is a woman. The *Proceedings* of the Rome Conference lists some sixty members of a rather large "Executive Council" (of the "Society of African Culture" instituted by the conference) of which only three are women. The 1956 documents in fact contain a "Message from the Negro Women" which is remarkable only in how unremarkable it is. The strong suspicion that it was probably drafted by some of the male organizers of the conference is reinforced by the obvious factitiousness of sentiments in the "message" like the following: "Can you cite a single *Negro man of culture* who in his writings has not exalted the Negro woman, the Mother?" The "Negro man of culture" was the then-current Francophone-derived term for the African, African-American, and Afro-Caribbean artist and intellectual considered as a "representative" of the race. The documents from these conferences and the tropes and topoi of discourse they inscribed and enshrined for a long time consolidated the "representative" figure of the postcolonial artist, intellectual, or nationalist statesman as ineluctably male. See *Presence Africaine* (1956, 1959).

4. On the subject of arrested decolonization see Jeyifo, "The Nature of Things."

5. Barbara Harlow in *Resistance Literature* deploys one of these "women's stories" in *Things Fall Apart* as an "allegory for an African strategy for independence" (xv).

6. On the notion of a "moral economy," see James C. Scott (1976).

7. I hasten to add that this thesis is not uniformly applicable to all of precolonial African social formations. The feudal and semifeudal centralized states of the Sahel and the Western Sudan obviously entailed considerable division and hierarchization of gender differences. Indeed

Ifi Amadiume errs in more or less generalizing her thesis to all of African societies and cultures.

8. Introduction, *Women in African Literature Today* 2.

9. There is of course an extensive, elaborate critical and theoretical discourse on the metaphorization of the womb as *the* ultimate site of creation and creativity, far more potent and superior to typical male-originated metaphors of creativity. The following exhortation from Anais Nin is representative: "All that happens in the real womb, not in the womb fabricated by man as a substitute.... woman's creation far from being like man's must be exactly like her creation of children, that is, it must come out of her own blood, englobed by her womb, nourished by her own milk. It must be a human creation of flesh, it must be different from man's abstraction." Consider Trinh T. Minh-ha's comment on this statement of Anais Nin: "Man is not content with referring to his creation as his child, he is also keen on appropriating the life-giving act of child-bearing. Images of men 'in labor' and 'giving birth' to poems, essays and books abound in literature. Such an encroachment on woman's domain has been considered natural, for the writer is said to be either genderless or bisexual" (37). On this *uterocentrism* I have two comments to make, rather self-consciously as a male critic. First, uterocentrism courts, and even sometimes embraces, the occultation of gynocritics considered as a perceptible female aesthetic. Second, however, it is not impossible for this mystique to coexist with very progressive, socially conscious works of literature, theater, or film. Nana, the matriarch of Julie Dash's acclaimed *Daughters of the Dust*, says: "The ancestors and the womb, they are the same." This connects with the strain of the over mythologization of history and memory in the film, a strain not incompatible with the film's equally powerful secular and demythologizing exploration of the violent clashes of the contending sacred narratives and epistemologies in the Gullah community.

10. Achebe's critique of neoliberal universalism in "Colonialist Criticism," dated as a timely response, a contextual intervention at the originary moment of the "Commonwealth Literature" rubric, remains pertinent. See his *Morning Yet On Creation Day*.

11. Gayle Rubin, "The Traffic in Women: Notes on the 'Political Economy' of Sex."

12. On this point consider the fact that the "sisterhood" which binds the griot woman, Farmata, to Ramatoulaye, the middle-class protagonist of Mariama Ba's novel *So Long a Letter*, is compounded by strong structures

of class and caste inequalities. For the influence of colonial French education on Mariama Ba's views on women and education, see Riesz.

13. For very informative analyses of national liberation and gender politics in various locations in the Third World see Evelyne Accad, "Sexuality and Sexual Politics: Conflicts and Contradictions for Contemporary Women in the Middle East"; Angela Gilliam, "Women's Equality and National Liberation"; and Nayereh-Tohidi, "Gender and Islamic Fundamentalism: Feminist Politics in Iran," all in Mohanty, Russo, and Torres, *Third World Women and the Politics of Feminism.* See also Cobham.

Works Cited

Accad, Evelyne. "Sexuality and Sexual Politics: Conflicts and Contradictions for Contemporary Women in the Middle East." In *Third World Women and the Politics of Feminism,* edited by Chandra T. Mohanty, Ann Russo, and Lourdes Torres, 237–50. Bloomington: Indiana University Press, 1991.

Achebe, Chinua. *Things Fall Apart.* London: Heinemann, 1962.

———. "Colonialist Criticism." In Achebe, *Morning Yet on Creation Day,* 3–18. New York: Doubleday, 1975.

Amadiume, Ifi. *Male Daughters, Female Husbands: Gender and Sex in an African Society.* London: Zed, 1989.

Chodorow, Nancy. *The Reproduction of Mothering: Psychoanalysis and the Sociology of Gender.* Berkeley: University of California Press, 1978.

Cobham, Rhonda. "Boundaries of the Nation, Boundaries of the Self: African Nationalist Fictions and Nuruddin Farah's *Maps." Research in African Literature* 22, no. 2 (Summer 1991): 83–98.

Davies, Carole Boyce. "Motherhood in the Works of Male and Female Igbo Writers: Achebe, Emecheta, Nwapa and Nzekwu." In *Ngambika: Studies of Women in African Literature,* edited by Carole Boyce Davies and Anne Adams Graves, 241–66. Trenton, NJ: Africa World Press, 1986.

Fanon, Frantz. "The Pitfalls of National Consciousness." *The Wretched of the Earth,* edited by Eldred D. Jones, 148–205. New York: Grove, 1968.

Gilliam, Angela. "Women's Equality and National Liberation." In *Third World Women and the Politics of Feminism,* edited by Chandra T. Mohanty, Ann Russo, and Lourdes Torres, 215–36. Bloomington: Indiana University Press, 1991.

Harlow, Barbara. *Resistance Literature.* London: Methuen, 1987.

Jeyifo, Biodun. "The Nature of Things: Arrested Decolonisation and Critical Theory." *Research in African Literature* 21, no. 1 (Spring 1990): 33–48.

Minh-ha, Trin T. *Woman, Native, Other.* Bloomington and Indianapolis: Indiana University Press, 1989.

Mohanty, Chandra T., Ann Russo, and Lourdes Torres, eds. *Third World Women and the Politics of Feminism.* Bloomington: Indiana University Press, 1991.

Ngugi wa Thiong'o. *Devil on the Cross.* London: Heinemann, 1982.

Ogundipe-Leslie, Molara. "The Female Writer and Her Commitment." In *Women in African Literature Today*, 5–13. London: Curry, 1987.

Ogunyemi, Chikwenye. "The Dynamics of the Contemporary Black Female Novel in English." *Signs* 2, no. 1 (Autumn 1985): 63–80.

Presence Africaine 8–10 (June–November 1956); 24–25 (February–May, 1959).

Riesz, Janos. "Mariama Ba's *Une si longue lettre.*" *Research in African Literatures* 22, no. 1 (Spring 1991): 27–42.

Rubin, Gayle. "The Traffic in Women: Notes on the 'Political Economy' of Sex." *Toward an Anthropology of Women*, edited by Rayna R. Reiter, 157–210. New York: Monthly Review Press, 1975.

Rudebeck, Lars. *Guinea-Bissan: A Study in Political Mobilization.* Uppsala: Scandinavian Institute of African Studies, 1974.

Schipper, Mineke. "Mother Africa on a Pedestal: The Male Heritage in African Literature and Criticism." In *Women in African Literature Today*, 35–54. London: Curry, 1987.

Scott, James C. *The Moral Economy of the Peasant: Rebellion and Subsistence in Southeast Asia.* New Haven, CT: Yale University Press, 1976.

Stratton, Florence. "Periodic Embodiments: A Ubiquitous Trope in African Men's Writing." *Research in African Literatures* 21, no. 1 (Spring 1990): 111–26.

Tohidi, Nayereh. "Gender and Islamic Fundamentalism: Feminist Politics in Iran." In *Third World Women and the Politics of Feminism*, edited by Chandra T. Mohanty, Ann Russo, and Lourdes Torres, 251–67. Bloomington: Indiana University Press, 1991.

Fire and Transition in *Things Fall Apart*

BU-BUAKEI JABBI

◆　◆　◆

ALTHOUGH CHINUA ACHEBE'S fundamental theme as
a beginning novelist was the neo-Negritude assertion of dignity in the African past,[1] which was of course legitimate as a
matter of historical necessity, the focus of drama in his first novel
may, rather, be said to be a society's response to the complex
challenge of contact with a colonizing cultural force. For the
impressively proud African past which he depicts in *Things Fall
Apart* shows a people caught in the initial throes of contact with
an imperial force which is self-righteously bent upon a "civilizing"
mission. The impact of that force on the host culture, especially
on the minds and lives of the indigenous Africans, is the plane
of action on which the story unfolds its tragic drama. Culture,
like life itself, is a dynamic or continuing process, and its quality
often depends upon a people's responses to evolutionary pressures
from within or to stresses generated from outside through friction
with new sets of values and institutional structures. Transition
and change, and seldom stasis, usually result from such meetings
between different cultures and peoples. For both society and the

individual, the intriguing process of relative acculturation is often fraught with a good variety of modes of responses and consequences. Achebe himself has suggested the tragic possibilities inherent in such encounters: "life just has to go on; and if you refuse to accept change, then tragic though it may be, you are swept aside."[2] And that, more or less, is the source of the tragedy of Okonkwo, the main character in the novel. Throughout the story Okonkwo indulges without restraint a personal misoneism which he seeks to impose upon the clan; he is hell-bent to avert change, to nip in the bud all new influences from outside, lest they enervate his society's values. His sustained incapacity for adjustment or compromise sparks off his final tragedy.

Okonkwo's attempts to stand in the way of change and resist transition spring from the peculiar conditions of his character, shaped partly by communal elements in his environment, for some of his characteristic shortcomings are also shared by the clan as a whole. In spite of relative individual exceptions and the many evident values of Igbo traditional society in the novel, Umuofia still betrays a few traits or symptoms of rigidity and moral indifference in some of its customs. The shows of manliness which characterize Okonkwo's actions are only one shade of a general streak in the beliefs and customs of his clansmen as a group. We may call it the manliness complex, but it involves a whole gamut of other attitudes and sociocultural features over and above a mere preoccupation with strength and physical prowess as such. A complete embodiment of that complex, both in some of its best and some of its worst attributes, is Okonkwo himself. And, in connection with him, the image for it in the minds of the people is the "roaring flame" or "flaming fire."[3] Achebe borrows this image from the popular speech of the village and works it into a central artistic symbol with which to explore his subject and convey its meaning.

The imagery of fire or elemental heat accumulates considerable expressive and organizing power as the story unwinds. It symbolizes not only Okonkwo's pride of strength and dignity, but his personal shortcomings as well. It is associated at points with the people's own grandeur of achievements and aspirations, but here as well it lights up some of their areas of cultural weakness, namely, the streaks of violence and destructiveness which are finely ingrained in the traditional philosophy and institutions of these people. In both spiritual and secular affairs the image functions in this basically dual way. By means of it, especially as it relates to Okonkwo, the novel manages to suggest how, unchecked or indulged, the manliness complex may blaze into a veritable *edax rerum*, working out a sinister scheme of suicide and disintegration from within. The novel's main thematic expression also seems to be achieved through the same symbol, that is, to put it crudely, the inevitability of change in a people's cultural life, for *Things Fall Apart* seems to affirm transition as a historical imperative in the dynamics of culture. Human values, Achebe says elsewhere, are never "fixed and eternal. . . . values are relative and in a constant state of flux."[4] But this imperative, demanding a delicate responsiveness or flexible tolerance of mind, does not function as a didactic or overt statement in the novel; it is at once the springboard of its dramatic conflicts and the source of its tragic consequences.

Above all, the fire imagery interacts with a symbolism of water to define the desired quality or direction of that inevitable change. The occurrence of these interacting images in Achebe's thinking outside the novels may serve to reinforce their significance. This is how he explains the relevance (to the verbal artist, as it were) of folkloric raw material in the society:

> The good orator calls to his aid the legends, folklore, proverbs, etc., of his people; they are some of the raw material with which he works. . . . They are like dormant seeds lying in the dry-season earth, waiting for the rain.[5]

As is suggested in the imagery of this final sentence, the generative symbolic interaction of these twin elemental phenomena in the novel is unlikely to be merely fortuitous.

Achebe's treatment of the image of fire in *Things Fall Apart* is just one measure of his artistic discipline and reaching after excellence in his narrative art. Among all the characters in that novel, it is Okonkwo whose nature and circumstances are most consistently depicted through an imagery of fire. The similes and metaphors which describe his deeds and thoughts spring from fire and related elements. Indeed, fire yields a steady flow of verbal imagery in which Okonkwo's character is forged for us, gradually shaping our attitude toward him. His habitual temper and recurrent outbursts of feeling often find expression in fire imagery. His own thinking and speech are profusely strewn with metaphors from this basic stock. When the novel opens, his fame and prestige have seen a meteoric rise into lordship of the clan. The image is invoked here for the first time to describe this ascendance: "Okonkwo's fame had grown like a bush-fire in the harmattan" (p. 1). That he is chosen not only to go as "the proud and imperious emissary of war" to Mbaino (p. 10), but also to take care of the sacrificial hostage lad he brought back with him, is a mark of that fame and greatness.

But the description of his greatness and achievements is perhaps the only instance where the fire imagery relates to Okonkwo without a smoke trail of pejorative suggestions. Almost all other uses refer to his character and temper, and with them an ironic eye is invited. Through them as well a tragic mood is increasingly conjured, for they evoke possibilities which seem to hover menacingly over almost every deed of Okonkwo. For instance, his wives and children "lived in perpetual fear of his fiery temper" (p. 10). And throughout, he can hardly check his brusque impatience toward less successful men and his own family, which lives under a big-stick discipline at home. Okonkwo scorns humility and open displays of gentle emotions. Of course, this lopsided personality was rooted in the shameful memory of a lazy father, a feckless debtor who had lived an improvident life and died an ignoble death, leaving his son none of the customary legacies to start him off. "And so Okonkwo was ruled by one passion—to hate everything that his father Unoka had loved. One of those things was gentleness and another was idleness" (p. 11). Even before his father's death Okonkwo had already started his grim struggle with life in search of success and prestige. His great strength and an "inflexible will" (p. 21) were weapons. But a basic human reaction of ambition soon gave way to a cultic obsession with manliness, especially in its harsher manifestations. Not only did anger and violent strength become, for him, the hallmarks of manliness; they also had to be repeatedly enacted as its own proof and assurance. All other emotions, he thought, should be repressed: "Okonkwo never showed any emotion openly, unless it be the emotion of anger. To show affection was a sign of weakness; the only thing worth demonstrating was strength" (p. 24).

It is no wonder then that his characteristic utterances take shape in metaphors of thunder and threats of destruction. The open-air *ogbanje* therapy is rife with them. The understanding patience of Okagbue Uyanwa, true to the veteran psychiatrist, contrasts pointedly with Okonkwo's impatient threats toward his own daughter. He either "swore furiously" or "roared at her." "Okonkwo stood by, rumbling like thunder in the rainy season" (pp. 73–76). On many other occasions we see him either threatening somebody or almost breathing fire (e.g., pp. 28, 136). Amadiora of the thunderbolt, by whom he often swore or cursed, was obviously Okonkwo's most favored deity in the Umuofia pantheon. For Okonkwo is a loaded cannon of bottled-up emotion, easily ignited into a roaring flame, often by trivial happenings and seldom with due regard to circumstance or ceremony: "He, Okonkwo, was called a flaming fire" (p. 138). It is through his indulgence of the manliness complex that flaming fire comes to symbolize the clan's own tendencies to violence and destructiveness. But he is more generally oblivious of the overall balance which the clan ideally maintains between manliness and its opposing principle, an ideal which can be traced from some of their customs and social structures. There is, for instance, the more or less consistent pattern of every male deity mediating with the people through a priestess and every female deity through a male agent. And there is also the custom of return to the motherland (for burial or consolation) in cases of death, misfortune, or exile from the fatherland (pp. 118–20). It is Okonkwo's ignorance of this balance that makes him overvalue manliness, setting up a false system of values as a personal ethic.

Those moments when his fury erupts openly in the novel trace a general pattern of potential or realized violence. They are a hierarchical scheme of aberrations, which increase in enormity with every succeeding incident. And each one is an adumbration of his ultimate suicide, that final tragic "offence against the Earth" (p. 184) in which they all culminate. In addition, not only is each an assuring show of manliness, each is also almost irresistible, proceeding from the force of his character. They are also proof that Okonkwo is not completely at one with his own society. For, somehow, whenever there is a communal festivity, a public gathering, or an observance of sacred rites, Okonkwo commits some act of indiscretion or violence which blights the occasion and draws public disapproval upon his head. From his beating of his wife Ojiugo during the Week of Peace, through the accidental killing of Ezeudu's son, to his killing of the white man's messenger, that is the pattern of Okonkwo's tragedy. Obierika and Ezeudu disapproved of his part in killing Ikemefuna for the same reason that these other deeds were abominable: "What you have done will not please the Earth. It is the kind of action for which the goddess wipes out whole families" (pp. 58–59). And, as Achebe says in another context, these people believe that "there is a fundamental justice in the universe and nothing so terrible can happen to a person for which he is not somehow responsible."[6] Sometimes Okonkwo incurs a more painful and tragic punishment than mere condemnation—as in the case of the messenger, when he has to commit suicide, the crowning irony of an end he had struggled against all his life. Indeed, a relentless inevitability hangs over Okonkwo's life, earning him deep sympathy without redeeming him. He may be a champion or embodiment of his clan's customs, but he is not a complete epitome of their more or less rounded system of values, a balance which he tends to subvert. He is like the candle wick which burns out its own pith, but this time without giving much light.

Still, his inadequacies exemplify to some extent the clan's own central cultural malaise, that is, those cruel customs of ignorance perpetuated by them. Their attitude toward twins, or the dead *ogbanje* child, or the lads offered by offending neighbors who would avoid the bloodshed of war is evidence of this: "The Earth had decreed that they were an offence on the land and must be destroyed" (112). Like Okonkwo's own shows of strength, these are also "silent and dusty chords in the heart of an Ibo man" (p. 131). They are shades or manifestations of the general manliness complex which gnaws at the heart of Umuofia civilization. Here, however, Achebe is only presenting "the past with all its imperfections."[7] But those imperfections are not just testimony to "the writer's integrity,"[8] they also enter actively into the novel's imaginative logic and its general scheme of plot development. These weaknesses play an important part in the acceptance and spread of Christianity among the people. They are a moral blind spot which the missionaries soon discover as an object for attack, thereby providing the initial paths or inroads into the people's cohesiveness. And the place of the white man's appearance in the moral scheme of the novel is that, in spite of its considerable long-term havoc, it helps to spark off a crisis of values in the cultural life of the people, one which constantly calls for a kind of resolution or reconcilement. It seems that this is a legitimate way to assess the aesthetic relevance of a writer's background. Its unfamiliar or esoteric nature should not be allowed to put off a critic too soon, for unfamiliarity is no intrinsic attribute of things, but is always in relation to, or a reflection of, some observer's own ignorance. In a work of literary art, therefore, the role of a so-called unfamiliar element may be assessed in its relationship to the style and structure, its contribution to the distinctive tone and quality of the work in question and to its place in the drama of values which is enacted.

So far, we have discussed fire mainly as a source of verbal imagery, that is, as a mine for similes and metaphors which help to reveal and evaluate both character and theme. But this presupposes no presence of actual fires in the novel's world itself. A novel, however, usually deals with literal details of background and living experience, in visible or tangible elements which may or may not be prodded to yield images. That is, sometimes the details are purely for "that effect of concrete particularity which is a staple of the novel form."[9] Obviously, fire and thunder were as much a part of the tropical rural life of Umuofia as they are for us today. But sometimes such physical details in a novel may function beyond the superficial level of realistic description and literal fact. To quote David Lodge:

> The selection and ordering of these surrogates must have an aesthetic motive and an aesthetic effect, though both writer and reader may be to some extent unconscious of the processes involved.[10]

Perhaps "must" implies here too much of an imperative in a matter which is more or less relative. However, while elements of background, setting, or atmosphere need not operate extraliterally in a work of art, they do sometimes reveal a tempting tendency in that direction in the hands of certain craftspeople.

These are some of the details which Achebe calls "the supporting scenery" of a story.[11] This phrase probably implies that they may also support the story aesthetically, say, by helping it to attain internal structural coherence and evocative depth, or perhaps merely instilling a distinctive quality and timbre associated with the society being depicted. They may therefore be used with changing effects from story to story. It is partly in such a sense that Achebe may claim to have utilized in both *Things Fall Apart* and *Arrow of God* basically the same background or scenery to write about the same society and yet produce stories which are the "exact opposite."[12]

In the rest of this essay, therefore, we will try to investigate at least one example of Achebe's use of the realistic physical surface of life in the novel for such nonliteral effects of art. Generally, it is a use of *concrete* imagery, as distinct from mere *verbal* imagery. It may consist, among other things, in real happenings, gestures, or deeds and also in features of landscape, weather, the elements, or physical objects, which are present in the novel primarily as obvious literal facts, but which are also invested with symbolic dimensions through the artist's contextual handling of them, Garrett says:

> "Symbolism" here means not a theoretical outlook but the use of symbols, which, as they appear in the novel, I take to

be images, objects, events, or complexes of these which are both literal and suggestive of further, usually more abstract, meaning. Such meaning may range from the most explicit to the most ambiguous and indefinite. I shall consider a symbol's associations as primarily grounded not just in universal human experience (which would define the symbol as archetype), or in particular historical conventions, but in the context created by the individual work. A symbol's meaning will be considered primarily as the function of its place in the structure of the internal relations between the component elements of a novel.[13]

One discovers in Achebe's *Things Fall Apart* that its realistic details sometimes become symbolic without giving up their literal or physical bases, for surface fact is hardly ever completely sacrificed on the altar of symbolic propensity. His art is ever so concealed!

Before we analyze the novel's use of purely concrete symbolism, however, we may mention a set of references to fire and water which oscillate delicately in a sort of no-man's land between the two types of imagery we have outlined. In these cases, one is not so sure which of them is operating, whether it is only one of them, or both of them at once. These innominate uses refer mainly to certain points of glory and grandeur in the life of the clan, and some of them further on show how Okonkwo is sometimes closely identified with, but at other times distanced from, the life of the community. Wrestling, war, and the *egwugwu* cult, all of them preeminent sources of pride and achievement for these people, are illustrative instances.

First, their martial life. In times of peace, war dresses are usually hung over the fireplace. And during ceremonial observances, and probably in war as well, the warriors "all wore smoked raffia skirts and their bodies were painted with chalk and charcoal" (pp. 108, 177). War, as we know, was both Okonkwo's personal vocation and the greatest single cause of Umuofia's fearful fame abroad. But it is wrestling, their other brand of physical prowess, that reveals a more significant relationship with the element of fire in the novel. Wrestling is even more properly Okonkwo's natural and vital element. And it is communally cultivated as a true virtue of manliness in Umuofia. Deft moves and corresponding shouts of applause at a wrestling contest are described in metaphors of thunder and fire. Here is the final moment of a memorable contest:

> Quick as the lightning of Amadiora, Okafo raised his right leg and swung it over his rival's head. The crowd burst into a thunderous roar. Okafo was swept off his feet by his supporters and carried home shoulder-high. (p. 44)

It is through such effects of imagery and shared experience that points of identity between Okonkwo and his society are lit up from time to time. Then, there is between Okonkwo, Ekwefi, an Ezinma a bond of fondness, understanding, and rapport which sometimes subdues his tantrums of fury and also bears out his warmth of heart. There is an interesting but minor relation between this rapport and the general imagery of fire (pp. 34–39). Ezinma is making a fire for Nwoye's mother, and we are aware of her eagerness to go to the New Year's wrestling contest, as her idea of the "twitching eye-lid" (p. 35) shows:

> She went on fanning it until it burst into flames. . . . Just then the distant beating of drums began to reach them. . . . The drums beat the unmistakable wrestling dance. . . . Okonkwo cleared his throat and moved his feet to the beat of the drums. It filled him with fire as it had always done from his youth. . . . It throbbed in the air, in the sunshine, and even in the trees, and filled the village with excitement. (pp. 36–38)

The contest itself has always been for Ekwefi, Ezinma's mother, the climactic point in each year's round of festivals (p. 34). For Okonkwo, it had been both a means of self-realization (p. 1) and an obvious influence on his view of life. Ezinma's flaming fire seems to be an outward index to her own growing (and even her parents' accustomed) anxiety to see the wrestling match. And that mutual eagerness is only an instance of the entire society's ever-intense ritual involvement with this traditional ceremony of transition.

A more balanced oscillation between verbal and concrete imagery appears in the treatment of the *egwugwu* cult. Here again, the points of identity and difference between Okonkwo and Umuofia are underscored through the imagery. As custodians of law and order and the ultimate dispensers of justice in the clan, the *egwugwu* are sometimes superior instruments of punishment or vengeance (pp. 164–70). Each of them had a "smoked raffia body" and "charred teeth." Their leader, Evil Forest, often "roars." Also, a "steady cloud of smoke rose from his head." But, significantly Evil Forest was also called "Fire-that-burns-without-faggots" (pp. 79–83). This smoldering fire is unlike Okonkwo's own sobriquet, "Flaming-fire." The leading *egwugwu* is also a traditional restorer of order and moderation (pp. 108–10). Another *egwugwu* is a one-handed spirit, "carrying a basket full of water" (p. 110). He would pour this as it were on aberrant tendencies and violent frenzies during public rituals, for they always abated on his entry. We thus see enshrined in this cult an awe-inspiring power and glory, an ethos of moderation and a restorative influence, all of which inhere in a faintly suggestive fire-water imagery. Ajofia's offer of tolerance to the white man (p. 170) is as typical of the clan itself as it is uncharacteristic of Okonkwo as a person. Even the people's initial offhand or amused resignation, with the blind trust that the clan's gods would fight their own offenders, is only a manifestation of their patience and general spirit of accommodation (pp. 129–45). Ironically, however, this popular temper will help to speed up their "falling apart" and its attendant moral crisis. In any case, this instance of symbolism is another way of assimilating the esoteric to art in fiction. Of course, as we have already said, unfamiliarity itself is more a function of the observer's own state of knowledge than an intrinsic attribute of social customs. A writer who parades it for mere advertisement is an exhibitionist, together with the critic who is awake to this mode of depiction alone. But, equally, a critic who scorns or ignores it simply because it is strange to *him* is abandoning his role out of a type of prejudice.

When we come to the instances of purely concrete symbolism of fire, we see that they either occur at a point of crisis or may merely presage some impending change in the life of a character or the clan as a whole. These are instances where the fire is obviously a literal presence, and yet it also serves a distinctively nonliteral function without merely being a source of simile or metaphor. It may be the fire for cooking or for warming oneself in the home, as in Ezinma's flaming fire above, or it may be perhaps the funeral glowing brand, paying the last respects to great men of the clan (p. 109). The use of fire for communal vengeance is perhaps more pertinent here as an instance of symbolic resonance. For example, when Okonkwo inadvertently killed a clansman:

> They set fire to his houses, demolished his red walls, killed his animals and destroyed his barn. It was the justice of the earth goddess. . . . They were merely cleansing the land which Okonkwo had polluted with the blood of a clansman. (p. 111)

This is an act of effacement which underscores the fact of exile and leaves it in no doubt. And here we see how the spiritual and the mundane are often so closely connected in Umuofia. For this punitive vendetta is also an act of purification, a virtual fertility rite in the customary farming life of the community. But the ritual is also a symbolic enactment of what we have already diagnosed: a predilection to violence and destructiveness. It will become the first cause of direct humiliation by the white man (pp. 168–77).

The hearth place is conventionally the setting for handing down the wisdom and literary heritage of the clan. But this domestic phenomenon is imbued with religious overtones when we see its counterpart in the shrine of Agbala, the Oracle of the Hills and the Caves. The fire is unlike that associated with Okonkwo, but it is essentially like the leading egwugwu's head of smoldering fire: "The fire did not burn with a flame" (p. 13). It is a sacred fire which lights up crucial moments of insight, revelation, and foreknowledge for the worshiping onlooker. It lends an awe-inspiring aura and a divine infallibility to the proclamations of the priestess. As had been the case with Unoka, Okonkwo's father, these are sometimes moments of acute self-analysis or disenchantment (p. 14). And Okonkwo's own domestic fire serves a similar function in one of the novel's central effulgences of meaning. It is the night following Nwoye's desertion or conversion:

> As Okonkwo sat in his hut that night, gazing into a log fire, he thought over the matter. A sudden fury rose within him and he felt a strong desire to take up his matchet, go to the church and wipe out the entire vile and miscreant gang. But on further thought he told himself that Nwoye was not worth fighting for. . . . Now that he had time to think of it, his son's crime stood out in its stark enormity. . . . He saw himself and his fathers crowding round their ancestral shrine waiting in vain for worship and sacrifice and finding nothing but ashes of bygone days, and his children the while praying to the white man's god. If such a thing were ever to happen, he, Okonkwo, would wipe them off the face of the earth.
>
> Okonkwo was popularly called the "Roaring Flame." As he looked into the log fire he recalled the name. He was a flaming fire. How then could he have begotten a son like Nwoye, degenerate and effeminate? . . . He, Okonkwo, was called a flaming fire. How could he have begotten a woman for a son? . . .
>
> He sighed heavily, and as if in sympathy the smouldering log also sighed. And immediately Okonkwo's eyes were opened and he saw the whole matter clearly. Living fire begets cold, impotent ash. He sighed again, deeply. (pp. 137–38)

Okonkwo obviously associates flame with manliness, and the smoldering fire with its passing away. Like the whole clan, he is sitting here on the promontory of a dilemma, face to face with inevitable change, but unable to arrest or direct its drift. The smoldering log suddenly crystallizes into a symbol of that historical process. It seems to lend Okonkwo some clairvoyance, though what he sees takes the color of his befogged hyperpatriotic lens. He "saw clearly in it" the threatened extinction of the clan's cultural heritage; it was a "terrible prospect, like the prospect of annihilation" (p. 137). He sees the impending change as too radical a shift of cultural center, a necessary enervation of moral fiber, and a devaluation of spiritual fervor: "Living fire begets cold, impotent ash." If this should not be denied the name of insight, it is at least fuzzy and stilted, for Okonkwo is blind to any prospects of a balanced synthesis or accommodation.

In fact, the conversion of Nwoye, toward which Okonkwo reacts with these temptations to violence, is a positive step toward that synthesis. For a long time Nwoye has been disturbed by instances of insensitivity in the life of the clan. The inward impact of conversion in his soul is presented with sharp symbolic force:

> The hymn about brothers who sat in darkness and in fear seemed to answer a vague and persistent question that haunted his young soul—the question of the twins crying in the bush and the question of Ikemefuna who was killed. He felt a relief within as the hymn poured into his parched soul. The words of the hymn were like the drops of frozen rain melting on the dry palate of the panting earth. Nwoye's callow mind was greatly puzzled. (p. 132)

Nwoye has not at all reached a final synthesis, nor is he even conscious of deliberately moving toward such an ultimate goal. But his conversion, though it is neither requisite nor adequate in itself in the search for an adjustment of values, is nevertheless a first step toward it. The image of rain water falling with relief on the sun-baked earth, which describes the import of that step, is one of the recurring images in the novel. Its previous occurrences are, in fact, symbolized foreshadowings of that ultimate denouement toward which Nwoye has started himself. Just as Okonkwo's tragic end had been prefigured a few times before, so is Nwoye's effort at a reconcilement of values anticipated repeatedly in a few symbolic incidents. The first drought in the novel (pp. 19–21) is a joint symbolization of the two types of anticipation. The "blazing sun" (p. 10) of the drought is imaginatively associated with Okonkwo's "flaming fire." So are both of these with the subsequent "violent torrents" (p. 20), that is, within the total structure of the novel. And what is emphasized in each case is the life-destroying propensity of all three through sheer immoderation, Okonkwo being someone "who never did things in halves" (p. 148). For only if "the rain became less violent," followed by the usual "spell of sunshine which always came in the middle of the wet season," would a good yield be assured (p. 20). Indeed, that year "the harvest was sad, like a funeral. . . . One man tied his cloth to a tree branch and hanged himself" (p. 20). But this is obviously adumbrative more of Okonkwo's suicide than of Nwoye's crucial conversion.

By far the most powerful anticipation of that spiritual rebirth is the second miniature drought, which greeted Okonkwo's initial efforts at rehabilitation in Mbanta:

At last the rain came. It was sudden and tremendous. For two or three moons the sun had been gathering strength till it seemed to breathe a breath of fire on the earth. All the grass had long been scorched brown, and the sands felt like live coals to the feet. Evergreen trees wore a dusty coat of brown. The birds were silenced in the forests, and the world lay panting under the live, vibrating heat. And then came the clap of thunder. It was an angry, metallic and thirsty clap, unlike the deep and liquid rumbling of the rainy season. A mighty wind arose and filled the air with dust. Palm trees swayed as the wind combed their leaves into flying crests like strange and fantastic coiffure.

When the rain finally came, it was in large, solid drops of frozen water which the people called "the nuts of the water of heaven." They were hard and painful on the body as they fell, yet young people ran about happily picking up the cold nuts and throwing them into their mouths to melt.

The earth quickly came to life and the birds in the forests fluttered around and chirped merrily. A vague scent of life and green vegetation was diffused in the air. As the rain began to fall more soberly and in smaller liquid drops, children sought for shelter, and all were happy, refreshed and thankful. (p. 116)

There is an irony inherent in Okonkwo's struggles against these droughts as a farmer. An elemental counterpart of his own life's guiding principle poses a dilemma or threat of failure to him from time to time. But as a man of action rather than thought, he is nowhere aware of the sinister possibilities cryptically suggested in the irony. Here, however, we see once more his twin favorites: the breath of flame of fire and thunder, again with their scorching effects upon life. And there is the rain cloud, bringing its promise of welcome change, and, finally, the life-inspiring rain itself, with its relief as it begins "to fall more soberly and in smaller liquid drops." This is the ideal planting season in both Umuofia and Mbanta when sunshine and rain alternate without being violent. All of the main symbols in the novel coalesce into this fabulous vignette in order to achieve a microcosm of the novel's wider structure of events. The entire passage is a veritable paradigm, an enacted drama almost, of the novel's moral cosmogony. It is an effective imaginative projection of that ultimate adjustment and accommodation toward which Nwoye would start himself off through conversion. But, of course, conversion itself is neither a necessary means nor a sufficient guarantee or proof of that process.

That synthesis of values is achieved nowhere in the novel, at least not in the sense of a historical event. Nwoye may embrace Christianity, or we may find the people becoming increasingly accommodating toward the white religion and influences. But these are budding signs which only presage, rather than realize, that final synthesis. If anything, we see that realization only in the interactions between the fire and water images, in the procreative intercourse of these elements which symbolizes and repeatedly foreshadows Nwoye's conversion. This is realization in a preeminently aesthetic or imaginative sense. It is more a pointer to possibilities than a dramatization of observable social facts. And that is probably because, to work a synthesis of values out of a conflict of different cultures requires in the long run a real force of imagination. Achebe himself has said that such processes can hardly be completed either immediately or in a straight progression. He holds out a cautious optimism about the evolution of values in a society:

Unfortunately when two cultures meet, you would expect, if we were angels shall we say, we could pick out the best in the other and retain the best in our own, and this would be wonderful. But this doesn't happen often . . . and I am not being so naive as to think that the progress is in one direction. You see, there are halts, there are even backward steps and so on. . . . But if you take a long view of society, you will see . . . that society is, in fact adjusting.[14]

The "wonderful" and the "long view" are depicted through the symbolic interactions we have outlined, for they define for us the direction and quality of the needed change. Even by the time of the final crisis in the novel, the process of adjustment is still in its infancy.

THIS ESSAY ARGUES and attempts to present a balance between two critical approaches to African literature, that is, through the analysis of content or themes and through a close examination of the writer's craftsmanship. That balance is actually an intrinsic blend in literature itself, and we have had to go to one of the earliest works of African writing in order to make our points. This essay thus identifies the inevitability of transition as a controlling theme in Achebe's *Things Fall Apart*, and then it tries to see how imagery and symbolism help to convey this theme together with the characters and dilemmas of those people who have to come to terms with it or duck under. The direction and quality of the change itself are also defined, again as these appear to be expressed through elements of style in the novel. The whole effort has been partly defensive, suggesting that this novel is a work of literary art which demands, indeed deserves and sustains, attention from the critic.

In addition, however, one hopes the effort will be of general relevance not only to the canon of Achebe's novels, but to the wider cause of modern African writing. Hitherto, African literature has often had to be defended against either the critic who had little faith in it or those who innocently regard it as a mere sociological handmaid, and sometimes even against those well-meaning patrons who accord it a mere gratuitous compliment. But, certainly, there is now an appreciable body of serious literature by African writers for the criticism of it to give riddance to a mere defensive pose. That is, criticism of African literature can surely afford to become truly literary and exploratory. Of course, here and there this trend has already set in, though it has yet to be firmly established or be widely applied to the various areas of African writing today. In this process it would be rewarding to appropriate at least one assumption in the criticism of fiction proposed by Mark Schorer:

> Criticism must begin with the simplest assertion: fiction is a literary art. It must begin with a base of language, with the word, with figurative structures, with rhetoric as skeleton and style as body of meaning.[15]

Criticism would do well to remember that a work of fiction is a structure of meaning. Life and experience are, of course, its native subject matter, but it is seldom a mere transcription of them. But this goes as much for the writer himself as for the critic of his literary artifacts. Both of them owe that as a debt to the growth of a strong tradition of African writing today.

Notes

1. Chinua Achebe, "The Role of the Writer in a New Nation," *Nigeria Magazine* 81 (1964): 157.

2. *African Writers Talking: A Collection of Radio Interviews*, edited by Cosmo Pieterse and Dennis Duerden (London: Heinemann, 1972), 14.

3. *Things Fall Apart* (London: Heinemann, 1958), 137–38. All page references are to this edition.

4. "The Role of the Writer in a New Nation," 158.

5. Foreword to *A Selection of African Prose*, vol. 1, edited by W. H. Whiteley (Oxford: Clarendon, 1964), viii.

6. *Morning Yet on Creation Day: Essays* (London: Heinemann, 1975), 97.

7. "The Role of the Writer in a New Nation," 158.

8. Ibid., 157.

9. David Lodge, *The Language of Fiction* (London: Routledge and Kegan Paul, 1966), 122.

10. Ibid., 46.

11. *African Writers Talking*, 16.

12. Ibid.

13. P. K. Garrett, *Scene and Symbol from George Eliot to James Joyce* (New Haven: Yale University Press, 1969), 9–10.

14. *African Writers Talking*, 13, 14, 17.

15. Mark Schorer, "Fiction and the 'Matrix of Analogy'," *Kenyon Review* 11 (1949): 539.

Realism, Criticism, and the Disguises of Both

A Reading of Chinua Achebe's Things Fall Apart with an Evaluation of the Criticism Relating to It

ATO QUAYSON

◆ ◆ ◆

> It is only when we go to the riverside that we
> can gauge the size of the water pot.
> —Ewe proverb

> No matter how well the hen dances, it cannot
> please the hawk.
> —Akan proverb

THE PROVERBIAL EPIGRAPHS to this essay seek to integrate the enterprise of criticism into a traditional African cultural context. The first points to the relativity at the heart of all critical pursuits: it is mainly in relation to the literary enterprise that the critical one is validated. Furthermore, no criticism can hope to completely encompass the total significance of the literary artifact, just as no water pot can hope to take in all of the river's water. On the other hand, all critical enterprises harbor a certain predatoriness, which the relationship between the dancing hen and the hawk can be taken to figure. The critical enterprise is never completely satisfied with the work of its predecessors and thus continually seeks to tear open previous critical discourses to make space for its own activity.

These two proverbs are recalled to contextualize my own critical exercise. In offering a critique of the general evaluation of

Things Fall Apart, I am conscious of the perceptive work that has been undertaken on the novel since its publication decades ago. Much of the criticism relating to the novel, however, shares implicit assumptions about the nature of the "realism" that the work itself offers. These assumptions subtly valorize the hermeneutical and exegetical approaches to the work without paying attention to the fact that its "realism" is a construct whose basic premises cannot be taken unproblematically. To help problematize the nature of the novel's realism, I shall, in the second part of this essay, focus on its construction of women and the feminine. This specific reading is offered as a model open to further modification and an alternative to the dominant tendencies in the area of the criticism of African literature. Ultimately, I intend to suggest that the representationalist readings that relate to his work are, though valid, grossly inadequate and that it is preferable to adopt a multitiered approach to his work and to African literatures in general that will not take them as merely mimetic of an African reality but will pay attention to them as *restructurations* of various cultural subtexts. This will hopefully liberate more exciting modes of literary analyses that would pay attention to the problematic relationships that African literary texts establish with their cultural backgrounds. This will also pave the way for a proper examination of other works that do not rely on realist modes of discourse for their (re)presentations of Africa. I bear in mind that if I now "hawk" other critiques, mine will soon be "hen" for subsequent ones; that is exactly as it should be, for it is impossible to say a last word on a writer as fine as Achebe.

I

Achebe's work, particularly *Things Fall Apart*, has inspired a great amount of criticism. In surveying this criticism, it is useful to bear in mind that the nature of that criticism is symptomatic of the evaluation of African literature in general.[1] The issues posed in relation to Achebe often pervade the critical practice relating to African literature. But perhaps, it is only Biodun Jeyifo and Chidi

Amuta who have attempted to define a typology of the criticism in the field. Jeyifo's two-tier typology holds greater potential for elaboration, and it is to his view that I turn to contextualize criticism of Achebe's work. Jeyifo defines the purview of postcoloniality as the dismantling "of bounded enclaves and subjectivities" (Jeyifo 52). He shares in this definition the tendency evident in *The Empire Writes Back* to perceive postcolonial practice as a discourse concerned with a self-definition that foregrounds the tensions with the imperial power and emphasizes the differences from the assumptions of the imperial center (Ashcroft, Griffiths, and Tiffin 2). The implicit assumption that postcolonial literatures are in a perpetual umbilical dance with the metropolitan center, counterproductive though it is, will not be taken on here. Jeyifo divides postcolonial writing and criticism into two distinct fields, which he names the postcoloniality of "normativity and proleptic designation" and the "interstitial or liminal" postcoloniality. The postcoloniality of normativity and proleptic designation is one in which the writer or critic speaks to, for, or in the name of the post-independence nation-state, the regional or continental community, the panethnic, racial, or cultural agglomeration of homelands and diasporas (Jeyifo 53).

The normativity in this conception of postcoloniality often entails a return to cultural sources, the projection of a futurist agenda, and the celebration of cultural authenticity. Indeed, Achebe himself espouses such an agenda in relation to his work. In his famous words:

> I would be quite satisfied if my novels (especially the ones I set in the past) did no more than teach my readers that their past—with all its imperfections—was not one long night of savagery from which the first Europeans acting on God's behalf delivered them. ("Novelist as Teacher" 45)

Ignoring for the time being the implications of these remarks for constructing the social role of the writer,[2] I note the implicit confidence expressed about the role of realism in the project of recovering cultural authenticity. Realism is so powerful as a conduit for social criticism that it is taken to pass on the verities available to other empiricist social discourses. Perhaps it is David Lodge, in *The Modes of Modern Writing*, who offers a definition of realism closest to that implied in Achebe's confident assertions on the role of his work:

> [Realism is] the representation of experience in a manner which approximates closely to descriptions of similar experience in non-literary texts of the same culture. (25)

The assumption that realism shares a community of values with other nonliterary discourses was particularly important in the general conceptions of the role of literature in the newly emergent African nations. Especially in the period just before and after independence in West Africa when a burgeoning newspaper culture and the Onitsha market literature[3] emphasized an empiricism and rationalism embodied in a recourse to "facts" and factual reporting, the perceived affinities between the economy of realism and those of other nonliterary discourses were taken for granted in the espousals of cultural authenticity. A remark by an early reviewer of Achebe's *A Man of the People* to the effect that the novel was "worth a ton of documentary journalism" (*Time*, 19 August 1966, 84, cited in Larson 16) encapsulates the expressed confidence in the shared "factuality" of the protocols of both novelistic realism and newspaper reportage in general.

The confidence Achebe expresses in the realism of his early novels was shared by his critics and led to several critical formulations which sought to elucidate the representationalist aspects of his work. The critical tendency that seemed to take the novels most evidently as in a one-to-one relationship to reality was that which sought to recover anthropological data about the Igbo from the novels. Charles Larson elicits such an anthropological reading from *Things Fall Apart*, though he introduces his work by deprecating that same tendency in Achebe's earliest reviewers. "What is clearly needed," writes Larson, "is the reviewer equipped to examine African fiction both from a cultural (anthropological) and an aesthetic (literary) point of view, though I am not trying to suggest that the two are ever totally separated" (Larson 16). He goes on to affirm that the first part of the novel is "heavily anthropological, but contains the seeds of germination for the latter half of the book" (Larson 30). Proceeding from such a premise, it is not difficult for him then to conclude that there is very little scenic description related to the building of mood and atmosphere in the Western sense, and that Achebe's descriptions are used directly for functional rather than for aesthetic purposes. In discussing the passage in which Ikemefuna is led into the forest to be murdered, Larson asserts that the description of the forest is given just to let the reader know where he is; the boy could not have been killed in the village anyway, so the forest scene is an inescapable necessity imposed on Achebe. In other words, the novel is intent on giving only factual information. Because of his anthropological biases, Larson fails to see that the whole scene is rich with meanings and can be read as an important symbolic expression of the darkness at both the center and margins of all cultures.

Obiechina duplicates this tendency from an insider's perspective. In his *Culture, Tradition, and Society in the West African Novel,* he sees the novel as reflective or mimetic of traditional beliefs and practices in an almost unmediated way, being interested, as he is, in showing how the cultural and social background "gave rise to the novel there, and in far-reaching and crucial ways conditioned the West African novel's content, themes and texture" (Obiechina 3). Within Obiechina's formulation, "culture," "tradition," and "society" become paradigmatic of the real West African world reflected in the novels he studies. In this way the novels become amenable to an "anthropological harvest" in which details are read from cultural background to fictional world and back again.

These readings of Achebe are better understood in the context of a general rhetoric that sought to define an authentic African world view opposed to the Western one. Criticism, in this context, tried to demonstrate the extent to which the narrative had "naturalized" the borrowed form of the novel by its specifically African discursive strategies. Several critics devoted themselves to arguing the "Africanness" of the text such as was evident in proverb use (Egudu; Lindfors; Shelton), in the oral rhythms concealed in the text (McCarthy), or in the patterns of temporality that are arguably relatable to African cultural sources (JanMohamed).

A more subtle version of the Africanness rhetoric seems to be offered by criticism that sees Achebe's work as setting itself against the construction of the African available within Western fiction. In her recent book on Chinua Achebe, C. L. Innes undertakes a contrastive pairing of Achebe with Joyce Cary, in which she establishes a typology of the "preferred." She draws inspiration for this from Achebe's own remarks about the factors that led him to write novels as a corrective to some of the jaundiced images about the African that were purveyed in writings by Westerners. Achebe's fictionalization of African reality is to be preferred to Cary's because Achebe is closer to the reality of Africa:

> In challenging Cary's "superficial picture," a representation to be observed on the surface without critical intervention, Achebe challenged not only the vision depicted but also the manner of the depiction, not only the story, but the mode of story-telling, and the consequent relationship between reader and writer. (Innes, *Chinua Achebe*, 18)

Innes explores the novel's Africanness in relational terms, and this suggests that it is the construction of different representations of the same world that is at stake. It is necessary to be alerted to the modes of perception of the African encrusted in reactionary discourses such as those of Cary. Representation is a subtle process imbricated within the textual strategies deployed by realist discourse. But it is important to note how such an approach privileges the realism of the preferred version and ignores the potential exclusions of such a version. In Achebe's specific evocation of the Igbo world, it is possible to further contrast him with other Igbo writers, such as Buchi Emecheta, to show that his version of African reality requires as much interrogation and qualification as those proffered by the Carys.

Side by side with this type of criticism was another which

sought to identify Africanness as a first step toward coralling the rural novels into a more radical political agenda. Indeed, the position of Chinweizu and colleagues in *Towards the Decolonization of African Literature* can be taken to represent the most radical expression of this agenda. They attacked many of the leading African writers and critics for obscurantism and a divorce from African oral sources and advocated a return to a traditional Afrocentrist literary and critical practice. The reactionary essentialism concealed in this position was quickly discovered and attacked by both writers and critics. It is now fashionable to address the *bolekaja*[4] formation in surveys of African literature in derogatory terms, but it seems to me that the nature of the *bolekaja* radicalism derives precisely from an unquestioning confidence in the capacity of realism for reflecting the real. Their fear was that, if the wrong "reality" were reflected, it would have a corrupting influence on readers, and ultimately militate against the larger processes of political decolonization, which were at the center of their concerns. In this sense they share the same attitudes that inform all criticism accepting realism at face value and ignoring its constructedness as an "ism."

All these critical formulations in relation to Achebe's work can be perceived as united in subtle maneuvers that take the culture of the realist novel as most truthfully inscribing the space and time of history. Palmer can be taken to be representative of this notion:

> Broadly speaking, the African novel is a response to and a record of the traumatic consequences of the impact of western capitalist colonialism on the traditional values and institutions of the African peoples. (Palmer 63)

It is interesting how such a formulation, and the critical practice informed by it, defines a novelistic agenda that emphasizes "record," grounding it in rationalism and empiricism. Furthermore this type of formulation permits the exclusion or underprivileging of the counterrealist and nonrationalist. In Palmer's own practice, when he engages with Tutuola, he is at pains to show that Tutuola is merely a teller of tales and not a novelist. His work thus requires a different level of seriousness:

> Tutuola is not strikingly original, but we can then go on to assert that whereas *realism* and *originality* are expected of the formal novel, the teller of folk tales is expected to take his subject matter and the framework his tales from the corpus of his people's traditional lore. (Palmer 12; emphases added)

Since Palmer has already suggested that the African novel is supremely concerned with "record," it is easy to see how his conception of Tutuola's work underprivileges the type of mythological discourse in which his writing engages. But more important, it serves to institute a subtle dichotomy between realism and nonrealism, with the added suggestion that the nonrealist is not properly the staple of the novel form. All the debates around Tutuola seem to me to adumbrate what Karin Barber ("African-language Literatures and Post-colonial Criticism") detects at the center of postcolonial and commonwealth literary criticism: the desire to bracket out certain forms of discourse, and to underplay or dismiss the vital activity of oral literature. Much of the criticism of African literature, she says, seeks to give oral tradition only an originary role in the construction of typologies of the Europhone African literatures. The oral tradition is seen mainly as a reservoir of materials to be exploited by the modern writer. This maneuver forecloses the possibility of seeing oral literature as vitalizing its own traditions of writing as expressed in indigenous language literatures. It seems to me that, additionally, the elements of oral literature employed by writers and elucidated by critics are seen mainly in the role of subserving an essentially rationalist and empiricist realist discourse. The African novel is made to yield reflections of Africa, and there is often an unconscious urge to read them as recording an "African" reality that comes without mediation. Thus, when a Tutuola gives full vent to the transgressive potential inherent in oral literary traditions, his work can only be seen in terms of the problematic. His work disturbs the process of establishing mimetic adequacy in the representation of the African world view.

It is perhaps fruitful at this stage to note Hayden White's general skepticism about the definitions of realism to make room for a contextualization of the relationship between realist and non-realist discourses in the representations of Africa:

> In my view, the whole discussion of the nature of "realism" in literature flounders in the failure to assess critically what a generally "historical" conception of reality consists of. The usual tactic is to set the "historical" over against the "mythical," as if the former were genuinely *empirical* and the latter were nothing but *conceptual*, and then to locate the realm of the "fictive" between the two poles. Literature is then viewed as being more or less *realistic*, depending upon the ratio of empirical to conceptual elements contained in it. (3n)

Realism is ultimately a construction that is privileged because it is seen as reflecting History and Truth in its engagement with empirical data. But it is a construction that needs to be interrogated. In the context of African literature, the myths and legends are important sources for the construction of an African world view. It is in fact significant that from the very inception of African literature, a tradition that draws dominantly from oral literature and its modes of perception has grown alongside the more realist tendency. We can number writers like Soyinka, Awoonor, Armah, and lately Laing, Okri, and Bandele-Thomas in the ranks of those who draw mainly on a mythic consciousness, but it is still disturbing that no full-length study has yet been made in which these writers are seen as together exemplifying a specific mode of literary consciousness.[5] The crucial thing though, is to regard their works as drawing from the wealth of cultural materials to produce *re/structurations* of the culture within a general mythopoeic practice. But it is a type of *re/structuration* in which realism itself participates so that any representationalist reading of realism is a maneuver that, consciously or unconsciously, ignores the problematic status of the realist text.

In order that African novels, be they realist or counterrealist, are not rapidly incorporated into an anthropological-representationalist reading of African reality, it is important to regard them all as symbolic discourses that continually restructure a variety of subtexts: cultural, political, historical, and at times even biographical.[6] And it is useful to bear in mind that a palpable gap is forever instituted between the narrative text and the subtexts it appropriates. It is then fruitful to regard the African novel as only partially reflecting a "reality" beyond itself, one reflected in a highly problematic way, forever struggling to be self-sufficient within itself, but always involved in various relationships with its informing matrix. It then becomes possible to endorse Homi Bhabha's desire to see a shift in the criticism of postcolonial literatures from the perception of the text as representationalist to seeing it as a *production*. But it seems to me also important not to privilege the textual as solely generative of meanings. The text is meaningful partly in relation to the culture from which it borrows its materials and with which it establishes varying relationships. This view of the text permits the recovery of a cultural matrix for the text, and at the same time opens up a space for an interrogation of the assumptions upon which it is grounded.

Perhaps this strategy would satisfy someone like Chidi Amuta, who is radically opposed to what he sees as a hegemonic traditionalist aesthetic that governs the criticism of African literature. In relation to *Things Fall Apart* and *Arrow of God*, he makes the assertion that they have become axiomatic reference points for diverse interests and opinions intent on rediscovering and commenting on "traditional African society" and "the culture conflict" inaugurated by the advent of colonialism, stock concepts which have since been adumbrated into a "mini-catechism" (Amuta 130). The "traditionalist aesthetic" can be incorporated into a multitiered activity of recovering significance for the text without necessarily lapsing into either a febrile essentialism or a constrictive formalism.

We can return finally to address Jeyifo's second formulation of postcoloniality. For him, interstitial or liminal postcoloniality defines an ambivalent mode of self-fashioning of the writer or critic which is neither First World nor Third World, neither securely and smugly metropolitan, nor assertively and combatively Third Worldist. The very terms which express the orientation of *this* school of post-colonial self-representation are revealing: diasporic, exilic, hybrid, in-between, cosmopolitan. (Jeyifo 53)

In short, this literature is acutely aware of the antinomies that riddle existence. It is interesting that Jeyifo *names* those he thinks are the dominant figures of this formulation of the postcolonial (Gabriel García Márquez, Salman Rushdie, Edward Said, Homi Bhabha), suggesting that the consciousness of the antinomic began with them. This, I think, is mistaken. "The African writer's very decision to use English," writes JanMohamed, "is engulfed by ironies, paradoxes, and contradictions" (JanMohamed 20). I agree with him and add that the very choice of the metropolitan language for the writing of postcolonial literatures secretes liminality into the inaugural act of postcolonialist representation itself. Furthermore, in the most sensitive of postcolonial writers, the representation is done with an uneasy awareness of the subtle contradictions inscribed in an emergent syncretic culture: on the one hand, the loss of a pristine traditional culture is regretted, but this is mingled with an awareness of its more reprehensible potential. On the other, the ruthless economic competition of urbanization and Westernization is deprecated while an awareness of the greater possibilities for vertical mobility, self-fulfillment, and freedom is registered. In that sense, the condition of interstitiality or liminality is the very essence of postcolonial writing, though each text establishes a different relationship to this conundrum. Jeyifo's typology breaks down and is particularly subverted by his own reading of Achebe's *Things Fall Apart* in which he emphasizes the novel's productive ambivalences and liminality in its continual relativization of *doxa* (represented by Okonkwo) as against paradoxa or irony (represented by Obierika and those at the margins of the text, such as *osus* and women).

What emerges, then, from the discourses of postcolonial criticism, is that it is new reading strategies that have come into being and are at issue, focusing on aspects of postcolonial texts that had hitherto been silenced. It is, to borrow an apt formulation of Irigaray's in another context, the "spaces that organize the scene, the blanks that sub-tend the scene's structuration and yet will not be read as such" (Irigaray 137–38) that have come into account in the readings of postcolonial literatures. And in the particular context of the criticism of African literature, the requirement that it move away from the dominant representationalist rhetoric to more nuanced approaches that will take account of the hitherto "silent spaces" and the subtle and often problematic relationships between text and context becomes patently imperative.

II

This reading of *Things Fall Apart*, then, is offered as a means of exposing the gap that exists between the realist African text and the reality that it is seen to represent. The novel is particularly useful for this enterprise because of its highly acclaimed (and well-deserved) literary status and the fact that it has been taken unproblematically since its publication in 1958.

It seems fruitful to conceive of the realism of *Things Fall Apart* as constructed on two levels simultaneously. At one level, the novel concerns itself with a description of Umuofian culture and its subversion by the contact with Western imperialism. This level of the novel can be perceived as metonymic of an Igbo or African reality. In Jakobsonian terms, the narrative progresses metonymically, with narrative elements selected for attention because they exist in discernible contiguous relation to one another. Significantly, however, the text frequently departs from the overarching narrative of the fall of Okonkwo and the division of the clan to pursue numerous anecdotes and digressions that are demonstrably not related to the main narrative but embody subtle qualifications of it. Furthermore, within the context of the unfolding events, the narrative generates a secondary level of conceptualization that can be seen as symbolic/metaphorical. This level subtends the metonymic text but gathers around itself all the antinomies associated with metaphor: ambiguity, contradiction, irony, and paradox.

The symbolic/metaphorical level of conceptualization reveals two closely related strata both at the level of content, the culture of Umuofia, and *also* at the level of the narrative's discursive strategies in general. On the one hand, Umuofia, as a culture, has institutions governed by a viable symbolic order. Though the narrative text itself reflects some of the central concerns of the culture, both in relation to the cultural institutions and more generally in relation to the culture's governing symbolic system, it employs certain discursive strategies that articulate a symbolic/metaphorical system not relatable solely to the symbolic order reflected by the actual culture. The narrative's own order is derivable from the various configurations of significances and in its structuration of the narrated events. It is at this strategic level of symbolic structuration that the novel's hierarchization of gender and the subtle subversion of its proffered hierarchy are played out, showing that the novel's realism, in the characteristic manner of a *writing*, continually produces excessive meanings. Taking it at face value then becomes inadequate and problematic.

Several critics have rightly pointed out that Okonkwo's downfall is mainly due to a neurotic concern with "manliness." Okonkwo pursues distinction, in the words of Abiola Irele, with an "obsessive single-mindedness that soon degenerates into egocentricity, until he comes to map out for himself very narrow limits of action or reflection" (Irele 11). Almost every critic of the novel pays attention to the nature of Okonkwo's tragic character, relating it to the narrow limits of action defined by his society as "manly" and showing how his character precludes the exercise of the more "feminine" virtues of tolerance, tenderness, and patience. Innes argues that it is a flaw encoded in the very symbolic order of Umuofian society and purveyed by its linguistic codes. Okonkwo's attitudes are framed by the culture's language and its implications, and it is this that makes him "unable to acknowledge the mythic implications of femininity and its values" (Innes,

Chinua Achebe, 117). What seems to have been ignored, however, is the fact that in totally focusing the narrative through Okonkwo and the male-dominated institutions of Umuofia, the novel itself implies a patriarchal discourse within which women, and much of what they can be taken to represent in the novel, are restricted to the perceptual fringes. In spite of this demonstrable patriarchy, however, Okonkwo is at various times ironized by the text, suggesting the inadequacy of the values he represents and ultimately those of the hierarchy that ensures his social status. It is important to stress that it is not just Okonkwo's values that are shown as inadequate, but those of the patriarchal society in general; he represents an extreme manifestation of the patriarchy that pervades the society as a whole.

Part of the structuration of the male-female hierarchy in the novel derives from what Chantal Zabus, in talking about the use of proverbs in *Things Fall Apart*, refers to as the "ethno-text." She defines the term in relation to "the discursive segments that belong to the vast corpus of African traditional oral material" (Zabus 20). Her focus is mainly on the implications for the demise of orality that the transposition of traditional discursive elements into the Europhone novel implies, but it is useful to expand the term ethno/text to embrace all of the traditional cultural practices that are depicted in a novel, be they linguistically based or not. It is the structuration derivable from Igbo culture itself that arguably offers the raw materials for the construction of the fictional world of Umuofia.[7] It is noticeable, for instance, that the female principle has a very important part to play in Umuofia's governing cosmogony. Ani, goddess of the earth, "played a greater part in the life of the people than any other deity" (26). The Week of Peace set aside for her before the celebration of the New Yam Festival is a time of tolerance, relaxation, and peaceful coexistence. So important is Ani that all of the society's activities are judged in terms of what is or is not acceptable to her; indeed, she is "the ultimate judge of morality and conduct" (26). G. D. Killam has been led to suggest, from an examination of the role of Ani in the lives of the people, that "a powerful 'female principle' pervades the whole society of Umuofia" (20). It is important to note, however, that this powerful female principle is most potent at a symbolic/metaphorical level. It finds its most powerful expression at the level of the clan's governing cosmogony. And, at all times, the female principle attracts some masculine essentiality in its definition. Ani has constant communion with the "fathers of the clan" because they are buried within her. She has a male priest, while Agbala, Oracle of the Hills and Caves, has a priestess as spokesperson. And in the arena of the traditionally most masculine-centered activity, war, the governing principle of Umuofian war medicine is believed to be an old woman with one leg, *agadi-nwayi* (9). The clan's cultural values institute the feminine in a very powerful position within the governing symbolic system, taking care to suggest a subtle interfusion of the two principles of male and female. In that sense, Umuofia's governing symbolic system suggests a necessary balancing of the two principles, so that the notion of a pervasive, single "female principle" requires qualification.

At the level of the metonymic realist description of the institutional practices of Umuofia, however, the ethnotext yields a completely different reality. Umuofia is a male-dominated society, and the narrative reflects this aspect of the culture. The continuing emphasis in the text is on depicting male-dominated activities—the oratory of men before the gathered clan, the acquisition and cultivation of farmlands, courage and resourcefulness in sport and war, and the giving and taking of brides. The text's focus on the patriarchy inscribed in the ethnotext is particularly evident in the portrayal of the political institution of justice. Since the Umuofians are acephalous, their central political power is invested in the *ndichie*, council of elders, and in the *egwugwu*, masked spirits of the ancestors who come to sit in judgment over civil and criminal disputes.

It is in the attitude of women toward the *egwugwu* that the hierarchy of power is unmasked. The *egwugwu* emerge to sit in judgment with "guttural and awesome" voices. And the sounds of their voices are no less mystifying than the sounds that herald their entry:

> *Aru oyim de de de dei!* flew around the dark closed hut like tongues of fire. The ancestral spirits of the clan were abroad.

The metal gong beat continuously now and the flute, shrill and powerful, floated on the chaos.

And then the *egwugwu* appeared. The women and children sent up a great shout and took to their heels. It was instinctive. A woman fled as soon as an *egwugwu* came in sight. And when, as on that day, nine of the greatest masked spirits in the clan came out together it was a terrifying spectacle. Even Mgbafo took to her heels and had to be restrained by her brothers. (63)

It is interesting that in its presentation of the scene the narrative betrays its attitude toward the relationship between women and power. Significantly, the *egwugwu* are described in an idiom of grandeur, the "tongues of fire" recalling the dramatic events of Pentecost recorded in the Acts of the Apostles (2:1–4). And the women's "instinctive" flight at their emergence can be read as the awestruck response to these masked ancestral spirits. A few lines later, however, the women reveal that they have more knowledge of the reality behind the masked spirits than they care to express: "Okonkwo's wives, and perhaps other women as well, might have noticed that the second *egwugwu* had the springy walk of Okonkwo. . . . But if they thought these things they kept them within themselves" (64–65). The narrative paints the scene with so much detail, objective distancing, and humor that it is impossible not to regard it as of the clearest "realistic" vintage. But the "thoughtful silence" of the women before this all-important masculine institution is ironic. The narrative works both to reveal the "natural" and "instinctive" female attitude toward power and also to ironize the pretensions of the masculine social institutions. But it is important to note that the irony does not work to radically undermine the hierarchy at the center of the power structure because the women constrain themselves to "thinking" their knowledge, but leave it unexpressed.

Some aspects of the narrative can be construed wholly as fictional constructions and not as trajectories of the ethnotext. Here it is the narrative, in terms of its own discursive strategies, that is responsible for any impression of patriarchy that comes across.

In the relationships in Okonkwo's household, for instance, we find a subtle definition of his masculinity that depends on a particular view of the women in his domestic set-up. Twice we are told Okonkwo beats his wives. The first time, it is Ojiugo, his last wife. The narrator's preface to the incident must be noted:

> Okonkwo was provoked to justifiable anger by his youngest wife, who went to plait her hair at her friend's house and did not return early enough to prepare the afternoon meal. (21)

If Okonkwo's anger is "justifiable" then the narrative has passed judgment on Ojiugo's "irrationality' " and "thoughtlessness" from her husband's perspective. And it is significant that the text does not bother to let Ojiugo explain herself on her return. It is just reported that "when she returned he beat her very heavily" (21). In his anger Okonkwo forgets that it is the Week of Peace, and even when he is reminded, he does not stop because, as we are told, he "was not the man to stop beating somebody half way through, not even for fear of a goddess" (21). In earning a severe reprimand from Ani's priest for flouting the rules governing the observance of the Week of Peace, his "manly" values are clearly shown as inadequate, but his character as derivable from this scene is as significant in terms of his attitudes toward his wives as it is in his attitudes toward the cultural mores he violates. In this segment of the narrative, however, there is a tacit but emphatic foregrounding of the social as against the private, because the beating occurs during a period of heightened cultural consciousness due to the Week of Peace.

At another time, it is Ekwefi who is to suffer the brunt of her husband's violent temper. In this instance it is only to satisfy his suppressed anger at the enforced laxity that precedes the New Yam Festival (27–28). Both of these instances are explications of what the text has already told us earlier on but only now depicts:

> Okonkwo ruled his household with a heavy hand. His wives, especially the youngest, lived in perpetual fear of his fiery temper, and so did his little children. (9)

The importance of this method of characterization for the patriarchal discourse inscribed in the text is that it depends on a binary opposition being established between Okonkwo and the other characters. And it is a binarism that frequently takes him as the primary value. When the binarism works to undermine Okonkwo and his relative values, it regularly foregrounds other men around whom alternative values in the text can be seen as being organized. Obierika and Nwoye are important nuclei of alternative values in this sense. In relation to Okonkwo's wives, however, the binarism implies a secondary role for them. Whatever significance is recovered for them must be gleaned from their silence, for they are not portrayed by the narrative as contributing to the *action* and its outcome.

The essential discursive operation of containing the significance of the women is most evident in relation to the handling of Ekwefi and Ezinma. The text builds them up until they seem to be alternative centers of signification, but it frustrates the completion of these significations by banishing them out of the narrative at some point. Ezinma and her mother, Ekwefi, are the only female characters developed by the narrative. We are told that Ekwefi ran away from her first husband to marry Okonkwo (28). By focusing on the relationship between her and her daughter, the narrative reveals the joys of motherhood and the closeness that mother and daughter enjoyed:

> Ezinma did not call her mother *Nne* like all children. She called her by her name, Ekwefi, as her father and other grown-up people did. The relationship between them was not only that of mother and child. There was something in it like the companionship of equals, which was strengthened by such little conspiracies as eating eggs in the bedroom. (54)

The warmth depicted in the relationship between mother and daughter aids in eliciting the reader's empathy with them, and thereby opens up a space for possible significations around these two. The significations, however, seem to be limited to a definition of maternal and filial instincts only. The episodes around

Ekwefi's pursuit of Chielo when her daughter is taken on a nocturnal round of the villages by the priestess are significant in that respect (72–76). And when she stands with tears in her eyes at the mouth of the cave into which Chielo has entered with her daughter and swears within herself that if she hears Ezinma cry she will rush into the cave to defend her against all the gods in the world, we know we are seeing terribly courageous maternal, and indeed human, instincts at play. Indeed, the scene even gains wider significance if perceived in contrast to Okonkwo's handling of Ikemefuna, who called him "father." In both instances where parental instincts are put to the test, the central characters are, significantly, taken outside the village into the forest. In Ekwefi's case, as in Okonkwo's, an element of eeriness governs the atmosphere, with Ekwefi's situation being the more frightening of the two. Both episodes involve the enigmatic injunction of deities, but whereas Ekwefi is prepared to defy the gods in defense of her daughter, Okonkwo submits to cowardice and participates in Ikemefuna's ritual murder. Ekwefi has been given admirable but limited stature by the text, and this is partly because it refuses to lend her a more crucial role in the action.

In Ezinma, we see a tough-minded and questioning personality. When her mother tells her the tale of the Tortoise and the Birds, she is quick to point out that the tale does not have a song (70). She joins the ranks of other male characters who pose questions of varying interest in the narrative: Obierika, Nwoye, Mr. Brown, Okonkwo, the district commissioner. Interestingly, her questions are posed in relation to what is not of great consequence in the narrative, the tales of women told in their huts at night to children, a context from which Okonkwo thinks his sons should be excluded, the better to ensure the growth of their manliness. At another time, Ezinma ventures to carry her father's stool to the village *ilo*, a move she is reminded is the male preserve of a son (32). And when she sits, she often fails to adopt the proper sitting posture prescribed for her sex and has to be forcefully reminded by her father in his characteristic bellowing command (32). When, in the quest for her *iyi-uwa*, she calmly takes her impatient father, a renowned medicine man, and indeed much of the village on a circular "treasure hunt," we see she enjoys the momentary leadership position that the situation permits her (56–60).

It is also significant that Ezinma comes to take the place of a boy and someone who can be trusted in her father's eyes.[8] At periods when he is in the greatest emotional crises, Okonkwo instinctively turns to his daughter. Such is the case, for instance, after his participation in the murder of Ikemefuna. After the boy's sacrifice, "he does not taste food for two days" and drinks palm wine "from morning till night." His eyes were "red and fierce like the eyes of a rat when it was caught by the tail and dashed against the floor" (44). On the third day, he asks Ekwefi to prepare him roast plantains, and these are brought by Ezinma. We notice the filial attachment between the two:

> "You have not eaten for two days," said his daughter Ezinma when she brought the food to him. "So you must finish this." She sat down and stretched her legs in front of her. Okonkwo ate the food absent-mindedly. "She should have been a boy," he thought as he looked at his ten-year-old daughter. He passed her a piece of fish. (44)

The narrative further registers a crucial position for Ezinma in our eyes when it tells us that during his enforced exile Okonkwo "never stopped regretting that Ezinma was a girl" and that of all his children "she alone understood his every mood. A bond of sympathy had grown between them" (122). It is to her that her father gives the task of convincing her other sisters not to marry any eligible men from Mbanta, but to wait until they return to Umuofia to make a better social impact on arrival. Thus, the space for registering significations around Ezinma and for exploring a viable notion of manliness that would offer a possible contrast with Okonkwo's notions of manliness are clearly built by the narrative. It is then highly problematic that Ezinma vanishes from the story after the return from exile and is never referred to again. It is as if to suggest that in the crucial exercise of delineating the climactic consequences of the meeting of the two cultures at the end of the novel, there is no space for women.

How, we might speculate, would the novel have been different if it had focused on Ezinma's reactions to the changes in Umuofia from the specific standpoint of the institution of marriage? Or how would the society's value systems have been perceived if their interrogation had been focalized through Ezinma instead of Nwoye and Obierika? And what would our attitudes toward Okonkwo's death have been if Ezinma's reaction to the event had been registered alongside Obierika's? In fact, is it not valid to ponder what the reaction of the women in general was to the mores of the society and the radical changes that unfold in the course of the narrative? There seems to be an unconscious recognition of the potential inherent in Ezinma and Ekwefi's characterizations for subverting the patriarchal discourse of the text. The significations around them go to join the various meanings around those "othered" by Umuofia and the narrative, such as twins, *osu*, and those who die of abominable ailments. These come briefly into the perceptual horizon, and though marginalized, remain potentially disruptive, partly because the mere fact of their presence constitutes a qualification of what has been centralized by the narrative. Though it has foregrounded the masculine in the male-female hierarchy inscribed at the level of the description of events, the narrative has also opened the hierarchy to a subtle interrogation of its values, even if ultimately leaving it intact. Considering the ways in which women are handled in the novel, it is possible to perceive *Things Fall Apart* as operating a mode of realism that does not just "name" an African reality; it also seeks to fix certain concepts, such as those around "woman," within a carefully hierarchized system of values that underprivileges them. In this light, *Things Fall Apart* would almost answer to the charges leveled by Hélène Cixous at the language of philosophical systems in general: they are all phallocentric and seek to privilege the masculine in the patterns of male-female binary pairs often proffered as "natural." Cixous's charge requires some qualification in the context of *Things Fall Apart*, however, particularly because its hierarchization of the masculine-feminine undergoes a continual subversion, revealing a more profound contradiction at the heart of its construction of the "natural" relations between "masculine" and "feminine."

If, on the one hand, patriarchy is privileged by both the ethnotext and the narrative itself, then this same patriarchy is alternatively shown as sitting uneasily within the general discourse of symbolization that the text constructs. It is in the area of the political themes of the novel that this is most evident. The contact between the colonizing and the traditional cultures is attended by a subtle construction of the male-female polarities which this time are not hierarchical but rather intermingle and change places in restless slippage.

When the white man first appears on the perceptual horizon of Umuofia, he is naturalized by being linked to the marginal. The white man is first referred to as an albino (52). Later, when his violent intrusion into the perceptual horizon through the riot of Abame has to be confronted, Obierika reflects other previous self-satisfied attitudes toward these white men in his reporting of the rout:

> I am greatly afraid. We have heard stories about the white men who made the powerful guns and the strong drinks and took slaves away across the seas, but no one thought the stories were true. (99)

In other words, they were harmless because they inhabited what was thought to be the realm of the fictive. When white men make their first physical appearance in the shape of Christian missionaries, they are first confined to the Evil Forest in which were buried "all those who died of the really evil diseases, like leprosy and smallpox" (105). They are not wanted in the clan and so are given land that is thought to be only marginally useful to the clan. But the early Christianity is depicted by the narrative as embodying and stressing qualities considered womanish— love, tolerance, affection, and mercy.[9] Okonkwo characteristically evaluates the missionaries as a "lot of effeminate men clucking like old hens" (108). A feminine "valence" attaches to the Christians. In this sense, the early relationship between Umuofia and Christianity describes a male-female hierarchy in which Umuofia is masculine and privileged. In effect the narrative suggests that the white missionary vanguard of the colonizing enterprise possessed an initial effeminacy which was amusing and, in effect, tolerable.

The effeminacy turns out to be highly contradictory and sinister, however. The church succeeds in attracting to itself all those marginalized by the society, *efulefus*, *osus*, and the men of no title, *agbala*. In doing this, it emasculates the society, making it incapable of standing as one. And as Obierika observes with uncanny perspicacity, "the whiteman has put a knife on the things that held us together" (124). In figuring the white man's intrusion first in terms of "effeminate clucking," and now in terms of an invading knife, the narrative prepares the way for an inversion of the implied male-female hierarchization that it suggested in describing the first contact between the missionaries and the culture of Umuofia. Indeed, it is significant that at the crucial point when Okonkwo seeks to assert the possibilities of a violent rebellion, his own clan breaks into a catatonic, "effeminate" confusion. At that point the text transfers the feminine valence with which it first constructed the white man onto the Umuofians. The shift of the feminine valence from the invaders to the invaded helps to define an important contradiction at the heart of the text's attitudes toward the colonial encounter. Colonialism is perceived at one and the same time as feminine (in the missionaries) and masculine (at the level of the British administration and its ruthless exercise of power). For colonialism to be able to succeed, Umuofia has to be transformed from the essential masculinity which has governed the textual construction of the society to an enervated femininity at the crucial point when rebellion was an option. In that sense, the narrative depicts Umuofia's "castration," with Okonkwo's suicide representing the ultimate overthrow of its masculinity.[10]

It is arguable, then, that the textual strategies have ascribed different values to the male-female hierarchy at two different levels of the text. At the level of metonymic realistic description, a certain ironized patriarchy governs the construction of the fictional Umuofia that derives its impulse partly from the ethno-text. But at the level of symbolic conceptualization, the narrative has hinted at its own patriarchal discourse which it has pro-

ceeded to undermine most powerfully when describing the colonial encounter. Then, the male-female hierarchy that has governed the text completely collapses, and its place is taken over
by an exchange of the "masculine" and "feminine" between the
two poles of the contending cultures. *Things Fall Apart* thus explores a loving image of Umuofia at the same time as it reveals
a dissatisfaction with the values of the society it describes in such
detail. And this is undertaken at a more subtle level than the
mere explication of content can reveal. In a very important
sense, the "naming" of a precolonial culture and the depiction of
its subversion by a marauding imperialism has involved the necessary construction of philosophical categories both *within* the
precolonial culture and *between* it and the invading one which fail
to stand still, involving a doubling back of the categories such as
to problematize the very assumptions on which the enterprise of
"naming" was undertaken in the first place. The novel thus reveals that its own realism is a construction traversed by both
sensitivity and ambivalence so that it cannot be addressed unproblematically.

What is important, in the context of criticism relating to *Things
Fall Apart* and the African novel in general, is that critics often
take novelistic realism at face value. They thus fail to perceive
the more subtle workings of the texts with which they engage
and fail to interrogate the assumptions on which they are based.
Even more crucially, they fail to see that "realism" is an "ism"
and a careful *restructuration* of various subtexts, so that its relationship to the Real cannot be taken for granted. In focusing on the
novel's handling of patriarchy, women, and the feminine, I have
tried to suggest that reading "culture" out of a novel is valuable
but inadequate, and that this needs to be supplemented with an
awareness that *Things Fall Apart*, like African novels in general,
possesses a richly ambivalent attitude toward its culture that can
only be discovered by paying attention both to the reality processed and to the larger discursive strategies employed. Every
"ism," to echo Soyinka in *Kongi's Harvest*, is an "absolutism," and
that is true of realism as well as criticism in all its disguises.

Notes

All page references to *Things Fall Apart* are from the African Writers series edition of 1962.

1. I focus attention mainly on the criticism of Achebe's novels set in the past, though the attitudes relating to them are pertinent to the novels set in the post-independence era. Indeed, James Olney and also Eustace Palmer see Achebe's novelistic career as paradigmatic of the development of the African novel in general. See Olney; Palmer 63.

2. In varying degrees this was the informing sentiment behind the general accounts of African critics in the 1960s and 1970s, such as Obiechina, Gakwandi, Ogungbesan, and Palmer.

3. It is significant that romance seems to have dominated the discourse of Onitsha market literature. But romance is in fact rationalism of a different order because modern romance generally depicts victory over the tribulations of the "real" world. Indeed, the market literature was an expression of a "Mills and Boon" reading culture that has become very powerful in the whole.

4. *Bolekaja*, which literally means "come down and fight," was borrowed from a phrase used by the conductors of Nigerian passenger lorries in their fiercely competitive touting for passengers and was adopted as a description of the Chinweizu et al. type of critical stance.

5. Soyinka perceived this tendency toward the mythopoeic in African literature as early as 1963 and tried to account for it in "From a Common Backcloth." Richard Priebe also assessed the general attitudes toward this mythopoeic tendency and argued for the perception of a specific literary tradition deriving from Amos Tutuola and growing around the mythopoeic, but the insights these two suggested do not seem to have been taken up in later critical assessments of African literature. The mythopoeic tendency in writers like Awoonor and Armah were recognized, but the critical assessments of their work were not integrated within an analysis of what relationships their efforts had with the discursive universes of Tutuola and even Soyinka.

6. The terms in which Frederic Jameson defines narrative as a socially symbolic act are very useful in this context, except that I do not think it is necessary to always grasp the narrative text as an essentially strategic confrontation between classes.

7. Several studies have been devoted to uncovering the Igbo back-

ground of Achebe's novel but perhaps the most wide-ranging and systematic is Wren's *Achebe's World*.

8. It is significant that in seeing her as a "son," Okonkwo attempts to erase his daughter's femininity. This then becomes a manifestation of his neurotic concern with "manliness," and his attitude toward his daughter opens up a further space for a criticism of his values.

9. Weinstock and Ramadan make the same point in relation to the symbolic structure of masculine and feminine patterns inscribed at the level of folktales and proverbs in the novel, suggesting that Christianity represents an apotheosis of the feminine values.

10. Other critics interpret the ambivalence in the novel's description of the colonial encounter as a function of the improper "targeting" of its readership. The novel is then unfavorably contrasted with the more politically aggressive novels of Armah and Ngugi. For a careful statement of this position, see Tayoba Tata Ngene's "Gesture in Modern African Narrative."

Works Cited

Achebe, Chinua. "The Novelist as Teacher." In Achebe, *Morning Yet on Creation Day*, 42–45. London: Heinemann, 1975.

Amuta, Chidi. *The Theory of African Literature: Implications for Practical Criticism.* London: Zed, 1989.

Ashcroft, Bill, Gareth Griffiths, and Helen Tiffin. *The Empire Writes Back: Theory and Practice in Post-Colonial Literatures.* London: Routledge, 1989.

Barber, Karin. "African-Language Literatures and Post-Colonial Criticism." *Research in African Literatures* 26 (1995): 3–30.

Bhabha, Homi K. "Representation and the Colonial Text: A Critical Exploration of Some Forms of Mimeticism." In *The Theory of Reading*, edited by Frank Gloversmith, 93–120. Sussex: Harvester, 1984.

Chinweizu, Onwuchekwa Jemie, and Ihechukwu Madubuike. *Towards the Decolonization of African Literature.* Enugu, Nigeria: Fourth Dimension, 1980.

Cixous, Hélène. "Sorties." In *Modern Criticism and Theory: A Reader*, edited by David Lodge, 286–93. London: Longman, 1988.

Egudu, R. N. "Achebe and the Igbo Narrative Tradition." *Research in African Literatures* 12, no. 1 (1981): 43–54.

Gakwandi, Shatto Arthur. *The Novel and Contemporary Experience in Africa.* London: Heinemann, 1977.

Innes, C. L. *Chinua Achebe.* Cambridge: Cambridge University Press, 1990.

————. "Language, Poetry and Doctrine in *Things Fall Apart.*" In *Critical Perspectives on Chinua Achebe,* edited by C. L. Innes and Bernth Lindfors, 111–15. London: Heinemann, 1979.

Innes, C. L., and Bernth Lindfors, eds. *Critical Perspectives on Chinua Achebe.* London: Heinemann, 1979.

Irele, Abiola. "The Tragic Conflict in the Novels of Chinua Achebe." In *Critical Perspectives on Chinua Achebe,* edited by C. L. Innes and Bernth Lindfors, 10–21. London: Heinemann, 1979.

Irigaray, Luce. *Speculum of the Other Woman.* Translated by Gillian Gill. Ithaca, NY: Cornell University Press, 1985.

Jameson, Frederic. *The Political Unconscious: Narrative as a Socially Symbolic Act.* Ithaca, NY: Cornell University Press, 1981.

JanMohamed, Abdul. "Sophisticated Primitivism: Syncretism of Oral and Literate Modes in Achebe's *Things Fall Apart.*" *Ariel* 15, no. 4 (1984): 19–39.

Jeyifo, Biodun. "For Chinua Achebe: The Resilience of Obierika." In *Chinua Achebe: A Celebration,* edited by Kirsten Holst Petersen and Anna Rutherford, 51–70. Plymouth, NH: Dangaroo, 1991.

Killam, G. D. *The Writings of Chinua Achebe.* London: Heinemann, 1977.

Larson, Charles. *The Emergence of African Fiction.* London: Macmillan, 1978.

Lindfors, Bernth. "The Palm-Oil with Which Achebe's Words Are Eaten." In *Critical Perspectives on Chinua Achebe,* edited by C. L. Innes and Bernth Lindfors, 47–66. London: Heinemann, 1979.

Lodge, David. *The Modes of Modern Writing: Metaphor, Metonymy and the Typology of Literature.* London: Routledge, 1977.

McCarthy, Eugene B. "Rhythm and Narrative Method in Achebe's *Things Fall Apart.*" *Novel* 18, no. 3 (1985): 243–356.

Ngene, Tayoba Tata. "Gesture in Modern African Narrative." Ph.D. diss., University of Texas, 1987.

Obiechina, Emmanuel N. *Culture, Tradition, and Society in the West African Novel.* Cambridge: Cambridge University Press, 1975.

Ogungbesan, Kolawole, ed. *New West African Literature.* London: Heinemann, 1979.

Olney, James. "The African Novel in Transition: Chinua Achebe." *South Atlantic Quarterly* 70 (1970): 299–316.

Palmer, Eustace. *The Growth of the African Novel.* London: Heinemann, 1979.

Petersen, Kirsten Holst, and Anna Rutherford, eds. *Chinua Achebe: A Celebration.* Plymouth, NH: Dangaroo, 1991.

Priebe, Richard. "Escaping the Nightmare of History: The Development of a Mythic Consciousness in West African Literature." *Ariel* 4, no. 2 (1973): 55–67.

Shelton, Austin. "The Palm-Oil of Language: Proverbs in Chinua Achebe's Novels." *Modern Language Quarterly* 30, no. 1 (1985): 86–111.

Soyinka, Wole. "From a Common Backcloth." *American Scholar* 32, no. 4 (1963): 387–97.

Weinstock, D. J., and Cathy Ramadan. "Symbolic Structure in *Things Fall Apart*." In *Critical Perspectives on Chinua Achebe*, edited by C. L. Innes and Bernth Lindfors, 126–34. London: Heinemann, 1979.

White, Hayden. *Metahistory: The Historical Imagination in Nineteenth-Century Europe*. Baltimore, MD: Johns Hopkins University Press, 1973.

Wren, Robert. *Achebe's World: The Historical and Cultural Context of the Novels of Chinua Achebe*. Harlow: Longman, 1981.

Zabus, Chantal. "The Logos-Eaters: The Igbo Ethno-Text." In *Chinua Achebe: A Celebration*, edited by Kirsten Holst Petersen and Anna Rutherford, 19–30. Plymouth, NH: Dangaroo, 1991.

An Interview with Chinua Achebe

CHARLES H. ROWELL

◆ ◆ ◆

C HARLES H. ROWELL: Mr. Achebe, here in the United
States, those of us who read twentieth-century world literature think of you as one of the most important writers in this
era. We view you as an artist—and for us the word *artist* has a
certain kind of meaning. In the African world, does *artist* have the
same meaning as that conceptualized in the Western world? Or,
more specifically, what do Nigerians conceive the writer to be? Is
he or she thought of as an artist, a creator of the kind that we
think of here in the United States when we speak about writers?

Chinua Achebe: Well, I think that there are obviously certain
common factors when anybody talks about an artist, whether in
America or in Africa. I think there are certain factors which
would apply to either place—and so we can leave those aside, if
you like. But there are differences definitely, in emphasis if not
absolute, and it is these that one should draw attention to. The
artist has always existed in Africa in the form of the sculptor, the
painter, or the storyteller, the poet. And I suppose the role of
the writer, the modern writer, is closer to that of the *griot*, the

historian and poet, than to any other practitioner of the arts. But I think one can find, even from the other forms of art, fundamental statements, cultural statements, made about art in general which seem to me to be peculiarly African in their emphasis.

What I mean, for instance, is this. The ceremony which is called *Mbari* among the Igbo people is a festival of art, a celebration of humanity. It is not a festival of oral arts; it is more a festival of the visual arts, the plastic arts, though drama and songs are presented there as well. There you will find, I think, what our people thought of art—and that's the reason I am referring to it. Some of the statements made by *Mbari* are very profound. One is that art is in the service of the community. There is no apology at all about that. Art is invented to make the life of the community easier, not to make it more difficult. Artists are people who live in society. The professional artist, the master artist and craftsman, is a special kind of person, but he is not the only person who is expected to practice art.

For this celebration, this *Mbari* celebration, ordinary people are brought in to work under the supervision of professional artists, because we assume that everybody has art in themselves. So ordinary people are brought in, and they are secluded with the professionals for a period—months and sometimes even years— to create this celebration of life through art. So what this says to me is that art is not something up there in the rarified reaches of the upper atmosphere but something which is down here where we live. Art is not something which is beyond the comprehension of ordinary people. It is something which ordinary people not only can understand and use, but even take part in making. So these are ideas which I don't find very much in the West, you see. These are some of the ideas we have that one should specify and draw attention to. If one looked at what we do and compared it with what our contemporaries do in the West, these ideas would explain some of the differences and some of the puzzlement that certain Western critics have, for instance, when they encounter African literature and say: "Why do they do that? Why are they so political?" And they ask these questions to the point of irritation. If only they understood where we were coming from, then perhaps they would not be so puzzled. Perhaps they would even be open to persuasion on this score.

Rowell: At the University of Virginia last April [19, 1989], you responded to a question from the audience which I think describes further what you have just said or is related to it. I can't quote you directly. However, I do remember that you implied that art, in Nigeria, is intimately linked to social responsibility and that it is connected to that which is moral, that which is ethical, that which is right, or that which is good. I think you made that statement in response to a question about Joseph Conrad—and I'm not trying to get into a Joseph Conrad discussion here. Will you say more about art?

Achebe: Yes. The festival which I have just been talking about, the *Mbari* festival, is commanded from time to time by the goddess of creativity, the earth goddess, called Ala or Ani by the Igbo people. This goddess is not only responsible for creativity in the world; she is also responsible for morality. So that an abomination is described as taboo to her, as *nso-ani*. That's the word for something which is not supposed to be done—not just a wrong doing, but an abomination—something which is forbidden by this goddess. So obviously by putting the two portfolios, if you like, of art and morality in her domain, a statement is being made about the meaning of art. Art cannot be in the service of destruction, cannot be in the service of oppression, cannot be in the service of evil. We tend to be a little apologetic about that. You know, if you talk about "good," people will get uneasy. They become uneasy. I don't know why that should be so, but we work ourselves into all kinds of corners from which we then become uneasy when certain words are mentioned. That's not the fault of the words; there is perhaps something wrong with us.

So there is no question at all, in the view of my people, that art cannot serve immorality. And morality here doesn't mean "be good and go to church." That's not what I'm talking about. I'm talking about manifest wickedness like murder. There is no art that can say that it is right to commit murder. I remember, I think it was Yevtushenko who once said that "you cannot be a poet and a slave trader." It seems to me fairly obvious that you

cannot combine those particular professions, because they are an-
tithetical. And this is not something which only the Africans or
the Igbo people know. I think it is there, embedded also in the
minds of other people. The difference is that our culture makes
no bones about it, and I think this comes through too in our
writing. It does not mean that our heroes have to be angels. Of
course not. It means, in fact, that heroes will be as human as
anybody else, and yet the frontier between good and evil must
not be blurred. It means that somewhere, no matter how fuzzy
it may be to us, there is still a distinction between what is permissible and what is not permissible. One thing which is not
permissible is to stereotype and dehumanize your fellows. That is
not permissible in our art. You celebrate them, their good and
their bad. You celebrate even rascals, because they abound in the
world and are part of its richness.

Rowell: You just said that this conceptualization of art comes
through "in our writing." Will you talk about how this is exemplified in your own work or that of other African writers,
either consciously or unconsciously?

Achebe: Well, I think if you took a tape recorder and went
around African writers, I bet you will find them making rather
large statements for what they do. You'll find them saying, for
instance, "I am writing so that the life of my people will be
better." I even found a modern story in Hausa which ended: "And
so they married and they produced many sons and daughters
who helped to raise the standard of education in the country."
That's the way the story ends, imitating the format of the folk
story but obviously turning it into something very practical for
today, you see. And I said elsewhere, if anybody reads this story
and says, "Oh now, this is an anticlimax," he could not possibly
know anything about Africa, because the story of today has to
do with raising the standards of education of the country, you
see. We are engaged in a great mission, and we attempt to bring
this into our storytelling. It is this mission that our storyteller
brings into his tale without the slightest inclination to discuss it
self-consciously in the way we are doing now. He instinctively
felt a need for his story and supplied it. This is why we get letters

saying to me, for instance, "Why did you let Okonkwo fail in *Things Fall Apart*? Why did you let a good man or a good cause stumble and fall?" At another time, I remember a letter from a woman in Ghana saying, "Why did Obi, in *No Longer at Ease*, not have the courage to marry the girl he loved instead of crumbling?" People are expecting from literature serious comment on their lives. They are not expecting frivolity. They are expecting literature to say something important to help them in their struggle with life.

That is what literature, what art, was supposed to do: to give us a second handle on reality so that when it becomes necessary to do so, we can turn to art and find a way out. So it is a serious matter. That's what I'm saying, and I think every African writer you talk to will say something approaching what I have just said—in different forms of words—except those who have too much of the West in them, and there are some people, of course, who are that way. But the writer I am referring to is the real and serious African writer. I think you will find him saying something which sounds as serious, as austere, or as earnest as what I have just said.

Rowell: You've mentioned the *griot*. I have read many things about what a *griot* is. And sometimes these texts seem to contradict each other. What is a *griot*? The word itself sounds Francophone.

Achebe: It's a word that comes from somewhere; I don't even know where it comes from. I know it certainly is not a Nigerian word. It's not an Igbo word. But it is a word which concerns us, because we know roughly what kind of person we are talking about. We are talking about the traditional poet and historian. The function of this person would not be exactly the same thing in all cultures. Where you have a monarchical system, for instance, the chances are that the *griot* or the poet, this historian, would be connected with the history of the dynasty. This is supposedly where problems immediately arise, you know. How reliable, then, is this poet, who resides in the court of the emperor, reciting the history? There are problems there. And the greatest *griots*, I think, have managed to find a way around those problems.

How they do it we cannot go into here. It suffices to remind us that seven hundred years after the life and death of Sundiata, the first emperor of Mali, the *griots* in West Africa were still reciting the story of his birth and life and death. It was only in the fifties, the 1950s, that this story was finally put down in writing. And the person who put it down in writing went to different and widely separated places and compared the versions given by various *griots* and discovered that the core of the story remained the same, you see. This is quite remarkable over a period of seven hundred years . . . because we tend to think that unless something is scribbled down on some piece of paper it cannot be true. I don't know who told us that. And we have come to believe it ourselves, that our history should be measured in terms of paper. So whenever you don't have a piece of paper, somebody says there is no history. And we seem to be quite ready to accept it. So you would find our historians going to archives in Portugal, for instance, to see what some sailor from Portugal had said when he came to Benin in the fifteenth century. We don't ask the condition of this sailor when he was making his entry, whether he was drunk or sober. He is on a piece of paper and therefore reliable— and more reliable than what you might gather in the field by asking people: "What do you remember? What do your people remember about this?"

Anyway, I think we are learning. We know a little better now than we used to. Thanks to the work of people like the late Professor Kenneth Onwuka Dike, who helped to create a new historiography of Africa using the oral tradition. We know now that we can find some of the truth in oral traditions. Now, to get back to the problem of the *griot*, let me tell the story of one short fable in Hausa, which I think exemplifies the way a *griot* might approach his problem obliquely, because if you are dealing with the emperor who is so much more powerful than yourself, you have to have your wits around you. If you start telling a story which puts him in a bad light or a bad mood, your career will be very short indeed! So you have to find a way of getting around this problem.

Now this is a story, a very simple animal story, from the Hausa language, which I encountered years ago. And I have used it again and again because I think it is a marvelous little story. In my own words, it goes something like this: The snake was riding his horse, coiled up in his saddle. That's the way the snake rode his horse. And he came down the road and met the toad walking by the roadside. And the toad said to him, "Excuse me, sir, but that's not how to ride a horse." And the snake said, "No? Can you show me then?" And the toad said, "Yes, if you would step down, sir." So the snake came down. The toad jumped into the saddle and sat bolt upright and galloped most elegantly up and down the road. When he came back he said, "That's how to ride a horse." And the snake said, "Excellent. Very good. Very good, indeed. Thank you. Come down, if you don't mind." So the toad came down, and the snake went up and coiled himself in the saddle as he was used to doing and then said to the toad, "It is very good to know, but it is even better to have. What good does excellent horsemanship do to a man without a horse?" And with that he rode away.

Now, the Hausa, who made this story, are a monarchical people. They have classes: the emir, the upper class, the nobility, etc., down to the bottom, the ordinary people, the *talakawa*. As you can see, the snake in this story is an aristocrat, and the toad a commoner. The statement, even the rebuke, which the snake issues is, in fact, saying: "Keep where you belong. You see, people like me are entitled to horses, and we don't have to know how to ride. There's no point in being an expert. That's not going to help you." Now that's very nice in that kind of political situation. And we can visualize the emir and his court enjoying this kind of story and laughing their heads off—because, you see, it's putting the commoner in his place. But also if you think deeply about this story, it's a two-edged sword. I think that's the excellence of the *griot* who fashioned it. To put this other edge to it, which is not noticed at first . . . this other side is that the snake is incompetent, the snake is complacent, the snake is even unattractive. It's all there in the story, you see, and the time will come in this political system when all this will be questioned. Why is it that a snake is entitled to a horse? Why is it that the man who knows how to ride does not have a horse to ride? You see. This questioning will come in a revolutionary time, and when it comes you don't need another story. It is the same story that will stand ready to be used; and this to me is the excellence of the *griot* in creating laughter and hiding what you might call the glint of steel. In the voluminous folds of this laughter, you can catch the hint of a concealed weapon which will be used when the time comes. Now this is one way in which the *griot* gets around the problem of telling the emperor the truth, you see. That is very, very important. Of course, if the *griot* is strong enough to say this to the emperor in his face, he will do it. But if he is not, he will find a way to conceal his weapon. Of course, there will be *griots* who sell out, but we're not talking about those, those who sing for their dinner.

Rowell: After your reading and lecture at the University of Virginia last April, one of my graduate students, a native of Mauritania, said to me: "In this culture, meaning the Western culture, you meet knowledge, you meet erudition, you meet expertise, but not wisdom. Mr. Achebe speaks and writes wisdom." That was what the student, Mohamed B. Taleb-Khyar, said, and I quote him directly.

Achebe: That was very kind of him.

Rowell: What I would like to ask of you is this: Does this speaking wisdom characterize, in any way, the sensibility of the African artist?

Achebe: Yes, I think it does. Wisdom is as good a word to use, I think, in describing the seriousness I was talking about, this *gravitas* that I'm talking about which informs our art. We can be as jovial, as lighthearted, even as frivolous as anybody else. But everything has its place and its measure. When you are dealing with art of the level at which we are dealing with it, it's a serious matter, a matter of clarification and wisdom.

Rowell: You are a teacher—in the United States we would say that you are a professor—of literature. What is the status of teaching literature in Africa? That's to say, does the teaching of literature contribute positively or negatively in the development, for example, of the new Nigeria? In other words, what is the role of the humanities in the African context?

Achebe: Well, we as writers and artists have or should have a central role in the society. We are not necessarily carrying the day in that way of thinking. For instance, when I gave the National Lecture in Nigeria (which you give if you win the Nigerian National Merit Award, which is our highest honor for intellectual achievement), the lecture I gave recently in Nigeria was entitled "What Has Literature Got to Do with It?" It was about the problem of development which concerns all of us. How do we develop, how do we raise our standard of living, how do we improve the life of our people, how do we modernize, and all of that which we aspire to like anybody else? How do we even raise the income per capita? All of these things are important. What I'm asking is: What has literature got to do with them? Has literature any relevance to all this or is it simply something we can perhaps forget for the time being? Are we to concentrate on the hard sciences, and then perhaps when we have become developed we can afford the luxury of literature? Is that what we want? There will be people who say so. There are attempts, for instance, to shift the emphasis in the universities in Nigeria from the humanities to the sciences, to limit the admissions for the humanities and increase the admissions for the sciences. Now all that, of course, may be necessary. I really don't know, but I think any people who neglect the importance of addressing the minds and hearts and the spirit of the people will find that they will be really getting nowhere at all in their development. One of the examples I gave was a story told us in Japan.

Some years ago I was taking part in a symposium in Japan. The Japanese would bring two foreign experts to Japan to meet with about half a dozen local experts in similar disciplines. They would talk and discuss for three or four days. On this occasion, the subject was culture and development. I remember the story which a Japanese professor told. His grandfather went to the University of Tokyo and graduated, he said, I think, about 1900. All of his notes, the notes he wrote in the university as a student, were written in English. His own father graduated about 1920. Half of his notes were written in English and half in Japanese. Then he, the man who was telling us the story, graduated in 1950 or thereabouts, from the same university. All his notes were written in Japanese. Now this profile is very interesting. The Japanese were becoming giants in the modern world, in technology and so on, surpassing those who began the industrial revolution. They were also, as it were, traveling back to regain their own culture through their language, you see. This is very important; I think this is an extremely important story. It says something about the relationship between technology and the humanities.

How far can you develop without dealing with certain humanistic problems, such as who am I, why am I here, what is the meaning of life, what is my culture? I believe that the relationship is close, important, and crucial.

Rowell: You teach literature courses. You told me that you teach African literature frequently. But when you teach a literature course that does not include an African literary text, what are some of the creative works or texts you select?

Achebe: No, I have never taught anything but African literatures, and I'm not really a professional literature teacher. The only reason I got into teaching at all is that I wanted to teach African literature. So I taught African literature from the start. I guess I've not done anything else in my teaching career.

Rowell: If you were teaching a course in twentieth-century literature, what are some of the texts you'd use? And why would you select them? I guess, ultimately, I'm asking this: What are some of the twentieth-century texts you consider to be important? For example, I couldn't imagine teaching a course in twentieth-century American literature without including Ralph Ellison's *Invisible Man* or William Faulkner's *Absalom, Absalom!* or Toni Morrison's *Sula*. In other words, what do you consider some of the most important texts for teaching twentieth-century world literature?

Achebe: Well, it's not really a question I can answer satisfactorily. The texts you mention are all very important—and there are other important ones as well. I wouldn't really be able to or want to rattle off a list just like that, but I would certainly try to cover the world. I would attempt to cover those writers who have written what you call "the landmarks" of the twentieth century. And I guess that would include people like T. S. Eliot, would include Ezra Pound, would include Faulkner, would include Hemingway. Then if you come nearer to our time . . . yes, yes, *Invisible Man* is an outstanding novel by any stretch of the imagination—and I would include it for that reason and also for the reason that Ellison is writing from a history and tradition which have a unique message for us. I would include one—at least one—Baldwin text. From African literature I would include *Ambiguous Adventure* by Cheikh Hamidou Kane; I would include Camara Laye and Amos Tutuola; I would include Alex La Guma and Nadine Gordimer. Then I would attempt to find, even in translation, some Arabic writers from Egypt, Naguib Mahfouz and Alifa Rifaat, for example. Then I would attempt to include writers from India, Raja Rao, for example. That doesn't cover the whole world. Then I would move to Latin America, you see. I would include Neruda and Márquez. Actually, some of the most interesting writing is taking place there. I would also go to the Caribbean which, for its size, is perhaps the most dynamic literary environment in the world in our time. There is a legion of people there I would want to include. So you see I would have really to end up with a very long list and then begin to pare it down. But the important thing I would attempt to do is not to limit myself to anybody's "great tradition," because that sort of thing limits you and blinds you to what is going on in the real world.

Rowell: Are there other reasons that you would not include "anybody's 'great tradition' "?

Achebe: No, no, I said I would go beyond anyone's "great tradition." Why? Because it is not the "great tradition." It cannot be. No way. One small corner of the world cannot wake up one morning and call its artifact the "great tradition," you see. Our people have a saying that the man who's never traveled thinks that his mother makes the best soup. Now we need to travel—

with all due respect to our mothers—we need to travel. So the question of a "great tradition" makes sense only if you're not aware of other people's traditions.

I had a very curious experience in Holland, where I was put up to run as president of International PEN. An older, much older, man, a Frenchman, was put up also—or he put himself up after he saw my name. And he won. But the interesting thing is that he had no conception—and didn't want to have any conception—of the literature of Africa. He kept quite clearly and studiously avoiding any mention of African literature, and at some point he said something like this: "How can we expect the Third World, with all of its problems, to produce great art?" Do you see what I mean? Now this is the kind of mind or mentality I'm talking about. It remains alien to me though I encounter it frequently. It is alien to me because my whole life has been ordered in such a way that I have to know about other people. This is one of the penalties of being an underdog: that you have to know about the overdog, you see. The overdog doesn't need to know about the underdog; therefore, he suffers severe limitations, and the underdog ends up being wiser because he knows about himself and knows about the overdog. So my reading list would be really catholic, would be catholic in every sense of the word. I haven't talked about the Far East, because I don't know enough, but I will try and find, for example, some good writers from Japan. One must read the Japanese novelists. Their contribution to the consciousness of the twentieth century is unique.

Rowell: Is the Third World writer presently participating in the ongoing revision of what one calls "the literary canon"?

Achebe: Oh yes, yes. By just being there. He/she is, in fact, the reason for the revision. He/she is the very reason for the revision.

Rowell: Isn't the Third World writer something else other than what we just said? The matter I'm thinking of here is linguistic. Let us assume for a moment that Percy Shelley was correct when he said that "the poet is the legislator of the world." The poet is indeed a person who shapes our vision of the world; he or she does that and provides us with a vocabulary, or new vocabulary, to describe it. I'm thinking of you and what you do for the

English-speaking world as a writer, and what Jorge Luis Borges does, or did, for the Spanish-speaking world, and what Aimé Césaire does linguistically, for example, for the French-speaking world. In other words, does the Third World writer alter or adapt the medium and, through a destruction of what is out there as— I'll call it this—"the parent language or dialect" itself, revise or reinvest the medium?

Achebe: Well, yes. My answer to the previous question was rather brief, but it was really intended to contain all of this. This Third World creature comes with an experience which is peculiar, including the linguistic experience. The use of French, in the case of Césaire, is the use of a French that has been in dialogue with other languages, you see. In my case, it is an English which has been in dialogue with a very rich alien linguistic milieu—that is, you have African languages strong in their own right, and an African history and experience. An English which has had this particular encounter cannot be the same as the English of Kingsley Amis writing in London. So this is something which the members of the metropolis have to deal with, and they don't always like it. But it is not really something for me to worry about. I know some people who are worried, and they say, "Look what they are doing to my language!" They are horrified.

We come with this particular preparation which, as it happens, actually enriches the metropolitan languages. But that's not why we do it; we're not doing it in order to enrich the metropolitan language. We're doing it because this is the only way we can convey the story of ourselves, the way we can celebrate ourselves in our new history and the new experience of colonialism, and all the other things. We have had to fashion a language that can carry the story we are about to tell.

It's not all so new, even though, perhaps, it's happening now on such a wide scale that we are paying more attention to it than before. But if you think, for instance, of all the great writers in English in our century, they are virtually all Irish. Why is that so? This is very important, and I think it is the same situation. James Joyce, of course, addresses it directly and talks about it in that famous passage in which Stephen Daedalus is talking about what the English language means to him and to his teacher, who is English. He muses on the fact that every word he says means something different to each of them—any word, "ale" or "Christ"—no word can mean the same thing to me as it does to him. Why? Because we colonials and excolonials come to the English language with a whole baggage of peculiar experiences which the English person doesn't have. This is what has made the English language, in our time, such a powerful force in literature. This is why we're talking about the Caribbean literature and about African literature.

Rowell: Will you elaborate on a statement you just made about using a new form of English? You said that it (the new form of the medium) was the only "way we can convey the history of ourselves." You said we use the language in the way we do because this is the only way we can convey the history or the story of ourselves. Apparently, you are talking about the nature of that revised form, or the new fabric, of English.

Achebe: Well, take Nigeria. Nigeria is a vibrant cultural environment. It has been for a long time. It has, literally, two hundred languages—not all of them important, but some quite big. The three main Nigerian languages are spoken by at least ten million people each, and some of them, like Hausa, cross beyond Nigeria's borders to other places. The English language arrives in Nigeria, then, and is thrown into this very active linguistic environment. Of course, it has the special privilege of being the language of administration, the language of higher education—the lingua franca, in fact—the language in which the various indigenous political and linguistic entities can communicate among themselves. Unless he learns the Igbo language, the Hausa man will communicate with the Igbo man in English. A Yoruba man communicates with a Hausa man in English. We're talking about Nigeria. And this has gone on for a number of generations. English, then, acquires a particular position of importance. You must recognize this, unless, of course, you agree with some of my friends who have said that we should ignore this history and ignore this reality and ignore whatever advantage of mutual communication

English has brought to our very complex situation. Unless you were to accept that extreme position, you would have to say, "What will we do with this English language that's been knocking around here now for so long?" Our people don't allow anything as powerful as that to keep knocking around without having a job to do, because it would cause trouble.

This is the whole point of that *Mbari* phenomenon that I was describing earlier, in which anything which is new and powerful, which appears on the horizon, is brought in and domesticated in the *Mbari* house with all the other things that have been around, so that it doesn't have the opportunity to stay out of sight and scheme to overthrow the environment. This is what art does. Something comes along and you bring it in—and even if you don't yet fully understand it, you give it a place to stand. This is the way in which we have been using the English language to tell our story. It's not the only way we can tell our story, of course. I can tell our story in the Igbo language. It would be different in many ways. It would also not be available to as many people, even within the Nigerian environment. So this is the reality: this English, then, which I am using, has witnessed peculiar events in my land that it has never experienced anywhere else. The English language has never been close to Igbo, Hausa, or Yoruba anywhere else in the world. So it has to be different, because these other languages and their environment are not inert. They are active, and they are acting on this language which has invaded their territory. And the result of all this complex series of actions and reactions is the language we use. The language I write in. And, therefore, it comes empowered by its experience of the encounter with me. One advantage it has is this: although it is thus different, it is not so different that you would have to go to school to learn it in America or in India or Kenya or anywhere English is already spoken. So it definitely has certain advantages which we can only ignore to our own disadvantage. It is a world language in a way that Hausa, Yoruba, Igbo are not. There is no way we can change that. Now that is not to say that we should therefore send these other languages to sleep. That's not what I'm saying. I am saying that we have a very, very complex and dynamic multilingual situation, which we cannot run away from but contain and control.

Rowell: *No Longer at Ease* addresses the problem of communication in particular terms. There are moments in the novel when there's a lack of communication. This problem revolves around Obi, your central character. Will you comment on the issues related to language and its failure as a medium in modern society?

Achebe: Well, yes, language is of course a marvelous tool of communication. This is what makes us different from cattle, that we have language and we are able to communicate with the precision that language brings. But even this is not enough. We all know that. Sometimes we say, "I know what I want to say, but I just can't find the words to say it." In other words, language is not absolutely perfect; there are still things we struggle to express. Sometimes we approach fairly close to what we feel, what we want to say, but at other times, no. So it's not surprising that there should be problems in communication, even though we've got language in the technical sense of just using words. But, of course, you can be using the same words and still not communicate, because of other blocks, of other factors. People can refuse to listen. People can for all kinds of reasons not want to accept the message.

That failure of communication, for instance, between Obi and Clara is interesting. They speak the same language but there is a communication breakdown. Obi is saying, "Just give me a little more time, my mother is sick. Let's wait, we'll get married later on." Now, Clara cannot understand that, you see, and it's not because she's unreasonable. She's very reasonable. She's so reasonable that she had foreseen this problem before and warned Obi about it, you see. She is not going to allow herself to be brutalized over and over again; this is why she'd taken the humiliating pains to say: "Do you know that you're not supposed to marry someone like me?" Obi says, "Nonsense, we're beyond that, we're civilized people." And now that Clara has invested her life in this civilization, she's being told: "Let's wait a minute." So this is an example of my own view of the breakdown in communication because it's not that either party does not understand the words being used, it's just that no words can solve their predicament. There's no way you can resolve this particular problem in any kind of language; we are at an impasse, and it's now beyond language. But we have no better tool than language to communicate with one another. So when language fails, what do we do? We resort to fighting, but that, of course, is destructive. So language is very important, it is a hallmark of our humanity, one of the hallmarks of our humanity, but it is never enough, even that is not enough. We work at it, we give it all the patience we have, but we must expect that even when all is said and done there will always remain those areas, those instances when we are unable to get across.

Rowell: What about Obi and communication with his family?

Achebe: Well, the same kind of thing is happening but not to the same degree, obviously. Between him and his mother there is a very peculiar relationship that has been built up from birth, which he's in no position to deal with at all. He can deal with his father quite abruptly, in fact, and overwhelm him, but he doesn't even try with his mother. This is a relationship we may not comprehend unless we come from a culture like his. There's no way he can argue with his mother when she says, "Well, if you're going to marry that girl, wait until I'm dead. You won't have very long to wait." In some cultures they say, "To hell with that. She's had her own life, this is my life." That's not the Igbo people, you know. There's no way Obi can respond like that. So that's communication again. One part of Obi knows that he can say, "Mother, I can't wait." Another part of him says, "You can't say that to your mother."

Rowell: Critics have often described Okonkwo in *Things Fall Apart* as representative of a kind of Aristotelian tragic hero. How do you respond to critics reading Okonkwo as a hero in terms of Aristotle's concept of tragedy?

Achebe: No, I don't think I was responding to that particular format. This is not, of course, to say that there is no relationship between these. If we are to believe what we are hearing these days, the Greeks did not drop from the sky. They evolved in a certain place which was very close to Africa. Very close to Egypt, which in itself was also very close to the Sudan and Nubia, which was very close to West Africa. So it may well turn out, believe it or not, that some of the things Aristotle was saying about tragedy were not really unheard of in other cultures. It's just that we are not yet ready to make these quantum leaps! For instance, it has been shown that one-third of the entire vocabulary of ancient Greek came from Egypt and the Middle East. And so obviously there were links with us which the Greeks themselves apparently had no problem acknowledging. It was only late, from the eighteenth century, that the Europeans began to find it difficult to accept that they owed anything to Africa. In any event, I think a lot of what Aristotle says makes sense. Putting it in a neat, schematic way may be peculiar to the Greek way of thinking about the hero. But that idea is not necessarily foreign to other people: the man who's larger than life, who exemplifies virtues that are admired by the community, but also a man who for all that is still human. He can have flaws, you see. All that seems to me to be very elegantly underlined in Aristotle's work. I think they are there in human nature itself and would be found in other traditions even if they were not spelled out in the same exact way.

Rowell: Would you agree that there are patterns of irony or an extensive use of irony in all of your first four novels, from *Things Fall Apart* all the way down to *No Longer at Ease*? If there are ironic situations or ironic characters, will you talk about that irony? I really don't like to ask writers to talk about their own work.

Achebe: I think irony is one of the most powerful (how does one say it?) . . . one of the most powerful conditions in human experience. And anybody who is a storyteller—I see myself as a storyteller—will sooner or later come to the realization that ironies are among the most potent devices available to them. Irony can raise a humdrum story to a totally new level of power and significance simply by the fact of its presence, the presence of ironic juxtaposition. That's really all I can say. Your question seems to me almost like asking what do I think about metaphors.

Well, you can't even begin to tell a story without saying, "*This thing* is like *that thing*." Or even, "*this thing is that thing*." Or, as in an almost grotesque proverb of Igbo, *the corpse of another person is a log of wood*. Of course, we know that somebody else's body is not a log of wood, but it could be so, for all we care. We don't seem to be able to put ourselves inside that box. We do not say, "There go I but for the grace of God." We lack the imagination to leap into that box. And if we didn't, the world would have been a much more wholesome place. The oppression in the world would not be as great as it is. The inhumanity we practice would be greatly reduced. But because we lack the metaphoric imagination we are unable to make that imaginative leap from out of our own skin into somebody else's. And so our storytellers jolt us with metaphor and irony and remind us that "there but for the grace of God go I." Without metaphor and irony things would be white or black, and not very interesting. It's only when you show that this white is also black that something very interesting and important begins to happen.

Rowell: In this interview, you have, I've noticed, in more than one instance, used a tale to illustrate your point. You have also used the proverb. I suddenly remember the narrator of *Things Fall Apart* talking about the importance of proverbs in Igbo conversation.

Achebe: Proverbs are miniature tales; they are the building blocks, if you like, of tales. They are tales refined to their simplest form, because a good proverb is a short story. It is very short indeed. What it demonstrates, first of all—before we go on to the why—is the clarity with which those who made these proverbs had observed their reality. A proverb is a very careful observation of reality and the world, and then a distillation into the wisdom of an elegant statement so that it sticks in the mind. You see it, you know it's true, you tell yourself, "This is actually true, why hadn't I thought of it," and you remember it. And there is a whole repertoire of these statements made by my people across the millennia. Some must have fallen out of use, others have remained and have been passed on from one generation to the next. And part of the training, of socialization of young people in this society, is to become familiar with these statements from our immemorial past. So that when we are dealing with a contemporary situation, when we are dealing with here and now, we have the opportunity to draw from the proverbial repertoire to support or refute what is said. It's like citing the precedents in law. This case before us is what we are talking about. But similar things have happened before; look at the way our ancestors dealt with them down the ages. So it gives one a certain stability, it gives one a certain connectedness. It banishes, it helps to banish the sense of loneliness, the cry of desolation: Why is this happening to me? What have I done? Woe is me! The proverb is saying, no, it's tough, but our ancestors made this proverb about this kind of situation, so it must have happened to someone else before you, possibly even to a whole lot of other people before. Therefore, take heart, people survived in the face of this kind of situation before. So proverbs do many kinds of things. They are, just for their elegance as literary forms, interesting and satisfying; then they ground us in our "great tradition"; they tell us something about the importance of observing our reality carefully, very carefully.

Rowell: We know you in the United States as a novelist mainly. But you're also a poet, a critic, and a short story writer. Does the poem, or the essay, or the short story do something for you that the novel cannot do?

Achebe: Yes, I think so, I think so. Though I hope you won't ask me what it is, because that would be more difficult. But suddenly I have not been writing short stories for some time; there was a period in my life when I wrote a lot of short stories. At that point I was not writing novels. There was also a period when I wrote much poetry, much for me. Now I rarely write poetry, and so it must mean these forms serve me at particular times or have served me at particular times. If I may be more specific, during the Biafran war, the civil war in Nigeria, I was not writing novels for years and years and years; after that I was not in a mood to write novels. I wrote most of my poetry at that period, many of the short stories. So without saying categorically that I only write poetry in times of war, I think that there is some connection between the particular distress of war, the particular tension of war, and the kind of literary response, the genres that I have employed in that period. I remember in particular one poem, "Christmas in Biafra," which actually came out of the kind of desperation which you felt hearing carols on short-wave radio and being reminded that there were places in the world where people were singing about the birth of the Prince of Peace, and you were trapped in this incredible tragedy. Now it's a very powerful feeling, a very powerful feeling indeed. It is analogous to that scene in *Things Fall Apart* just before those men kill Ikemefuna and they hear in the air the sound of music from a distant clan. I don't know how those men felt hearing it: the sounds of peace and celebration in the world and a horrendous event at home. So what I'm feeling at any particular time and what the world is doing impinge on the kind of writing I do, obviously.

Rowell: Earlier you said, "I see myself as a storyteller." What do you mean?

Achebe: Well, that's just a manner of speaking, of again relating myself in the manner of the proverbs we are talking about to something that had happened before. So even though I don't think I'll ever be in the court of the emperor, telling stories to him and his courtiers, still I am in that tradition, you see. The story has always been with us, it is a very old thing, it is not new; it may take new forms, but it is the same old story. That's mostly what I'm saying, and we mustn't forget that we have a certain link of apostolic succession, if you like, to the old *griots* and storytellers and poets. It helps me anyway; it gives me that sense of connectedness, of being part of things that are eternal like the rivers, the mountains, and the sky, and creation myths about man and the world. The beginning was a story, it is the story that creates man, then man makes other stories, you see. And for me this is almost like Ezeulu in *Arrow of God* who before he performs important functions in his community has to go to the beginning and tell how his priesthood came into existence. He has to recite that story to his community to validate his priestly rites. They know it already but cannot hear it too often. This is how stories came into being, and this is what they did for our ancestors, and we hope that they will continue to serve our generations, not in the same form necessarily, but in the same spirit.

Rowell: What is the role of the literary critic in the new Nigerian society?

Achebe: Well, that's a good question. I didn't want to speak for critics, but I dare say that there were ancestors of literary critics in the past; I mean, spectators who might get up and say: "I don't like that stuff!" Obviously modern critics could claim a certain apostolic succession but quite frankly I don't think the role of their ancestors was as elevated as that of the original creators. Today when the thing is down in print on paper, I think the role of the critic has become a lot more complex and thus a lot more important. It is important because there is need for mediation. Since I'm not going to go around and meet the people and answer their questions as a storyteller would do in the past, actually meet them face to face and experience their support or disagreement, somebody else is called into existence to perhaps explain difficult parts, or perform all kinds of functions of a mediating nature. Also, there is so much which is produced, there is so much that is written, all of it is not of the same quality and a certain amount of discrimination is necessary just to survive the barrage of production in the modern world, the sheer number of books. I think therefore the role of the critic is important. Also, I think the critic is there to draw attention to this continuity that I was talking about, to the tradition. How does this new work relate to what has happened before, how does it relate to writers who were here before, how does it even relate to those who did not write their stories but told them? So I think there is a new and necessary and important role for the critic.

Rowell: I'm going to ask one more question about art and literature. Then I want to turn to a handful of questions about your background. If you had to look back on your works and judge them, is there one text or one genre which allowed you to speak or write the best way you wanted to? Or is there one of them which is more representative of the kind of expression you wanted to make?

Achebe: Well, I think I can only talk about one genre, and the only reason I can talk about it is that I can lean on the simple fact of numbers. I've written more novels than I've done any other thing, and therefore that must be the one that as of now seems most congenial. But I really don't even try to think about that and even if I were tempted I would resist the thought. I would go out of my way to stop it because, as I've said, everything I have written has been useful to me at the time when I needed to write it, and I wouldn't want to say that this time is more important than that time. So apart from being able to say that obviously I have written more novels, I would not bother to rank my texts and genres, or award distinctions, even secretly.

Rowell: Did your education at the University of Ibadan direct you in any way toward a career in creative writing? I guess what I'm ultimately asking is, how did you come to write?

Achebe: Yes, well, I think I grew up in Ibadan in a way that pointed clearly in the direction of writing. That was the period when I was able to reassess what I had read, and all I had to go by at that point was the colonial novel written by white people about us. And so it was a very, very crucial moment in my career, that moment when I was reading these things again with a new awareness of what was going on, the subtle denigration, and sometimes not so subtle, that I had missed before. So in that sense it's at Ibadan that I grew up, and growing up is part of the decision to write. It did not give me the taste for writing; it was always there. Even in high school and before that, because the taste for stories was always there. I think it's simply encountering myself in literature and becoming aware that that's not me, you see. A number of texts helped; one of them was Joyce Cary's *Mister Johnson*, and I suppose one of them was Conrad's *Heart of Darkness*. There were a lot of other books not so well known and not worth remembering. But what I'm talking about is encountering the colonial ideology, for the first time in fiction, as something sinister and unacceptable. So if you add to this the weakness for stories anyway, you have the possibilities, even the incitement to become a writer, somebody who will attempt to tell his own story. Because we all have a story in us, at least one story, I believe. So in my case Ibadan was the watershed, a turning point.

Rowell: At the present time we have only a bit of biographical or autobiographical public information about you, the man and the writer, and I've always wondered whether or not the Christian component of your background (your father was a mission teacher) extracted you from Igbo culture in any way?

Achebe: I think it intended to, but I don't think it succeeded. Certainly it had its moments of success. But with my curiosity, my natural curiosity, I didn't allow it to succeed completely. And so there I was between two competing claims but not aware of any discomfort as a child. I was certainly aware of curiosity about the non-Christian things that were going on in my community, and I was not really convinced that because they were non-Christian they were therefore bad, or evil. And even though I met a lot of Christians who seemed to operate on the basis that everything in the traditional society was bad or evil or should be suppressed, I think that slowly, little by little, they realized too that that was really a lost hope, a wrong kind of attitude to adopt. I could see that a bit in my father. I know that he became less rigid as he grew older. The things he would not tolerate, when I was very little, I saw him not pay too much attention to later on—like traditional dancing and singing, you know. I never had any problem with those things. I was in a peculiar and an interesting position of seeing two worlds at once and finding them both interesting in their way. I mean, I was moved by the Christian message. I was moved by hymns in the church. I was moved by the poetry of Christianity. I was also moved by the thing that Christianity was attempting to suppress: the traditional religion, about which at the beginning I didn't know very much. But I was going to make it my business to listen and learn and go out of my way to find out more about the religion. This is how it happened. So I was not distressed at all by being born in that kind of crossroads. On the contrary, I thought it was one of the major advantages I had as a writer.

Note

This interview was conducted in Mr. Achebe's quarters at the International House in New York City on Sunday, May 28, 1989.

Suggested Reading

Achebe, Chinua. "Chi in Igbo Cosmology." In Achebe, *Morning Yet on Creation Day*, 159–75. New York: Anchor/Doubleday, 1975.

Ackley, Donald. "The Male-Female Motif in *Things Fall Apart*." *Studies in Black Literature* 5, no. 1 (1974): 1–6.

Adebayo, Tunji. "The Past and the Present in Chinua Achebe's Novels." *Ife African Studies* 1, no. 1 (1974): 66–84.

Cantu, Yolande, ed. *Chinua Achebe's "Things Fall Apart"*: A Critical View. London: Collins, 1985.

Carroll, David. *Chinua Achebe*. New York: St. Martin's, 1980.

Chinweizu. "An Interview with Chinua Achebe." *Okike* 20 (1981): 19–32.

Echeruo, Michael J. C. "Chinua Achebe." In *A Celebration of Black and African Writing*, edited by Bruce King and Kolawole Ogungbesan, 150–63. Zaria and Ibadan: Ahmadu Bello University Press and Oxford University Press, 1975.

Ezenwa-Ohaeto. *Chinua Achebe: A Biography*. Oxford: Currey, 1997.

Gachukia, Eddah W. "Chinua Achebe and Tradition." In *Standpoints on African Literature: A Critical Anthology*, edited by Chris Wanjala, 172–87. Nairobi: East African Literature Bureau, 1973.

Gikandi, Simon. *Reading Chinua Achebe*. London: Currey, 1991.

————. "Chinua Achebe and the Poetics of Location: The Uses of Space in *Things Fall Apart* and *No Longer at Ease*." In *Essays on African Writing I: A Re-evaluation*, edited by A. Gurnah, 1–12. Oxford: Heinemann, 1993.

Heywood, Christopher. "Surface and Symbol in *Things Fall Apart*." *Journal of the Nigerian English Studies Association* 2 (1967): 41–45.

Ihekweazu, Edith, ed. *Eagle on Iroko: Papers from the International Symposium, 1990*. Ibadan: Heinemann Nigeria, 1991.

Innes, C. L. *Chinua Achebe*. Cambridge: Cambridge University Press, 1990.

Innes, C. L., and Bernth Lindfors, eds. *Critical Perspectives on Chinua Achebe*. Washington, DC: Three Continents, 1978.

Irele, F. Abiola. "*Le monde s'effondre de Chinua Achebe: Structure et signification*." In *Litteratures africaine et enseignement*, edited by J. Corzani and A. Ricard, 171–86. Bordeaux, France: Presses Universitaires, 1985.

————. "The Crisis of Cultural Memory in Chinua Achebe's *Things Fall Apart*." In Irele, *The African Imagination: Literature in Africa and the Black Diaspora*, 115–53. New York: Oxford University Press, 2001.

Iyasere, Solomon, ed. *Understanding "Things Fall Apart": Selected Essays and Criticism*. Troy, NY: Whitston, 1998.

Killam, G. D. *The Novels of Chinua Achebe*. New York: Africana, 1969.

Lindfors, Bernth, ed. *Approaches to Teaching "Things Fall Apart."* New York: Modern Language Association, 1991.

————. *Conversations with Chinua Achebe*. Jackson: University of Mississippi Press, 1997.

Melone, Thomas. "Architecture du monde: Chinua Achebe et W. B. Yeats." *Conch* 2, no. 1 (1970): 44–52.

————. *Chinua Achebe et la tragedie de l'histoire*. Paris: Presence Africaine, 1973.

Njoku, Benedict. *The Four Novels of Chinua Achebe: A Critical Study*. New York: Lang, 1984.

Nnolim, Charles. "Form and Function of the Folk Tradition in Achebe's Novels." *Ariel* 14 (1983): 35–47.

Nwabueze, Emeka. "Theoretical Construction and Constructive Theorizing on the Execution of Ikemefuna in Achebe's *Things Fall Apart*: A Study in Critical Dualism." *Research in African Literatures* 31 (2000): 163–73.

Nwachukwu-Agbada, J. O. J. "Chinua Achebe's Literary Proverbs as Reflections of Igbo Cultural and Philosophical Tenets." *Proverbium* 10 (1993): 215–35.

Ogede, Ode. *Chinua Achebe and the Politics of Representation*. Trenton, NJ: Africa World, 2001.

Oko, Emilia. "The Historical Novel of Africa: A Sociological Approach to Achebe's *Things Fall Apart* and *Arrow of God.*" *Conch* 6, nos. 1–2 (1974): 15–46.

Osei-Nyame, Kwadwo. "Chinua Achebe Writing Culture: Representations of Gender and Tradition in *Things Fall Apart*." *Research in African Literatures* 30 (1999): 148–64.

Petersen, Kirsten H., and Anna Rutherford, eds. *Chinua Achebe: A Celebration*. Oxford: Heinemann, 1990.

Ravenscroft, Arthur. *Chinua Achebe*. Harlow, UK: Longman, 1977.

ten Kortenaar, Neil. "Beyond Authenticity and Creolization: Reading Achebe Writing Culture." *Publications of the Modern Language Association* 110 (1995): 30–41.

Traore, Ousseynou. "Why the Snake Lizard Killed His Mother: Inscribing and Decentering 'Nneka' in *Things Fall Apart*." In *The Politics of (M)Othering: Womanhood, Identity, and Resistance in African Literature*, edited by Obioma Nnaemeka, 50–68. London: Routledge, 1997.

Turkington, Kate. *Chinua Achebe: Things Fall Apart*. London: Arnold, 1977.

Winters, M. "An Objective Approach to Achebe's Style." *Research in African Literatures* 12 (1981): 55–68.

Wren, Robert. *Achebe's World: The Historical and Cultural Context of the Novels of Chinua Achebe*. Washington, DC: Three Continents, 1980.

Yankson, Kofi. *Chinua Achebe's Novels: A Sociolinguistic Perspective*. Uruowulu-Obosi, Nigeria: Pacific Printers, 1990.